RADIOHEAD AND PHILOSOPHY

Popular Culture and Philosophy® Series Editor: George A. Reisch

For full details of all Popular Culture and Philosophy® books, visit www.opencourtbooks.com.

Popular Culture and Philosophy®

RADIOHEAD AND PHILOSOPHY
Fitter Happier More Deductive

Edited by
BRANDON W. FORBES
and
GEORGE A. REISCH

OPEN COURT
Chicago and La Salle, Illinois

Volume 38 in the series, Popular Culture and Philosophy®, edited by George A. Reisch

To order books from Open Court, call 1-800-815-2280, or visit our website at www.opencourtbooks.com.

Open Court Publishing Company is a division of Carus Publishing Company

Printed and bound in the United States of America

Library of Congress Cataloging-in-Publication Data

Radiohead and philosophy : fitter happier more deductive / edited by Brandon W. Forbes and George A. Reisch.
   p. cm. -- (Popular culture and philosophy 38 ; v. 38)
 Includes bibliographical references and index.
 Includes discography.
 ISBN 978-0-8126-9664-6 (trade paper : alk. paper)
 1. Radiohead (Musical group) 2. Music and philosophy. I. Forbes, Brandon W. II. Reisch, George A.
 ML421.R25R33 2009
 782.42166092'2--dc22
              2008054658

Contents

v

Radiohead and the Music Industry. *(Rainbows and Arrows.)* 99

Radiohead's Existential Politics. *(First Against the Wall.)* 135

Radiohead, Heidegger, and Technology. *(Our Iron Lungs.)* 191

Radiohead and the Postmodern. *(Not Here. Isn't Happening.)*

1 Step

Phew. For a minute there, we lost ourselves. We were about to publish this book without a price and ask Radiohead fans to pay what they want for it. But then we remembered. While the music industry was up-ended in 2007 by the debut of *In Rainbows* and other albums distributed by artists themselves, the world of book publishing remains a few steps behind. For now, at least.

Philosophy, though, has no difficulty keeping up with Radiohead. We had a pretty good hunch going into it, but putting this book together made it plain to us that there are good reasons why Radiohead has succeeded The Clash as 'The Only Band that Matters'. Some of those reasons are philosophical. Not that Radiohead says much about competing theories of truth or subtleties of the mind-body problem (for humans or androids). Instead of abstractions, Radiohead's music points toward philosophical analyses of actual experiences in the world. Yes, some of these experiences were analyzed by Aristotle, Nietzsche, and Heidegger, but others belong exclusively to us, here and now. As Mark Greif put it in his groundbreaking essay, "Radiohead, or the Philosophy of Pop" (included here), Radiohead not only suggests the question, 'How should it really ever be possible for pop music to incarnate a particular historical situation?' They show how it's done.

Take the video for *In Rainbows'* "House of Cards." Because it uses cutting-edge three-dimensional modeling technology, we don't actually 'see' Thom Yorke's face as he sings the song and attends a neighborhood party. Instead, a rotating laser digitally captures the events, the people, and the houses. In our world, the video reminds us, only the underlying data matters—our very lives and selves, in many ways, are now digital. Radiohead pushes this insight to its artistic limit by making available the video's source code so that end users (previously known as "fans" before our digital age) can manipulate and re-image the data for themselves. This is one of many philosophical spaces Radiohead has opened for us—spaces in which their music, their worldview, and their encounter with the world can connect to our own.

Whether it's because of their Oxford pedigree or just raw talent and intelligence, Radiohead's effortless fusion of Joe Strummer's politics with the technological interrogation of the Talking Heads (to whom they owe their name) leads all of the scholars in this book to fascinating and new encounters with philosophy. From Heidegger's phenomenology and the manipulation of Yorke's voice on *Kid A*, to Marx's take on the "pay-what-you-want" model of distribution, to the pathos of Aristotelian tragedy unfolding in so many Radiohead songs, each of these encounters engages our understanding of our historical situation in all its beauty, its terror, and its unimagined possibilities.

This is philosophy in the twenty-first century. But judging by the philosophical visions of Radiohead in these chapters, the light has not gone out.

Anyone Can Play Philosophy. *(yes yes yes yes yes yes yes yes yes.)*

1.

Is Radiohead the Pink Floyd of the Twenty-First Century?

GEORGE A. REISCH

> The whole point of creating music for me is to give
> voice to things that aren't normally given voice to,
> and a lot of those things are extremely negative.
> Personally speaking, I have to remain positive
> otherwise I'd go fucking crazy.
>
> —Thom Yorke, Pitchfork Interview, August 16th, 2008
>
> All you touch and all you see is all your life will ever be.
>
> —"Breathe," *Dark Side of the Moon*

Watching Radiohead perform at an outdoor amphitheater, rock critic Jim DeRogatis flashed back to "Pink Floyd at Pompeii," a concert filmed inside an ancient amphitheatre near the famous village. "No other band today," DeRogatis said of Radiohead, "has the power to transport a crowd of more than 30,000 to foreboding alien landscapes and the shadowy places of their nightmares in quite the same way." Radiohead, he concluded, is "the Pink Floyd of Generation Y." Message boards and blogs are filled with similar comparisons. "Radiohead is the new Pink Floyd," they say, or, "Radiohead is *better than* Pink Floyd."

But neither Radiohead nor Pink Floyd—well, Roger Waters, at least—would agree that their music is about remote, interstellar spaces or imaginary, dreamlike experiences. These two bands have earned enormous respect and devotion because their music speaks to things in *this* world. Treating music as an escape, a mere occasion for a party, is *so* off-the-mark in Pink Floyd's case that Waters once became spitting mad at noisy, drunken fans. That episode in

1977 nudged Waters down a creative path that led to *The Wall*—a now classic, double-barreled, four-sided critique of war, cruelty, social conformity, looming madness, and alienation (not aliens).

True, there was a time when Pink Floyd was all about 'space-rock' and psychedelia. Legendary founder Syd Barrett, who died in 2006, pioneered the genre in the mid to late 1960s while Waters and David Gilmour were mainly along for the rocket ride, learning how to set the controls and write songs. Yet after Barrett's demise, Waters took the ship out of interstellar overdrive, turned it around, and headed back to the planet of his earthly obsessions.

Radiohead got their 'space-rock' reputation with *The Bends* (opening with "Planet Telex") and, mainly, *OK Computer*. Pitchfork said the album moves through "space at 1.2 light years per hour," while Qmusic said "the first three tracks (of a five-song, continuous, 25-minute suite that's as brilliant as any music of the last decade) all mention aliens or interstellar activity in some capacity." Amazon.co.uk agrees that "OK Computer heads out into the cold deep space of prog-rock and comes back with stuff that makes mere pop earthlings like Stereophonics tremble." If DeRogatis is right that Radiohead has taken over the 'space-rock' mantle from Pink Floyd, Syd Barrett's famous black cloak—the one he famously wore and sang about in "Bike"—is now draped over Thom Yorke's shoulders. Titles like "Sail to the Moon" and "Black Star" invite the comparison, while "Subterranean Homesick Alien" may even point to Barrett himself. Yorke sings about aliens who "take me onboard their beautiful ship, show me the world as I'd love to see it." When he returns to "tell all [his] friends," they would think that he'd "lost it completely"—"They'd shut me away, but I'd be alright."

But Yorke's interest in spaceships and aliens is like what Barrett said about his cloak. It's "a bit of a joke." As the chapters in this book show, Yorke's lyrics and music speak directly to our lives and times. Pink Floyd may have been "just fantastic" (as the suit in "Have a Cigar" bellowed), but Radiohead has little interest in fantasy, spaceships or aliens. These things which are "not normally given voice to" have long fascinated existentialist and, especially, phenomenological philosophers. They have to do with the world we know and experience, but they *can't* be effectively addressed using ordinary language in ordinary ways.

The Band Is Just Phenomenological

Why not? Because philosophical phenomenology studies first-person experience *itself,* experience that has not (or not yet) been parsed, chunked, shaded and spun into the words we use to communicate with others and think our private thoughts. Pioneered largely in the twentieth century by French and German philosophers Jean-Paul Sartre, Maurice Merleau-Ponty, Edmund Husserl, and Martin Heidegger, phenomenology studies experience in its pure forms, before it becomes reflected upon, rearranged, remembered and forced into typical models of experience (such as "good," "bad," "romantic," "exciting," "boring," "frightening," and so on). Coming *after* the original experience, all this clumsy discourse usually hides experience, or aspects of it, from our subsequent awareness and understanding. Phenomeno-logy aims to unearth, recover, and understand was we either lose or never pay attention to in the first place.

This phenomenological bent may be familiar if you were once grabbed, startled or terrified by Radiohead's music. Most fans, I suspect, don't gradually warm up to the band. Instead, the conversion is sudden and drastic. You probably heard *OK Computer* or *Kid A* and were struck by something vague yet powerful and real—as if Radiohead presented sounds and rhythms from a hidden, subliminal soundtrack that plays just beneath the surface of life. Before I discovered the band, I thought these sounds were subjective and private—the particular sound of my own brain, I figured, humming, popping, and stuttering through life. But when *OK Computer* plays, my neurons seem to hum along with music they have *always* known. However you try to describe it, Radiohead makes sense almost immediately—musically, despite complex time signatures, and emotionally, even though the words are often obscure and drenched in sound. It also makes political sense (and I don't mean simply *"Hail to the Thief"*) though I didn't realize that until reading and editing several of the essays in this book. Do you know that strangely menacing-yet-beautiful, scary-yet-uplifting sound the world makes? You're not alone.

Creeping toward Phenomenology

If you doubt this phenomenological quality of Radiohead's music, take stock of what their major albums are *not* about. Start with their breakthrough hit "Creep" from 1992. "Creep" is about adolescent despair and alienation over a girl. Indeed, there's no phenomenology here because the song is Radiohead's rewrite of a song written many times before about an unavailable goddess. She "floats like a feather" and her skin makes Yorke cry. But once she sees him, she runs away (because he's "a creep, a weirdo"). And that's it. There's no "Pretty Woman" change of fortune here. She just keeps running and does not "come walking back" (as she does for Roy Orbison).

With one exception, "Creep" has almost nothing to do with the phenomenological tilt of post-*Bends* Radiohead.[1] In *The Bends,* they began to move away from pop's usual concerns with standard, pre-packaged experiences and emotions (romance, sex, peace-and-love (or God), rejection, denouncement, infatuation). And by *Kid A*, they had entirely abandoned them to explore the original qualities and textures of the world we live in. It was as if they opened a musical trap door, hidden to most pop bands, leading down below life's ordinary stage—on which the Beatles, Stones and Roy Orbison sang about girls and Roger Waters sang about death, money, capitalism, and madness—where we can see the wires, conduits, and neuronal loops that make it possible for us perceive and have consciousness of *anything at all*. Down here, the 'space-rock' label is meaningless. Words are meaningless.

Standing on the Edge and Looking Underneath

What you hear there beneath these floorboards is often scary and intimidating. A friend of mine says the opening piano chords of "Karma Police" make the hairs on his neck stand up. I know exactly what he means. Radiohead is the only band that matters

---

1 The exception is Jonny Greenwood's brittle, abrupt, and arresting power chords that stumble into the song's chorus. Especially on first hearing, they sound as if your stereo or iPod is making strange noises. They push you closer to your original sensations to question or relocate the boundaries of the sound and your perceptions of it.

because their music, so oriented to these fundamental aspects of experience, often points to what is worrisome and foreboding in the very look and feel of modern life.

Take "No Surprises." At first, Yorke seems to offer a parody or satire, strung together out of political and cultural clichés about home, security, and routine:

> bring down the government, . . . they don't speak for us.
>
> A job that slowly kills you; bruises that won't heal.
>
> No alarms and no surprises; such a pretty house and such a pretty garden.

Yet wrapped in the plinkety-plink-plink music of a nursery rhyme or music box, the lyrics become less sarcastic (like The Kink's "Shangri-la") and more a study in the political infantilization—by cliché, chit-chat, conventional wisdom, and routine—of adults either unable or unwilling to live freely and creatively. Grant Gee's video (in which Yorke sings the song with his head inside a glass or plastic sphere—more diving bell than space suit—that slowly fills with water) shows that these voting, mortgage-holding, commuters are drowning in passivity, ignorance, and denial. The truth voiced here is breathtaking, literally, since no description or analysis can match its musical and visual punch.

Subterranean Homesick Technology

Next to these false promises of domestic happiness, Yorke's lyrics often point to the fragility of our advanced, technological civilization. "Infrastructure will collapse," he sings in "House of Cards," while *OK Computer* begins with a car crash—

> In a fast German car
> I'm amazed that I survived
> An airbag saved my life. ("Airbag")

Midway through the album, we fight depression and alienation fed by

> Transport, motorways and tramlines,
> starting and then stopping,
> taking off and landing,
> the emptiest of feelings. ("Let Down")

And, near the end, we find ourselves in a crashed airplane ("Lucky").

While clearly suspicious of technology, Radiohead still has a special credibility in this arena because they have so embraced technology as a creative tool. Their tastes in musical software, hardware and even antique electronic instruments (such as the Theremin-like Ondes Martenot that Jonny Greenwood plays) are omnivorous.

Pink Floyd were also renowned for their use of technology—projectors for their light shows, echo machines, Syd Barrett's famous cigarette-lighter guitar slide, *Dark Side*'s synthesizer-based "On the Run," and lots and lots of amplifiers. Part of Floyd's early musical innovation, as Edward Macan argued (in *Pink Floyd and Philosophy*), was their commitment to electronic musical experimentation.[2] Songs like "Set the Controls for the Heart of the Sun" and "Interstellar Overdrive" build to jarring, disorienting crescendos (Macan calls them "breakthrough" moments) that take away your musical roadmaps and preconceptions in a bid to shock, awaken, and rearrange your perceptual capacities. If "Karma Police" seems scary, listen to "Careful with that Axe, Eugene!"

But the messages about modern life and technology from Pink Floyd and Radiohead point in different directions and take their logic from different cultural circumstances. Barrett's penchant for musical exploration was embraced by the emerging LSD-thirsty London counterculture not many years after postwar rationing and bread lines had finally subsided in the 1950s. In postwar England, in other words, there were plenty of reasons to musically dream about far-away, fantastic places. Barrett and his band used far-out, fantastic electronics to do just that. Under Waters, as Macan explains, Floyd's radical *musical* explorations of alienation

---

2 "Theodor Adorno, Pink Floyd, and the Psychedelics of Alienation," in *Pink Floyd and Philosophy: Careful with that Axiom, Eugene!* (Open Court, 2007), pp. 95-119.

gave way to *lyrical* indictments of education, capitalism and other human institutions. With aggressive nuclear powers to the east and west eyeing each other suspiciously through the 1970s and 1980s, Waters was less interested in conjuring psychedelic, transformative possibilities than in directly criticizing the oppressive, limiting realities he observed around him.

But these realities had vanished by the time *OK Computer* took the world by storm, some twenty-four years after *Dark Side* was released. The Berlin Wall and the Soviet Union were gone, the Balkan nations felt liberated, and many hoped that cold-war fears and insecurities would be a merely sad chapter in modern history. But new threats and demons emerged (such as war and ethnic cleansing in the Balkans and Africa, climate change, persistent disease and poverty, and new extremes in corporate greed, Enron-style). What made the post-cold-war world seem especially sinister, however, was the continued growth of a new kind of technology—information technology—that made Moog synthesizers seem quaint and harmless. The computers, networks, and databases that once may have promised greater efficiencies and global prosperity (at least until Kubrick's *2001* planted some doubt), that promised to make us fitter, happier, and safer in our homes, in our pretty little gardens, and in our selves, instead seemed to take over and reshape the way the world looks and feels.

Everything Is Not OK, Computer

Worries about the corrosive social and political effects of technology are not new. The rise of television and mass media in the 1950s caused some people to worry that democracy would atrophy if so many were exposed to information presented and controlled by so few. Sociologist C. Wright Mills delineated the tacit partnership of the military, the government, and business corporations in his celebrated book, *The Power Elite*. Herbert Marcuse's *One-Dimensional Man* argued similarly that magazines, television, and radio promoted a consumerism that suppresses genuine political freedom:

> Our society distinguishes itself by conquering the centrifugal social forces with Technology rather than Terror, on the dual basis of an overwhelming efficiency and an increasing standard

of living. . . . In the medium of technology, culture, politics, and the economy merge into an omnipresent system which swallows up or represses all alternatives.[3]

More recently, Noam Chomsky has detailed the "manufacturing" of political consent in America and the West by elites who impose not only facts and figures on the public but that particular *feeling*, fed by technologically-enabled media, that ordinary citizens are incapable of criticism or dissent:

> It is an important feature of the ideological system to impose on people the feeling that they are incompetent to deal with these complex and important issues; they'd better leave it to the captain. One device is to develop a star system, an array of figures who are often media creations or creations of the academic propaganda establishment, whose deep insights we are supposed to admire and to whom we must happily and confidently assign the right to control our lives and control international affairs. . . . we poor slobs ought to just watch, not interfere.[4]

Chomsky's interest in this feeling takes him a step toward Radiohead (which is perhaps why this passage is quoted inside the *Airbag/How Am I Driving?* EP). The intellectual who has perhaps come closest, however, is Mills, who grounded his sociological and ideological analyses of modern life in what he called its "tang and feel." In a lecture from 1954, he asked his audience,

> What is the tang and feel of our experience as we examine the world about us today? It is clear that these feelings are shaping the way we ask and the way we answer all the questions of this conference.[5]

Mills had in mind two particular fears of cold-war life associated with technology and the national press—nuclear annihilation and rampant McCarthyism. But his own description of what it was like

---

3 Herbert Marcuse, *One-Dimensional Man* (Beacon Press 1964), pp. x, xvi.

4 J. Peck, ed., *The Chomsky Reader*, pp. 42-43

5 Mills and Mills, eds. *C. Wright Mills: Letters and Autobiographical Writings* (University of California Press, 2000), p. 184.

to be alive in the early 1950s expresses more broadly the anxiety of anyone who resists Marcuse's one-dimensional culture of conformity, of one who resists Chomsky's feeling that dissent implies incompetence, or of one who, like Yorke, worries that he's going crazy because important and disturbing things that *should* be said about life simply aren't. Mills said,

> We are often stunned and we are often distracted, and we are bewildered almost all of the time. And the only weapon we have—as individuals and as a scatter of grouplets—is the delicate brain now so perilously balanced in the struggle for public sanity. . . . We feel that we are living in a world in which the citizen has become a mere spectator or a forced actor, and that our personal experience is politically useless and our political will a minor illusion. . . . We feel that distrust has become nearly universal among men of affairs and that the spread of public anxiety is poisoning human relations and drying up the roots of private freedom. (pp. 184–85).

Who Are Your Real Friends?

Decades later, in the age of personal computers and the internet, this distrust and anxiety has found new, technology-based roots that seem to control and restrict our social, economic and emotional lives. One example is the word "friends" and the meanings, associations, and obligations lately accrued to it. Friends now refers to persons one has never seen or talked to in person. They have instead posted a few kilobytes of data or a hyperlink to the public advertisements of ourselves that most of us (under a certain age, at least) create online. To maintain those advertisements and the desirable contacts and social opportunities they bring, we must in turn maintain certain schedules (lest your inbox overflow, or friends feel unwelcome or alienated by a late response), regularly purchase (or usually re-purchase) software (since you must have an up-to-date version), wait (for batteries to recharge, operating systems to load, downloads to complete), and remain ever vigilant about being tricked or impersonated by thieves in far away places who continually scrutinize computer networks and patiently wait (like a wolf outside your door) for a slip-up, a password or credit card number revealed, allowing them to intercept your electronic payments, empty your bank account, and ruin your credit rating—essential, after all, for your continued participation in the consumer economy—that is monitored, adjusted, and sold for profit to interested parties by three large corporations known as Experian, Equifax and Transunion.

Yet, despite these and other interlinked anxieties of our internet-age (spam, phishing, cyber-stalking, cyber-bullying, and so on), very few (myself included) are willing to renounce the internet, cell phones, satellite downloads and live without the computers, email, instant messaging, countless channels of television, online games and all the other fixtures we are accustomed to. It seems, just as Marcuse predicted, that we can see no viable alternatives to the efficient, technologically rational system of life we are caught up in.

Paranoid or not, we may already be androids. One of phenomenology's basic insights is that the conscious self is connected to, shaped by, and possibly even *constituted by*, the intentionality and purposiveness of first person experience. We—our selves, our souls, our minds—do not exist independently of our bodies and our material experience in the world. Descartes, for instance, was wrong to reason as he did in his *Meditations* that "I exist" and *then, subsequently*, convince himself that the exterior world he saw around him was in fact real and that his senses could be trusted. Instead, the "I" that experiences the world is always embodied. Being, Heidegger insisted, must always be understood as "Being-in-the-world"; and for Merleau-Ponty, "the subject that I am, when taken concretely, is inseparable from this body and this world."[6]

Our ever deepening dependence and engagement with the technologies of modern life, therefore, may lead to changes in our selves, *to* ourselves, that we might in fact reject or regret were we to understand them and see them for what they are. Like the people in Jamie Thrave's video for "Just," we might all collapse in shock or despair were we to face some truths about ourselves—truths that we never paid attention to, that no one ever talked about, even though they were obvious and in front of our faces all along. What would really hurt, of course, is realizing that that we'd

---

6 *The Phenomenology of Perception* (Routledge, 2002), p. 475.

done it to ourselves. By embracing and immersing ourselves in technology, we'd turned ourselves into machine-like and soulless androids.

Where Pink Floyd Ends
and Radiohead Begins

Radiohead's music, then, points to concerns about contemporary technology that only partly overlap the foreboding and shadowy landscapes once conjured by Pink Floyd. For Radiohead, technology is not simply a tool to artistically depict a corrupted world in need of cultural and political reform (as it was for Waters) or to escape ordinary perceptions (as it was for Barrett). For Radiohead's classic albums are filled with a phenomenological curiosity about the technology that has become the medium through which we experience life itself, saturated as our senses are by information, appliances, antibiotics, advertisements, and videotape.

Yet there remains something in Radiohead rooted in that magical, nostalgia-inspiring decade of Syd Barrett and Pink Floyd, moon-landings, and the ecology movement sparked by Rachel Carson's *Silent Spring*.. In "The Bends," Yorke sings "I wish it was the Sixties," but, in fact, it still is. Stephen Still's iconic "There's something happening here/what it is ain't exactly clear" has become Yorke's "I'm not here, this isn't happening" (from *Kid A*'s "How to Disappear Completely") or "something big is gonna happen" (from *Hail to the Thief*'s "Go to Sleep"). Some of these chapters use existentialism, psychoanalytic theory, or theology to explore the possible transformations that may be afoot. Others take up the ethical complexities—environmental and economic, mainly—of the music industry and what it may evolve into (in light of the controversial pay-what-you-want model for *In Rainbows*). Others address the politics latent in *Hail to the Thief*, the human-machine interface explored by *OK Computer*, *Kid A*, and *Amnesiac*, and the ways that the band's music takes us from Aristotelian tragedy to what it might mean for Martin Heidegger to press a button on his postmodern iPod.

There may even be a small but important truth behind the 'space-rock' idea, after all. For if Yorke's occasional references to spaceships and planets are understood phenomenologically, as I've been suggesting, then the possibilities for experience, understanding and political engagement lurking in Radiohead's music and explored in these chapters may be a *metaphorical* space ship ride— not toward the insanity lurking on the dark side of the moon, however. Like early Pink Floyd, we've set the controls so the light of the sun will enlighten us about what kinds of worlds and what kinds of experience are out there. If we pay close enough attention, we may find our way to a better, less terrifying, and previously unknown planet Earth.

2.

Radiohead, or the Philosophy of Pop

MARK GREIF

I've wondered why there's no philosophy of popular music. Critics of pop do reviews and interviews; they write appreciation and biography. Their criticism takes many things for granted and does-n't ask the questions I want answered. Everyone repeats the received idea that music is revolutionary. Well, is it? Does pop music support revolution? We say pop is of its time, and can date the music by ear with surprising precision, to 1966 or 1969 or 1972 or 1978 or 1984. Well, is it? Is pop truly of its time, in the sense that it represents some aspect of exterior history apart from the path of its internal development? I know pop does something to me; everyone says the same. So what does it do? Does it really influence my beliefs or actions in my deep life, where I think I feel it most, or does it just insinuate a certain fluctuation of mood, or evanescent pleasure, or impulse to move?

The answers are difficult not because thinking is hard on the subject of pop, but because of an acute sense of embarrassment. Popular music is the most living art form today. Condemned to a desert island, contemporary people would grab their records first; we have the concept of desert island discs because we could do without most other art forms before we would give up songs. Songs are what we consume in greatest quantity; they're what we store most of in our heads. But even as we can insist on the seriousness of value of pop music, we don't believe enough in its seriousness of meaning outside the realm of music, or most of us don't, or we can't talk about it, or sound idiotic when we do.

And all of us lovers of music, with ears tuned precisely to a certain kind of sublimity in pop, are quick to detect pretension, overstatement, and cant about pop—in any attempt at a wider criticism—precisely because we feel the gap between the effectiveness of the music and the impotence and superfluity of analysis. This means we don't know about our major art form what we ought to know. We don't even agree about how the interconnection of pop music and lyrics, rather than the words spoken alone, accomplishes an utterly different task of representation, more scattershot and overwhelming and much less careful and dignified than poetry—and bad critics show their ignorance when they persist in treating pop like poetry, as in the still-growing critical effluence around Bob Dylan.

If you were to develop a philosophy of pop, you would have to clear the field of many obstacles. You would need to focus on a single band, to let people know you had not floated into generalities and to let them test your declarations. You'd have to announce at the outset that the musicians were figures of real importance, but not the "most" anything—not the most avant-garde, most perfect, most exemplary. This would preempt the hostile comparison and sophistication that passes for criticism among aficionados. Then you should have some breathing room. If you said once that you liked the band's music, there would be no more need of appreciation; and if it were a group whose music enough people listened to, there would be no need of biography or bare description.

So let the band be Radiohead, for the sake of argument, and let me be fool enough to embark on this. And if I insist that Radiohead are "more" anything than some other pop musicians—as fans will make claims for the superiority of the bands they love—let it be that this band was more able, at the turn of the millennium, to pose a single question: How should it really ever be possible for pop music to incarnate a particular historical situation?

Radiohead belong to "rock," and if rock has a characteristic subject, as country music's is small pleasures in hard times (getting by), and rap's is success in competition (getting over), that subject must be freedom from constraint (getting free). Yet the first notable quality of their music is that, even though their topic may still be freedom, their technique involves the evocation—not of the feeling of freedom—but of unending low-level fear.

The dread in the songs is so detailed and so pervasive that it seems built into each line of lyrics and into the black or starry sky of music that domes it. It is environing fear, not antagonism emanating from a single object or authority. It is atmospheric rather than explosive. This menace doesn't surprise anyone. Outside there are listeners-in, watchers, abandoned wrecks with deployed air bags, killer cars, lights going out and coming on. "They" are waiting, without a proper name: ghost voices, clicks of tapped phones, grooves of ended records, sounds of processing and anonymity.

An event is imminent or has just happened but is blocked from our senses: Something big is gonna happen / Over my dead body. Or else it is impossible that anything more will happen and yet it does: I used to think / There is no future left at all / I used to think. Something has gone wrong with the way we know events, and the error leaks back to occurrences themselves. Life transpires in its representations, in the common medium of a machine language. (Arrest this man / he talks in maths / he buzzes like a fridge / he's like a detuned radio.) A fissure has opened between occurrence and depiction, and the dam bursts between the technical and the natural. These are not meant to be statements of thoughts about their songs, or even about the lyrics, which look banal on the printed page; this is what happens in their songs. The technical artifacts are in the music, sit behind our lips, and slide out when we open our mouths—as chemical and medical words effortlessly make it into the lyrics ("polystyrene," "myxomatosis," "polyethylene").

Beside the artificial world is an iconography in their lyrics that comes from dark children's books: swamps, rivers, animals, arks, and rowboats riding ambiguous tracks of light to the moon. Within these lyrics—and also in the musical counterpoint of

chimes, strings, lullaby—an old personal view is opened, a desperate wish for small, safe spaces. It promises sanctuary, a bit of quiet
in which to think.

> Such a pretty house
> and such a pretty garden.
> No alarms and no surprises,
> no alarms and no surprises,
> no alarms and no surprises please.

But when the songs try to defend the small and safe, the effort
comes hand-in-hand with grandiose assertions of power and violence, which mimic the voice of overwhelming authority that
should be behind our dread-filled contemporary universe but
never speaks—or else the words speak, somehow, for us.

> This is what you get
> this is what you get
> this is what you get
> when you mess with us.

It just isn't clear whether this voice is a sympathetic voice or a
voice outside—whether it is for us or against us. The band's task,
as I understand it, is to try to hold on to the will, to ask if there is
any part of it left that would be worth holding on to, or to find out
where that force has gone. Thom Yorke seems always in danger of
destruction; and then he is either channeling the Philistines or,
Samson-like, preparing to take the temple down with him. So we
hear pained and beautiful reassurances, austere, crystalline, and
delicate—then violent denunciations and threats of titanic
destruction—until they seem to be answering each other, as
though the outside violence were being drawn inside:

> Breathe, keep breathing.

> > We hope that you choke,
> > that you choke.

> Everything
> everything
> everything in its right place.

You and whose army?

We ride—we ride—tonight!

And the consequence? Here you reach the best-known Radiohead lyrics, again banal on the page, and with them the hardest mood in their music to describe—captured in multiple repeated little phrases, stock talk, as words lose their meanings and regain them. "How to disappear completely," as a song title puts it—for the words seem to speak a wish for negation of the self, nothingness, and nonbeing:

> For a minute there
> I lost myself, I lost myself.

> I'm not here. This isn't happening.

❗🚋🚌🚐✂🔪📟📠☎✈

A description of the condition of the late 1990s could go like this: At the turn of the millennium, each individual sat at a meeting point of shouted orders and appeals, the TV, the radio, the phone and cell, the billboard, the airport screen, the inbox, the paper junk mail. Each person discovered that he lived at one knot of a network, existing without his consent, which connected him to any number of recorded voices, written messages, means of broadcast, channels of entertainment, and avenues of choice. It was a culture of broadcast: an indiscriminate seeding, which needed to reach only a very few, covering vast tracts of our consciousness. To make a profit, only one message in ten thousand needed to take root, therefore messages were strewn everywhere. To live in this network felt like something, but surprisingly little in the culture of broadcast itself tried to capture what it felt like. Instead, it kept bringing pictures of an unencumbered luxurious life, songs of ease and freedom, and technological marvels, which did not feel like the life we lived.

And if you noticed you were not represented? It felt as if one of the few unanimous aspects of this culture was that it forbade you to complain, since if you complained, you were a trivial human, a small person, who misunderstood the generosity and benignity of the message system. It existed to help you. Now, if you accepted the constant promiscuous broadcasts as normalcy, there were messages in them to inflate and pet and flatter you. If you simply said this chatter was altering your life, killing your privacy or ending the ability to think in silence, there were alternative messages that whispered of humiliation, craziness, vanishing. What sort of crank needs silence? What could be more harmless than a few words of advice? The messages did not come from somewhere; they were not central, organized, intelligent, intentional. It was up to you to change the channel, not answer the phone, stop your ears, shut your eyes, dig a hole for yourself and get in it. Really, it was your responsibility. The metaphors in which people tried to complain about these developments, by ordinary law and custom, were pollution (as in "noise pollution") and theft (as in "stealing our time"). But we all knew the intrusions felt like violence. Physical violence, with no way to strike back.

And if this feeling of violent intrusion persisted? Then it added a new dimension of constant, nervous triviality to our lives. It linked, irrationally, in our moods and secret thoughts, these tiny private annoyances to the constant televised violence we saw. Those who objected embarrassed themselves, because they likened nuisances to tragedies—and yet we felt the likeness, though it became unsayable. Perhaps this was because our nerves have a limited palette for painting dread. Or because the network fulfilled its debt of civic responsibility by bringing us twenty-four-hour news of flaming airplanes and twisted cars and blood-soaked screaming casualties, globally acquired, which it was supposedly our civic duty to watch—and, adding commercials, put this mixture of messages and horrors up on screens wherever a TV could only be introduced on grounds of "responsibility to know," in the airport, the doctor's office, the subway, and any waiting room. But to object was demeaning—who, really, meant us any harm? And didn't we truly have a responsibility to know?

Thus the large mass of people huddled in the path of every broadcast, who really did not speak but were spoken for, who received and couldn't send, were made responsible for the new Babel. Most of us who lived in this culture were primarily sufferers or patients of it and not, as the word had it, "consumers." Yet we had no other words besides "consumption" or "consumerism" to condemn a world of violent intrusions of insubstantial messages, no new way at least to name this culture or describe the feeling of being inside it.

So a certain kind of pop music could offer a representative vision of this world while still being one of its omnipresent products. A certain kind of musician might reflect this new world's vague smiling threat of hostile action, its latent violence done by no one in particular; a certain kind of musician, angry and critical rather than complacent and blithe, might depict the intrusive experience, though the music would be painfully intrusive itself, and it would be brought to us by and share the same avenues of mass-intrusion that broadcast everything else. Pop music had the good fortune of being both a singularly unembarrassed art and a relatively low-capital medium in its creation—made by just a composer or writer or two or four or six members of a band, with little outside intrusion, until money was poured into the recording and distribution and advertising of it. So, compromised as it was, music could still become a form of unembarrassed and otherwise inarticulable complaint, capturing what one could not say in reasonable debate, and coming from far enough inside the broadcast culture that it could depict it with its own tools.

❗🚋🚈🚟✈✦✎📼🗂📞✈

A historical paradox of rock has been that the pop genre most devoted to the idea of rebellion against authority has adopted increasingly more brutal and authoritarian music to denounce forms of authoritarianism. A genre that celebrated individual liberation required increasing regimentation and coordination. The development could be seen most starkly in hard rock, metal, hardcore, rap-metal—but it was latent all along.

Throughout the early twentieth century, folk musics had been a traditional alternative to forms of musical authority. But amplification alone, it seems, so drastically changed the situation of music, opening possibilities in the realm of dynamics and the mimesis of other sounds, that it created avenues for the musical representation of liberation that had nothing to do with folk music's traditional lyrical content or the concern with instrumental skill and purism. Specifically, it gave pop ways to emulate the evils liberation would be fighting against. Pop could become

Goliath while it was cheering David. One aspect of amplification by the late 1960s stands out above all others: it opened up the possibility, for the first time, that a musician might choose to actually hurt an audience with noise. The relationship of audience to rock musician came to be based on a new kind of primitive trust. This was the trust of listeners facing a direct threat of real pain and permanent damage that bands would voluntarily restrain—just barely. An artist for the first time had his hands on a means of real violence, and colluded with his audience to test its possibilities. You hear it in the Who, the Doors, Jimi Hendrix. In the 1960s, of course, this testing occurred against a rising background of violence, usually held in monopoly by "the authorities," but being manifested with increasing frequency in civil unrest and police reaction as well as in war overseas. All of which is sometimes taken as an explanation. But once the nation was back in peacetime, it turned out that the formal violence of rock did not depend on the overt violence of bloodshed, and rock continued to metamorphose. The extremity of its dynamics developed toward heavy metal during the 1970s—and some connected this to industrial collapse and economic misery. Later it was refined in punk and postpunk, in periods of political defeat—and some connected the music's new lyrical alternations of hatred of authority with hatred of the self to the political, economic, and social outlook.

Maybe they were right. But this is perhaps to give too much automatic credence to the idea that pop music depicts history almost without trying—which is precisely what is in question.

❗🚃🚌🚦✂✒📭✁☎✈

To leap all the way into the affective world of our own moment, of course, might require something else: electronic sounds. To reproduce a new universe, or to spur a desire to carve out a life in its midst, a band might need a limited quantity of beeps, repetitions, sampled loops, drum machines, noises, and beats. "Electronica," as a contemporary genre name, speaks of the tools of production as well as their output. Laptops, Pro Tools, sequencers, and samplers, the found sounds and sped-up breaks and pure frequencies, provided an apparently unanchored environment and a weird soundscape that, though foreshadowed in studios in Cologne or at the Columbia-Princeton Electronic Music

Center, didn't automatically fit with the traditions of guitars and drums that pop knew. But the electronic blips the music used turned out to be already emotionally available to us by a different route than the avant-gardism of Stockhausen or Cage. All of us born after 1965 had been setting nonsense syllables and private songs to machine noise, and then computer noise, since the new sounds reached our cradles. Just as we want to make tick and tock out of the even movement of a clock, we wanted to know how to hear a language and a song of noises, air compressors and washer surges, alarm sirens and warning bells. We hear communication in the refined contemporary spectrum of beeps: the squall of a microwave, the chime of a timer, the fat gulp of a register, the chirrups of cell phones, the ping of seatbelt alerts and clicks of indicators, not to mention the argot of debonair beeps from the computers on which we type.

Radiohead, up until the late 1990s, had not been good at spelling out what bothered them in narrative songs. They attempted it in their early work. One well-known and well-loved but clumsy song sang about the replacement of a natural and domestic world by plastic replicas ("Fake Plastic Trees"). That account was inches away from folk cliché—something like Buffy Sainte-Marie's "Little Boxes." Its only salvation may have been the effect observed rather than the situation denounced: It wears you out, describing the fatigue human beings feel in the company of the ever-replaceable. *The Bends*, the last album produced before their major period, had this steady but awkward awareness, as the title implies, of being dragged through incompatible atmospheres in the requirements of daily life. But the band didn't yet seem to know that the subjective, symptomatic evocation of these many whiplashing states of feeling—not overt, narrative complaint about them—would prove to be their talent.

On the first mature album, *OK Computer*, a risk of cliché lingered in a song of a computer voice intoning: "Fitter, happier, more productive"—as if the dream of conformist self-improvement would turn us artificial. But the automated voice's oddly human character saved the effect—it seemed automated things, too, could be seduced by a dream of perfection equally delusory for them; then the new commensurability of natural and artificial wasn't a simple loss, but produced a hybrid vulnerability when you had thought things were most stark and steely. The band was also, at that time, mastering a game of voices, the interfiling of inhuman speech and machine sounds with the keening, vulnerable human singing of Thom Yorke.

Their music had started as guitar rock, but with the albums *Kid A* and *Amnesiac* the keyboard asserted itself. The piano dominated; the guitars developed a quality of organ. The drums, emerging altered and processed, came to fill in spaces in rhythms already set by the frontline instruments. Orchestration added brittle washes of strings, a synthetic choir, chimes, an unknown shimmer, or bleated horns. The new songs were built on verse-chorus structure in only a rudimentary way, as songs developed from one block of music to the next, not turning back.

And, of course—as is better known, and more widely discussed—on the new albums the band, by now extremely popular and multimillion-selling, "embraced" electronica. But what precisely did that mean? It didn't seem in their case like opportunism, as in keeping up with the new thing; nor did it entirely take over what they did in their songs; nor were they particularly noteworthy as electronic artists. It is crucial that they were not innovators, nor did they ever take it further than halfway—if that. They were not an avant-garde. The political problem of an artistic avant-garde, especially when it deals with any new technology of representation, has always been that the simply novel elements may be mistaken for some form of political action or progress. Two meanings of "revolutionary"—one, forming an advance in formal technique, the other, contributing to social cataclysm—are often confused, usually to the artist's benefit, and technology has a way of becoming infatuated with its own existence.

Radiohead's success lay in their ability to represent the feeling of our age; they did not insist on being too much advanced in the "advanced" music they acquired. The beeps and buzzes never seemed like the source of their energy, but a means they'd stumbled upon of finally communicating the feelings they had always held. They had felt, so to speak, electronic on *OK Computer* with much less actual electronica. And they did something very rudimentary and basic with the new technologies. They tilted artificial noises against the weight of the human voice and human sounds. Their new kind of song, in both words and music, announced that anyone might have to become partly inhuman to accommodate the experience of the new era.

Thom Yorke's voice is the unity on which all the musical aggregations and complexes pivot. You have to imagine the music drawing a series of outlines around him, a house, a tank, the stars of space, or an architecture of almost abstract pipes and tubes, cogs and wheels, ivy and thorns, servers and boards, beams and voids. The music has the feeling of a biomorphic machine in which the voice is alternately trapped and protected.

Yorke's voice conjures the human in extremis. Sometimes it comes to us from an extreme of fear, sometimes an extreme of transcendence. We recognize it as a naked voice in the process of rising up to beauty—the reassurance we've alluded to in the lyrics—or being broken up and lost in the chatter of broadcasts, the destroying fear. In the same song that features a whole sung melody, the vocals will also be broken into bits and made the pulsing wallpaper against which the vulnerable pale voice of the singer stands out. Only a few other popular artists build so much of their music from sampled voice, rather than sampled beats, instrumental tones, or noises. The syllables are cut and repeated. A "wordless" background will come from mashed phonemes. Then the pure human voice will reassert itself.[1]

A surprising amount of this music seems to draw on church music. One biographical fact is relevant here: they come from Oxford, England, grew up there, met in high school, and live, compose, and rehearse there. Their hometown is like their music. That bifurcated English city, split between concrete downtown and green environs, has its unspoiled center and gray periphery of modest houses and a disused automobile factory. Its spots of natural beauty exist because of the nearby huge institutions of the university, and if you stand in the remaining fields and parks you always know you are in a momentary breathing space, already encroached upon. But for the musically minded, the significant

---

1 The philosopher Stanley Cavell used to say that the first impulse opera evokes is to wonder where in the physical singer the immaterial song can be located. In live performance, the striking thing about Thom Yorke is how small a person he is; not only is his voice excessive, beyond human averageness, it is moored to a smaller-than-average body and onstage persona that seem to dramatize the question, in his music, of where voices come from—from individual people or the techniques that surround and overmaster them.

feature of Oxford is its Church of England chapels, one in each college and others outside—places of imperial authority, home to another kind of hidden song. The purity of Yorke's falsetto belongs in a boys' choir at Evensong. And then Yorke does sing of angels, amid harps, chimes and bells:

> black-eyed angels swimming with me
> . . . and we all went to heaven in a little rowboat
> there was nothing to fear and nothing to doubt.

And yet the religion in the music is not about salvation—it's about the authority of voices, the wish to submit and the discovery of a consequent resistance in oneself. It is antireligious, though attuned to transcendence. The organ in a church can be the repository of sublime power: a bundling of human throats in its brass pipes, or all the instruments known to man in its stops. You can hear your own small voice responding, within something so big that it manifests a threat of your voice merely being played mechanically and absorbed into a totality. To sing with an organ (as Yorke does at the end of *Kid A*) can be to discover one's own inner voice in distinction to it; and at the same time to wish to be lost, absorbed, overwhelmed within it. A certain kind of person will refuse the church. But even one who refuses the church will not forget the overwhelming feeling.

Sublime experience, the tradition says, depends on a relation to something that threatens. Traditionally it depended on observing from a point of safety a power, like a storm, cataract, or high sea, that could crush the observer if he were nearer. (By compassing the incompassable power in inner representation, it was even suggested, you could be reminded of the interior power of the moral faculty, the human source of a comparable strength.) Radiohead observe the storm from within it. Their music can remind you of the inner overcoming voice, it's true. But then the result is no simple access of power. This sublime acknowledges a different kind of internalization, the drawing of the inhuman into yourself; and also a loss of your own feelings and words and voice to an outer order that has come to possess them.

‼️🚃🚌💥✂️〰️🖥️📄☎️✈️

The way Yorke sings guarantees that you often don't know what the lyrics are; they emerge into sense and drop out—and certain phrases attain clarity, while others remain behind. This de-enunciation has been a tool of pop for a long time. Concentrating, you can make out nearly all the lyrics; listening idly, you hear a smaller set of particular lines, which you sing along to and remember. It is a way of focusing inattention as well as attention.

The most important grammatical tic in Radiohead lyrics, unlike the habitual lyrical "I" and apostrophic "you" of pop, is the "we." We ride. We awake. We escape. We're damaged goods. Bring down the government, they don't speak for us. But also: We suck young blood. We can wipe you out anytime. The pronoun doesn't point to any existing collectivity; the songs aren't about a national group or even the generic audience for rock. So who is "we"?

There is the scared individual, lying to say he's not alone—like the child who says "we're coming in there!" so imagined monsters won't know he's by himself. There's the "we" you might wish for, the imagined collectivity that could resist or threaten; and this may shade into the thought of all the other listeners besides you, in their rooms or cars alone, singing these same bits of lyrics.

There's the "we," as I've suggested, of the violent power which you are not, the voice of the tyrant, the thug, the terrifying parent, the bad cop. You take him inside you and his voice spreads over all the others who—somewhere singing these words for just a moment—are like you. You experience a release at last, so satisfying does it feel to sing the unspoken orders out loud to yourself, as if at last they came from you. You are the one willing the destruction—like Brecht and Weill's Pirate Jenny the barmaid, washing dishes and taking orders, who knows that soon a Black Ship will come for her town, bristling with cannons. And when its crew asks their queen whom they should kill, she will answer: "Alle."

So the characteristic Radiohead song turns into an alternation, in exactly the same repeated words, between the forces that would defy intrusive power, and the intrusive power itself, between hopeful individuals and the tyrant ventriloquized.

It has to be admitted that other memorable lyrics sing phrases of self-help. Plenty of these important lines are junk slogans from the culture, and of course part of the oddity of pop is that junk phrases can be made so moving; they do their work again. In a desperate voice: You can try the best you can / if you try the best you can / the best you can is good enough. Or: Breathe, keep breathing / don't lose your nerve. Or: Everyone / everyone around here / everyone is so near / it's holding on. On the page, these lyrics aren't impressive, unless you can hear them in memory, in the framing of the song. Again, one has to distinguish between poetry and pop. The most important lines in pop are rarely poetically notable; frequently they are quite deliberately and necessarily words that are most frank, melodramatic, and unredeemable. And yet they do get redeemed. The question becomes why certain settings in music, and a certain playing of simple against more complex lyrics, can remake debased language and restore the innocence of emotional expression. (Opera listeners know this, in the ariose transformations of "Un bel dì" [One fine day] or "O mio babbino caro" [Oh my dear papa]. But then opera criticism, too, has a longstanding problem with lyrics.)

In the midst of all else the music and lyrics are doing, the phrases of self-help may be the minimal words of will or nerve that you need to hear.

❗🚃🚌☀✂✏🖼🕯☎✈

The more I try to categorize why Radiohead's music works as it does, and by extension how pop works, the more it seems clear that the effect of pop on our beliefs and actions is not really to create either one. Pop does, though, I think, allow you to retain certain things you've already thought, without your necessarily having been able to articulate them, and to preserve certain feelings you have only intermittent access to, in a different form, music with lyrics, in which the cognitive and emotional are less divided. I think songs allow you to steel yourself or loosen yourself into certain kinds of actions, though they don't start anything. And the particular songs and bands you like dictate the beliefs you can preserve and reactivate, and the actions you can prepare—and which songs and careers will shape your inchoate private experience, depends on an alchemy of your experience and the art itself. Pop is neither a mirror nor a Rorschach blot, into which you look and see only yourself; nor is it a lecture, an interpretable poem, or an act of simply determinate speech. It teaches something, but only by stimulating and preserving things that you must have had inaugurated elsewhere. Or it prepares the ground for these discoveries elsewhere—often knowledge you might never otherwise have really "known," except as it could be rehearsed by you, then repeatedly reactivated for you, in this medium.

!⌨🚋🚌✗✎💾🗂📞✈

But is the knowledge that's preserved a spur to revolution? There is no logical sense in which pop music is revolutionary. That follows from the conclusion that pop does not start beliefs or instill principles or create action ex nihilo. It couldn't overturn an order. When so much pop declares itself to be revolutionary, however, I think it correctly points to something else that is significant but more limited and complicated. There is indeed an antisocial or countercultural tendency of pop that does follow logically from what it does. That is to say, there is a characteristic affect that follows from a medium that allows you to retain and reactivate forms of knowledge and experience which you are "supposed to" forget or which are "supposed to" disappear by themselves—and "supposed to" here isn't nefarious, it simply means that social forms, convention, conformity, and just plain intelligent speech don't allow you to speak of these things, or make them embarrassing when you do. Pop encourages you to hold on to and reactivate hints of personal feeling that society should have extinguished. Of course this winds up taking in all classes of fragile personal knowledge: things that are inarticulable in social speech because they are too delicate or ideologically out of step, and things that should not be articulated because they are selfish, thoughtless, destructive, and stupid. That helps explain how these claims for "what I learned from pop" can go so quickly from the sublime to the ridiculous and back to the sublime. It explains why we are right to feel that so much of what's promised for pop is not worth our credulity. But, again, risking ridiculousness, I think the thing that pop can prepare you for, the essential thing, is defiance. Defiance, at its bare minimum, is the insistence on finding ways to retain the thoughts and feelings that a larger power should have extinguished.

❗🏠🚐🚋✳✖🔌📷🗂📞✈

The difference between revolution and defiance is the difference between an overthrow of the existing order and one person's shaken fist. When the former isn't possible, you still have to hold on to the latter, if only so as to remember you're human. Defiance is the insistence on individual power confronting overwhelming force that it cannot undo. You know you cannot strike the colossus. But you can defy it with words or signs. In the assertion that you can fight a superior power, the declaration that you will, this absurd overstatement gains dignity by exposing you, however uselessly, to risk. Unable to stop it in its tracks, you dare the crushing power to begin its devastation with you.

Power comes in many forms for human beings, and defiance meets it where it can. The simplest defiance confronts nature's power and necessity. In the teeth of a storm that would kill him, a man will curse the wind and rain. He declares, like Nikos Kazantzakis's peasant Zorba, "You won't get into my little hut, brother; I shan't open the door to you. You won't put my fire out; you won't tip my hut over!" This will is not Promethean, simply human.

In all forms of defiance, a little contingent being, the imperiled man or woman, hangs on to his will—which may be all he has left—by making a deliberate error about his will's jurisdiction. Because the defiant person has no power to win a struggle, he preserves his will through representations: he shakes his fist, announces his name, shouts a threat, and above all makes the statements, "I am," "we are." This becomes even more necessary and risky when the cruel power is not natural, will-less itself, but belongs to other men. Barthes gives the words of the French revolutionist Guadet, arrested and condemned to death: "Yes, I am Guadet. Executioner, do your duty. Go take my head to the tyrants of my country. It has always turned them pale; once severed, it will turn them paler still." He gives the order, not the tyrant, commanding necessity in his own name—defying the false necessity of human force that has usurped nature's power—even if he can only command it to destroy him.

The situation we confront now is a new necessity, not blameless like wind or water and yet not fatal as from a tyrant or executioner. The nature we face is a billowing atmospheric second nature made by man. It is the distant soft tyranny of other men, wafting in diffuse messages, in the abdication of authority to technology, in dissembling of responsibility under cover of responsibility and with the excuse of help—gutless, irresponsible, servile, showing no naked force, only a smiling or a pious face. The "they" are cowardly friends. They are here to help you be happy and make fruitful choices. (We can wipe you out anytime.)

At its best, Radiohead's music reactivates the moods in which you once noticed you ought to refuse. It can abet an impersonal defiance. This is not a doctrine the band advances, but an effect of the aesthetic. It doesn't name a single enemy. It doesn't propose revolution. It doesn't call you to overthrow an order that you couldn't take hold of anyway at any single point, not without scapegoating a portion and missing the whole. This defiance—it might be the one thing we can manage, and better than sinking beneath the waves. It requires the retention of a private voice.

❗🔥🚃🚌✂️ⁿ📟📁☎️✈️

One of the songs on *Hail to the Thief* has a peculiar counterslogan:

> Just 'cause you feel it
> doesn't mean it's there.

To sense the perversity of the appearance of these words in a pop song, you have to remember that they occur inside an art form monomaniacally devoted to the production of strong feelings. Pop music always tells its listeners that their feelings are real. Yet here is a chorus that denies any reference to reality in the elation and melancholy and chills that this chorus, in fact, elicits. Yorke delivers the lines with an upnote on "feel" as he repeats them, and if anything in the song makes your hair stand on end, that will be the moment. He makes you feel, that is, the emotion he's warning you against. Next he sings a warning not to make too much of his own singing: there's always a siren / singing you to shipwreck. And this song, titled "There There," was the first single released off the album, pressed in many millions of copies; it was played endlessly on radio and MTV.

The purpose of the warning is not to stop feelings but to stop you from believing they always refer to something, or deserve reality, or should lead to actions, or choices, or beliefs—which is, of course, what the messages you hear by broadcast like you to make of them. The feelings evoked by a pop song may be false, as the feelings evoked by all the other messages brought to you by the same media as pop songs may be false. You must judge. If leading you to disbelieve in broadcast also leads you to disbelieve in pop, so be it; maybe you believed in pop in the wrong way. You must distinguish. The broadcast messages are impersonal in one fashion. They pretend to care about you when actually they don't know or care that you, as a single person, exist. Impersonal defiance is impersonal in another way; it encourages you to withdraw, no longer to believe that there is any human obligation owed to the sources of messages—except when they remind you, truly, of what you already have subtly sensed, and already know.

You can see a closed space at the heart of many of Radiohead's songs. To draw out one of their own images, it may be something like a glass house. You live continuously in the glare of inspection and with the threat of intrusion. The attempt to cast stones at an outer world of enemies would shatter your own shelter. So you settle for the protection of this house, with watchers on the outside, as a place you can still live, a way to preserve the vestige of closure—a barrier, however glassy and fragile, against the outside. In English terms, a glass house is also a glasshouse, which we call a greenhouse. It is the artificial construction that allows botanical life to thrive in winter.

Radiohead's songs suggest that you should erect a barrier, even of repeated minimal words, or the assertion of a "we," to protect yourself—and then there proves to be a place in each song to which you, too, can't be admitted, because the singer has something within him closed to interference, just as every one of us does, or should. We'll all have to find the last dwellings within ourselves that are closed to intrusion, and begin from there. The politics of the next age, if we are to survive, will be a politics of the re-creation of privacy.[2]

2 This chapter was originally published in the journal *n+1*, issue 3, 2006, pp. 23-39.

3.

All the Argument We Need

John Sylvia

In early June of 2008, Radiohead teamed up with MTV's project EXIT (End Exploitation and Trafficking) and released a music video for the song "All I Need." Typical music videos follow a story element of the song, show clips of the members of the group playing their instruments, or just use intriguing visuals. This video's quite different. It does feature a story, but it has an edge.

The video features a split screen. On the left is presumably an American child going about his typical day. On the right is a child presumably from another country also going about his typical day. Despite similarities such as waking up, washing their faces, and eating, the video shows the stark contrast between the two lives. The American child is relatively comfortable. He watches television, goes to school, reads from a book, and colors a picture. In contrast, the other boy works in a shop. Near the end, this boy puts down an almost finished shoe just as the American child takes off his shoes to go to bed. The shoes are shown right next to each other on the split screens and look similar, if not identical. Because this video was made specifically for the EXIT program, the meaning is clear; however, even if we didn't know the reason the video was made, the message should be fairly clear in light of labor conditions around the world.

Because the shots are so similar, they contrast how different the lives of the two boys are.

Although there is by no means universal agreement, many people have been strongly affected by this video and made aware of the exploitation of child laborers in other countries. I've long thought about the issue from a political and philosophical perspective. Yet this video still made an incredibly strong impression on me—stronger than even some of the best philosophical arguments in western philosophy. My reaction struck me as somewhat strange. The little philosopher's voice raced in my head after watching the video. Traditional arguments about the things in the world are expected to be logical and clear. An argument should be carefully constructed and precise. Yet music, even lyrically, is very often vague, imprecise and fuzzy. What then could it offer about the matter which philosophy or logical discourse could not?

Arguing without Argument

Perhaps you've already guessed my answer. Music can elicit such a strong reaction precisely because it can cause an emotional response when we listen to it. This reaction seems to be somehow stronger than reactions to simply logical or rational philosophical arguments. We've already looked at this musical and emotional argument against child labor, so what would a more philosophical argument look like?

We can choose from many different ethical theories to make our case, but let's try to keep it simple. The basic principle of utilitarianism is that what is right is the action which produces the greatest good for the greatest number of people. We could spend a lot of time splitting hairs over different formulations of this principle and exactly what we mean by "greatest good." But if we accept the basic principle of utilitarianism, it does not seem like exploiting children for labor brings about the greatest good for the greatest number of people. The good of my being able to purchase cheap shoes does not outweigh the negative impact of this way of life for so many children. Therefore, the conclusion is: I should not purchase shoes from companies that exploit children, and of course, no company should exploit children.

Now, let's stop and ask some questions. First, were you convinced by the argument? Second, how did it make you *feel*? If you can accept the basic principle of utilitarianism, then you probably should be convinced that the argument is correct. (If you just don't like utilitarianism, we could easily make the same argument from another ethical theory.) Actually, we might not even need a theory to justify our thinking that this exploitation is bad. On some level, we just feel that it is. But what's the impact of a philosophic argument like this? Did it rile you up and cause the same feelings and thoughts that the "All I Need" video caused? Possibly for a few it did, but more than likely the somewhat vague "argument" of the video caused a much stronger reaction than the clear and precise philosophic argument. But how could that be? How can Radiohead argue about the way the world is without using anything like what we consider a traditional argument?

To answer that question, we're going to have to look back to Aristotle's conception of rhetoric—the practice of writing or speaking skillfully. He divides the art of rhetoric into three distinct categories: ethos, pathos, and logos. Ethos deals with the credibility of the one making the argument, pathos deals with the emotional appeal being made, and logos deals with the logical reasoning involved. This distinction gives us a much easier way to understand the difference between the two arguments we've been looking at.

The history of western philosophy has focused heavily on the importance of logos. In ancient Greece, the Sophists wrote about and went around teaching the art of rhetoric, often for a fee. For them, rhetoric meant giving a convincing speech—even if it wasn't necessarily accurate; in other words they ignored the logos aspect. This disregard for the so-called truth upset philosophers like Socrates and Plato, who were contemporaries very critical of the Sophists. Plato, especially, believed in a form of Truth that was eternal and unchanging, while Socrates would find it appalling to charge money for helping others discover truth. Because Socrates and Plato have been taken as the founding fathers of philosophy, their view of the Sophists has been mostly adopted, and therefore, at least for most of the history of western philosophy, the emphasis has been placed on logos while ethos, and especially pathos, have been downplayed.

In a lot of ways this emphasis on the logos makes sense. The scientific method is seemingly founded on reason and rationality. A focus on the logos might be understood as an emphasis on the tool that has allowed society to progress as far and as quickly as it has. There is no doubt that the way of reason is important and necessary; however, emphasis was placed so heavily on that method alone that the ethos and pathos were almost entirely excluded.

All I Need: All about the World

If music is able to offer arguments about the world, it seems to do it without this emphasis on logos. Consider the way television commercials utilize pathos and ethos form arguments. They play on basic needs and emotions of humans (pathos), and sometimes draw on celebrities (ethos) to make the point. These commercials do seem to have some power over us, even if it is subconscious, but it would be quite a stretch to say that they are *arguing* a point. Yet, I want to claim that Radiohead *is* able to argue a point outside of logos. What's the difference?

There's another philosophical distinction (usually associated with logical positivism) that I need to invoke—the difference between cognitive information and expressive information. Cognitive information tells us something about the world and it should be possible at least in theory to verify whether a cognitive statement is true or false. "The moon is made of cheese" is a cognitive statement because we can determine whether it is true or false by either using a powerful telescope or actually going to the moon to examine it. In Ancient Greece, they weren't able to actually do either of these tests, but the statement was still testable in principle and therefore cognitive.

Art, on the other hand, is typically taken to be expressive. It is not typically understood as saying anything testable about the world. We feel uncomfortable calling a painting or a song true or false because, the point is, a work of art *expresses* something the artist feels. While most think Radiohead and other bands create music that is mainly expressive and emotional, there is a way to see it as also being cognitive, as telling us something about the world.

At the very least we know from listening to "All I Need" something about how Thom Yorke feels about the world. But do we know this for certain? Are we positive that he wasn't writing ironically? Or that he tossed a bunch of words into a bag and drew them out randomly, arranging them into a song as he went? Unless Thom himself came right out and honestly explained his writing methods and thoughts in detail, we'd never really be certain that the lyrics truly expressed his feelings about something.

There's a simpler answer, however. We can learn about *ourselves* through a piece of music. Think back to the lyrics "I only stick with you because there are no others. You are all I need." When I hear these lyrics together with the slow and haunting music, I reflect on my own life. Am I only staying with my partner because there's no one else? Maybe they are all I *need* but do I *want* more? It could very well be that these thoughts were already dancing around in your subconscious, but it wasn't until you heard the song that they came welling up to the surface. The song focuses an idea or a question on which we can sit back, reflect, and apply to our own lives.

2 + 2 = 5

The "All I Need" video actually makes an argument about the world by combining all three elements of rhetoric: the logos, pathos, and ethos. First, the band has credibility, or ethos. (Whether or not this ethos is deserved or should apply to arguments about child exploitation can be debated, but I'm not going to do that here.) Second, we've already described the emotions the song elicits as a form of pathos. And the logic of its argument, that one child is a winner and the other a loser in our global economy, is clear. But it is the combination of the three modes of rhetoric that makes the video actually stronger and more convincing than a straightforward ethical argument. Consider a standard response in defense of the global economic conditions the video addresses: "So what? Children need to work—it teaches them proper values and instills a work ethic."

There's a well-known philosophical thought experiment which helps explain why "All I Need" is more powerful than any cognitive argument like this. Robert Nozick asks us to imagine an "experience machine" (Robert Nozick, *Anarchy, State, and Utopia*. New York: Basic Books, 1974). Suppose it were possible to plug ourselves into this machine and experience anything we choose. Always wanted to be a part of Radiohead? Plug into this machine and you can be a member of the band! You can go on the tours, experience the fame and glamour, get the women, or go to the best parties. Just program your particular fantasy and plug into the machine. The best part of it is that while you're *in* the machine, you don't even realize that this experience isn't real. If this is sounding familiar, the plot of *The Matrix* has often been related to this thought experiment. So, as Radiohead fans, this deal sounds pretty good to us, doesn't it?

Maybe not. Even in *The Matrix*, most characters choose *not* to experience the life inside the experience machine once they know there's a choice. Nozick argues that there are good reasons for their decision. The most important is the idea that we want to *actually* do things. But in the experience machine "there is no *actual* contact with any deeper reality, though the experience of it can be simulated" (p. 43). Consider the popular computer game *The Sims*, in which you create a character and control it through what amounts to a pretty mundane life (at least, compared to the action and adventure found in other video games). The character has to eat, go to the bathroom, stay clean, go to work to make money, and so on. The analogy isn't perfect, but it strikes me that a *Sims* character would resemble your own character inside Nozick's experience machine. So if your "sim" is able to become a rock star in the game, have you actually accomplished anything by plugging in? Do you somehow feel better about your own life, excluding the minor relaxation and enjoyment you'd get from playing any game? It doesn't seem that you would. And the same would hold true for the "you" that is in the experience machine. You're not actually doing or accomplishing anything at all. Sure, the experience machine might offer pleasure, but more important than that are our actual accomplishments and our struggles to live in and understand the real world.

You're Living in a Fantasy World, This Beautiful World

How might all this apply to the issue of child labor which "All I Need" addresses? It shows one of the reasons why the video's combination of ethos, pathos, and logos is so compelling. As many writers about Radiohead have noted, their work addresses and criticizes the Baudrillardian, *Matrix*-like quality of our media-saturated culture. In a way, we are all "plugged in" to Nozick's machine in the form of televisions, radios, movies, and the internet that constantly bombard us with images, stories, and claims that can seem credible and reasonable, if only because they survive a news cycle or appear in different venues. The quotation from linguist and political theorist Noam Chomsky featured on the "Airbag / How Am I Driving?" EP suggests how this interconnecting web of ethos, pathos, and logos (which I marked in brackets) works in politics:

> It is an important feature of the ideological system to impose on people the feeling [pathos] that they are incompetent to deal with complex and important issues [logos]: they'd better leave it to the captain. One device is to develop a star system, an array of figures who are often media creations or creations of the academic propaganda establishment, whose deep insights we are supposed to admire [ethos] and to whom we must happily and confidently assign the right to control our lives and to control international affairs. (Noam Chomsky, in J. Peck, ed., *The Chomsky Reader*, pp. 42–43)

This star system might even convince you that child-labor exploitation is not such a bad thing. Suppose you see a popular news story on rising prices that reminds you to appreciate how inexpensive imported shoes are. Suppose you've also seen a touching interview with families in Indonesia or Thailand who are happy to make any money at all in local factories. You might then question these arguments against child labor by asking: Is it *really* the greatest good for the greatest number if we don't exploit children? Maybe more people are better off if we do! Or, you might simply let the question fade into the background of modern life, with suffering children taking the part of just more images floating around "out there" somewhere in the world news cycles, head-lines and images. The "realness" of the suffering and unfairness, in other words, can be lost, regardless of how clear or rigorous our cognitive arguments about exploitive child labor may be.

That's why the video for "All I Need" is a slap in the face. It punctures the hyperreality we're all plugged into. The reality and problems with child labor become immediate and apparent through that split-screen analysis. Even though cognitively I'd already accepted that child labor was wrong, the video still served as a wake up call. It brought forth the reality and the nature of the problems of child labor in a way that no cognitive argument could.

The members of Radiohead themselves aren't actually doing philosophy, of course. But we can look philosophically at their work to understand how it is related to the world and our under-standing of the world in ways that can be more direct and persua-sive than traditional arguments. The video shows that pathos and ethos can work in harmony with logos to form an even stronger argument than logos alone could. We *care* about the world around us, so why shouldn't emotion play a part in arguing about the world, especially if it used appropriately. Radiohead gives us an example of how this can be done—a way of arguing about the world without really arguing at all.[1]

1 For helping me sort through the ideas in this article I would like to thank both my wife, Kim Sylvia, and Steven Smitherman, who helped guide my musical taste as we grew up. Also thanks go to George and Brandon for helping me tighten the focus of the essay.

4.

Radiohead and Some Questions about Music

EDWARD SLOWIK

There's an old joke about a stranger who, upon failing to get any useful directions from a local resident, complains that the local "doesn't know much." The local replies, "yeah, but I ain't lost."

Philosophers of music are kind of like that stranger. Music is an important part of most people's lives, but they often don't know much about it—even less about the philosophy that underlies music. Most people *do* know what music they like, however. They have no trouble picking and choosing their favorite bands or DJs (they aren't lost). But they couldn't begin to explain the musical forms and theory involved in that music, or, more importantly, why it is that music is so important to them (they can't give directions). Exploring the evolution of Radiohead's musical style and its unique character is a good place to start.

Radiohead and Rock Music

In trying to understand the nature of music, it might seem that focusing on rock music, as a category of popular music, is not a good choice. Rock music complicates matters because it brings into play lyrics, that is, a non-musical written text. This aspect of rock may draw people's attention away from the music itself. (In fact, I bet you know many people who like a particular band or song based mainly on the lyrics—maybe these people should take up poetry instead!) That's why most introductions to the philosophy of music deal exclusively with classical music, since classical music is often both more complex structurally and contains no lyrics, allowing the student to focus upon the purely musical structural components.

Radiohead is not your average rock band, needless to say, and their musical compositions have attracted the interest of many music lovers from the classical and jazz communities. As the composer Paul Lansky (whose electronic music directly inspired the song "Idioteque") puts it: "There is nobody else like Radiohead, and the band's work is interesting to many who are not among the cohort of rock fans, although these form its largest audience."[1] What is it about Radiohead's music that draws such interest from outside popular music?

I think it's safe to say that Radiohead's first two albums, *Pablo Honey* and *The Bends,* have limited cross-over appeal to other styles since these albums fit more closely the traditional mold of rock or pop music. The songs have straightforward lyrics, and employ the standard rock instrumentation of lead and rhythm guitars, bass, drums, with the possible addition of keyboards or extra guitars. More importantly, the melodies, rhythms, harmonies, and other components of popular song structure also seem comparable to much popular music of the time, despite many strong hints to their later style. Beginning with *OK Computer,* the structure and "sound world" of Radiohead's output grows increasingly more complex and experimental. Rather than employing the basic melodic format of most pop songs (verse, chorus, and connecting bridge passage), many songs have a much more elaborate structure that defies expectations. "Paranoid Android," from *OK Computer* has so many different parts, and transitions to new material, you might think that it is three separate songs rolled into one.

---

1 Paul Lansky, "My Radiohead Adventure," in *The Music and Art of Radiohead*, edited by J. Tate (Aldershot: Ashgate), p. 175. Also worth looking at is another article in the same book, "Public Schoolboy Music: Debating Radiohead," by Dai Griffiths.

In looking back, however, *OK Computer* may seem to be more of a transitional album for the group, since the album largely features the standard rock instrumentation that one doesn't always find in their later output. Many of the songs from the second half of the album seem like they could have been on *The Bends*. It's with the next two albums, *Kid A* and *Amnesiac,* that Radiohead reveal the most severe and startling changes. These two albums are really the two halves of an amazing double-album, since most of the tracks were recorded in the same sessions. Besides a much greater use of keyboards and other electronic sounds, there is the addition of orchestral instrumentation, as well as the incorporation of jazz, techno, and many other musical influences. What is really striking about the music, however, is the "more abstract harmonic and formal language" ("My Radiohead Adventure," p. 174). The music just sounds different from rock music, even in those songs that mainly use traditional rock instruments.

Hail to the Thief and *In Rainbows* both contain a number of songs that aim for a more traditional rock music sound, but much in these albums also follows the precedents set in *Kid A* and *Amnesiac.* Part of the explanation for the difference in the overall sound, starting with *Kid A,* lies in the more complex harmonic textures employed by the band, a process that is also common throughout most of *OK Computer* (such as in "Airbag"), together with the increasingly experimental sonorities and instrumentation. In your average pop song, there is a single melodic line, often sung or played by the lead guitar, which is accompanied by the other instruments. In numerous songs on *Kid A* and *Amnesiac,* on the other hand, there are several lines in the music, such that each instrument seems to have its own distinct melodic and rhythmic content. A nice example of this is "In Limbo" from *Kid A,* where the different rhythmic and thematic lines played by each instrument stand out fairly clearly. "One of Radiohead's great secrets," Lansky rightly says, "is the inventive use of rhythmic levels, simultaneous projections of different metric layers." This method of composition is common in classical music, too. Lansky likewise notes that "Radiohead's relation to harmony in general is sophisticated and unusual," and he compliments "the expansive and rich contours of [their] tunes" (p. 175). Lead guitarist Jonny Greenwood, who is classically trained, has cited the twentieth-century composers Olivier Messiaen (1908–1992) and Kryzysztof Penderecki (b. 1933), as some of his musical influences.[2]

There are numerous precedents throughout rock history for much of what Radiohead has accomplished, starting with the post-1965 music of the Beatles, and continuing through the classic art rock bands like Pink Floyd and beyond. One could argue that Radiohead continues the tradition of many of these "progressive" or "art rock" bands, but that they just do it better (excluding the Beatles, who started it all). The members of Radiohead have constantly denied these labels, probably because they fear that their music will be stereotyped or pigeonholed as some branch of avant-garde rock music with limited mass appeal. At the very least, one thing that Radiohead has in common with all great composers or song writers is their dedication to constantly breaking new barriers and creating new musical works, and not simply repackaging the ideas that were successful in the past. Much, if not most, pop music is dedicated to that very purpose, namely, cashing in on the latest trend. Like any great artist, Radiohead has paid for its explorations into new musical realms, as the many negative initial responses to *Kid A* made quite clear. In the end, however, many critics and fans began to see that their new musical creations were, in fact, a logical progression and extension of their past artistic successes. However logical, though, they may not be imitable. When asked about the many Radiohead-lite bands, like Coldplay, that continue to spin out watered down copies of their earlier music (up to 1997), Thom Yorke, putting his hands to his mouth, mockingly yelled out, "Good luck with *Kid A!*" (*Welcome to the Machine*, p. 238).

Finally, does Radiohead's musical output consist of songs? Some have wondered: "Where *OK Computer* featured twelve highly inventive and original takes on the concept of a rock song, *Kid A* saw Radiohead producing tracks that not only defied categorization as rock music but that, on occasion, also challenged per-

---

2 This section of the essay relies on, Tim Footman, *Welcome to the Machine: Radiohead and the Death of the Classic Album*, Chrome Dreams, 2007, for an analysis of history of the band and the reception of their music. See, also, Martin Clarke, *Radiohead: Hysterical and Useless*, Plexus, 2006.

ceived notions of 'song'."[3] First, if a song requires lyrics, then many tracks on their various albums are not songs; for instance, "Treefingers" and "Hunting Bears," would not be songs since they have no lyrics. But, many of Radiohead's greatest "songs" also have important sections that likewise do not present any words, such as, to take but one example, the "Pyramid Song," whose powerful, and wordless, last section brings together and develops much of the musical material in the song. This outro section is hardly a cute coda of the kind you sometimes find in the purely instrumental conclusions of classical songs. In "Pyramid song," it's perhaps the song's most important moment.

What Is Music?

A good way to think about philosophy is that it is an attempt to answer the deepest and most fundamental questions about any given subject. Therefore, probably the deepest question you can ask about music is "What is it?"[4] One response often given is that music is organized or structured sound. Yet, a lawnmower makes organized sound: so, is the sound of a lawnmower music? Many modern classical composers and music fans would say "yes," since the revolution in modern art has greatly expanded the category of art across the board. For example, many people have seen paintings in art galleries or museums that look like just a blotch of different colors splashed across a canvas with no discernable shape or intention. It seems as though the colors don't represent anything. And, of course, those creations are paintings, or so the art gallery owners would tell you!

The twentieth century practically admitted everything into the ranks of art, and that includes music, of course, although many philosophers and music-lovers might complain. John Cage, the

---

3 Allan F. Moore and Anwar Ibrahim, "'Sounds Like Teen Spirit': Identifying Radiohead's Idiolect" in *The Music and Art of Radiohead*, p. 145.

4 Here I'm drawing on some ideas from Andrew Kania, "The Philosophy of Music," in the online Stanford Encyclopedia of Philosophy; Peter Kivy, Introduction to a Philosophy of Music, Oxford University Press, 2002; and Noël Carroll, The Philosophy of Art, Routledge, 1999.

famous twentieth-century American composer, created a work entitled, *4' 33"*, which comprises, essentially, a pianist sitting at a piano and doing *nothing* for four minutes and thirty-three seconds—it's strange to say that he "composed" the work, but I guess he did. Cage didn't intend the silence to be the music, but he wanted to draw people's attention to the sounds that were occurring during the "performance" (and it's also strange to say that it was a performance, but I guess it is as well). A performance of *4' 33"* thereby challenges our definition that music is structured sound, since most of the sounds occurring during the performance are probably random and unorganized (such as people coughing, people squirming in their seats, and all the other things that you would hear when a lot of people are uncomfortably having to sit together in silence). Some of Radiohead's songs also sound like unorganized sounds, like "Treefingers." After many listens, however, it is clear that there actually are themes and musical structure in this work.

Music may be the most puzzling of all the arts, philosophically speaking, because it is difficult to point to—more so than painting or sculpture. We know what a painting or sculpture is: a painting is that rectangular thing hanging on the wall with colors on it. But what object is music? Where do we point to? This is a problem in the ontology—the being or existence—of music. Is it a sequence of vibrations in the air? Or is it a series of written markings on a musical staff, or an electronic code on a CD? In traditional classical music, which is written down to be performed by many musicians, this may seem a bigger problem than for recorded pop music. A rock song, such as "Like Spinning Plates" from *Amnesiac,* is a studio recording of individual performances by the band's members, and thus it would seem that there is only one thing (or a combined collection of things) to which we can point to when trying to locate that piece of music in the world, although that performance has been reproduced on countless CDs. But what about the live performances of "Spinning Plates," like the beautiful piano-based version on *I Might be Wrong: Live Recordings*? Clearly that's an instance of the song, likewise for any cover versions performed by other musicians.

There have been many attempts to answer the problem of the ontology of music. One approach, called *nominalism*, holds that a musical piece exists as, or is instantiated by, particular performances of that piece, or written scores or recordings of the music. There are many problems with this theory, though, such as those songs, symphonies, or other musical pieces, that are conceived by a composer but are never written down. Does a song, thought up by a song writer, fail to be a song if never actually performed or written down? That seems unintuitive, since most people would likely judge that it is still music, indeed, it is still a song, despite the lack of a performance or a written score. Another theory, *idealism*, holds that music is indeed a mental entity, that is, something that only exists in the mind (like an idea). But, if a Radiohead song, say, "All I Need," only exists as an idea in Thom Yorke's mind, then how do we know if the band's recording of that song successfully communicated that idea to us? Since we can't get into Thom's head to check, we can't be sure, and how do the other members of the band know if they've got the right idea (song) from Thom, too! Obviously, this is a bigger problem for those composers who are no longer alive, since we can't ask them (but even living composers might forget what idea they had earlier held). In addition, for an idealist, it almost seems as if the performance of the song is just a cumbersome method of transmitting ideas—but that demeans or underplays the sound or auditory experience of the music, which is an odd view of music, to say the least.

On the whole, the most common theory on the ontology of music is *realism*, which regards music as an abstract object similar to mathematics or concepts, but without requiring that they only exist in the mind (as does the idealist). Mathematical objects, such as numbers, are not physical objects: you won't bump into the number "9" while out taking a walk. But, most philosophers also reject the view that numbers are only mental entities: that is, if no people existed in our world, such that there were no minds, it still seems that numbers would exist (for instance, there would still be a particular *number* of trees, or oceans, and other objects in existence, although we're not there to count them). What's nice about the realist theory is that it avoids many of the problems of both the nominalist, since music isn't confined to only existing things, as well as the idealist, since music isn't only a mental thing. Yet, is the song "Optimistic" really like a number? And do we really know what a number is, anyway? The difficulty with stating that music is an abstract object, as the realist believes, is that we really don't understand abstract objects. So, while realism may have some advantages over the other two theories outlined above, it still possesses many deep philosophical puzzles of its own.

Music: Emotion or Form?

In trying to answer the question, "What is music?," one of the important related issues involves how music, to put it bluntly, works or functions. When a person listens to "15 Step," or enjoys any type of art form, what is happening? How do artistic experiences, called "aesthetic" experiences, differ from other kinds of experiences, like a sports or work experiences? What's the purpose or role of music in our lives?

When reflecting upon the experience of art, it's likely that most people would find our emotional responses to art to be the most significant or obvious factor. Music, in particular, can bring about powerful emotions. The "emotion (or expression)" theory of music is based on this insight, since most people find music to be happy, sad, or any number of other emotions. Turning to the music of Radiohead, many music critics and fans have linked their songs with a host of dark or anguished emotions, such as the despair in the lyrics of "Like Spinning Plates." Consequently, the emotion theory *defines* music as an expression of emotion by the composer. But, a song is not a living being that can possess emotions, so how can it be claimed to have or express emotions? Put another way, how can something which doesn't have emotions, like a song, nevertheless raise emotions in us?

This problem has long been the major concern of the emotion theory. An obvious reply to this difficulty is to claim that the music *in itself* doesn't express emotion, since only humans, or psychological agents, can do that. Rather than actually embodying emotion, music is the means or method by which the composer expresses his or her emotions. That sounds reasonable, but how does music accomplish this neat trick of expressing the composer's emotion? Furthermore, if the audience does not feel or experience the emotion that the composer intended to transmit through the song, does that mean it is not a song? If the emotion theory is correct, then a bad song writer cannot make art, since they've failed to express the emotions that they wanted to express (and, as you'll recall, art is defined as an expression of emotion). But that's absurd, for a botched song is still a song!

Likewise, can we really know the emotions that Thom, Jonny, and the rest of the group intended to express through their music? Take "Like Spinning Plates": while the lyrics seem to express anguish, and the music has a complex, regular rhythm, along with quirky harmonies and sound effects, it does not have the really harsh or dissonant tones and rhythms that one might expect if anguish were the sole intention. Indeed, the otherworldly or abstract character of the music in this song makes pinpointing the exact emotion very difficult. As some have commented, the lyrics of *Kid A* and *Amnesiac* are, in general, also fairly abstract. And since abstraction does not convey a straightforward or clear-cut emotional message, it's often difficult to know exactly what specific emotion was intended by the lyrics as well. Furthermore, even if we think we have a pretty clear idea on what type of emotion is being expressed in the music, such as anguish in "Like Spinning Plates," it's also true that these types of dark emotions can come in many different forms, and with many different nuances. So, which emotion was intended? Besides, what does anguish, or joy, anger, and so on, sound like when translated into music? If there are many disagreements among composers, as there is bound to be, then music is probably a pretty poor method of expressing emotion; therefore, music must have another purpose.

Another problem for the emotion theory is that many philosophers hold that the composer must have actually had the experience in their own life in order to transmit that emotion through their music. Yet, why should that be the case? Even if Thom's life had been really easy-going, and he had never experienced deeply sad or dark feelings, it seems perfectly reasonable to assume that he could still possess the musical skills required to write a sad song. Many novelists write convincingly about murderers or politicians, or other types of people that they've never been or maybe ever met. So, why can't song writers create songs about emotions that they haven't had?

Finally, one can raise a number of problems for the emotion theory that shows that this definition of music is too broad, that is, it allows things to count as music that aren't music. For instance, if music is a created and structured sound that expresses emotion, then it would seem that angry drivers who blast their car horns are also making music! An advocate of the emotion theory might reply by claiming that there must be an audience, and that the main intention of the created sound must be to express emotion (and not for another reason, like for the driver in front of you to wake up and start moving since the light has turned green). So, since blasting a car horn doesn't meet those last conditions, it can't be music. But, in response, not only do people honk their horns precisely because they have an audience, but often, especially when in a long traffic jam, some (unhinged) drivers must know that honking their horns won't accomplish anything. Their intention must be to express emotion, and thereby they are making music, at least according to the definition of emotion theory, which seems absurd since it's certainly not music (or is it?).

Another way of looking at how emotion factors into our experience of music is to claim that the structure of music—the combination of its rhythms, harmonies, melodies, and the rest—somehow brings about emotions in us. That is to say, we respond emotionally to the form of music. This view, that music is really all about the structure of its musical elements (tones, pitch, rhythm, and so on) is called *formalism*. As noted earlier, what sets Radiohead apart from other contemporary bands, and most past bands, is the way that they put together the elements of traditional rock music, along with other musical elements from outside rock music, to achieve truly unique results. Often, the emotions that people detect or feel in a Radiohead song will vary from person to person, but the structure of the music remains the same of course: people simply react to that structure, or form, differently. Therefore, a theory of music must base the definition of music on its formal structure to some degree. Just as painting is the structural arrangement of colors and shapes on a flat surface, and sculpture is the structural arrangement of shapes and figure in three dimensions, music is the structural arrangement of the elements of sound.

Formalism in music is clearly a powerful and intuitive theory, but we've already seen one of its problems: a lawnmower presents an arrangement of structured elements of sound, if somewhat simplistic and monotonous, as does the car horn of the road-raged driver, so the sound of a lawnmower and car horn are music according to formalism. However, if we return to the issues of audience and intention, then the formalist theory of music seems to fair better than the emotion theory. The main intention of both a lawnmower and a car horn is *not merely* the presentation of a structured sound but to, respectively, cut the lawn and alert other drivers or pedestrians. The intention of music, on the other hand, is the presentation of structured sounds for its own sake, and not for any other purpose. But what about birdsongs? Many people may enjoy the distinctive sound that a bird makes for its own sake, but the bird didn't create those sounds to be enjoyed for its own sake—it serves as the bird's method of communicating with other birds. Therefore, birdsongs are not music according to the formalist theory that we're considering. This outcome may strike people as somewhat too limiting, needless to say, because many people do experience the sounds of birds, or even car horns, aesthetically in the same way that they enjoy human songs: so why can't birdsongs be art, too? (In response, can it be claimed that they're art but not music?)

A more obvious problem concerns music with lyrics. Most Radiohead songs have a written text, which presents a complication for the formalist theory since lyrics are not merely structured sounds: they also communicate a non-musical message. The formalist theory thus seems to work best for music that has no written or non-musical text, such as symphonies and other classical pieces for instruments alone. Some Radiohead's song are also wordless, like "Treefingers" and "Hunting Bears," as was mentioned earlier, but most are not. Therefore, the formalist definition of music is too narrow in that it leaves out many things that are music, like the lyrical component of songs (and maybe birdsongs, too).

Are Musical Experiences Universal?

Many philosophers have hoped that investigations into the psychological or social experience of music might find that human beings tend to react to music in the same way, probably at a deep unconscious level, such that the same types of musical structures are associated with the same types of emotions. For example, a slow downtrodden beat may evoke sadness for most people and in most societies, while a light fast beat is linked to happy feelings. If this is correct, it may show that human beings have certain types of psychological reactions and emotions hard-wired into us given the same musical experiences, thereby demonstrating the strong connection between our experience of musical structures and our emotions. One of the reasons, among many, for the importance of these findings is that it would show that our musical experiences are universal (that is, the same for all people), even if only to a very minimal degree. Other philosophers and musicologists, on the other hand, have argued that different people and cultures could have totally different psychological responses to the same music. This debate remains an open question.

But, if we all do have similar experiences given the same music, then music may be a more fixed, and possibly central, aspect of human experience than many have thought. One of the fascinating implications of these findings, if true, is the extent to which music criticism could gain a certain degree of validity or objectivity. If all people naturally react to music in similar ways, can we then claim that our judgments of music are also built into us? David Hume, the famous eighteenth-century Scottish philosopher, argued in his essay "Of the Standard of Taste" that the test of time is the only way to judge which art is truly great. If the vast majority of critics and music lovers, over a long stretch of time, praise and value the music of, say, a particular rock band, does that show that the band is really, objectively better than the competition? It's too early to tell whether or not the investigations into the philosophy and psychology of music will confirm Hume's theory, since there are many problems with this view. Yet, it does show that the consequences of the study of music could be very far-reaching indeed—it might even suggest that, when you and your friends argue about whether *OK Computer* or *In Rainbows* is a better disc, one of you might be actually right!

Art and Belief. *(Show Me The World As I'd Love To See It.)*

5.

New Shades

JERE O'NEILL SURBER

To really appreciate and understand Radiohead you need a new 'aesthetic', which is a lot like putting on a new pair of sunglasses. Here's why: The field of philosophy called Aesthetics is, in several ways, like buying sunglasses. Sure, price and UV protection are important, but we usually get these matters out of the way pretty quickly. It's other questions we generally spend most of our time considering.

We know that the tint of the glasses will make a big difference on what sort of contours and details we'll be able to see. For instance, any skier will know that orange-tinted goggles allow the contours of the snow to be seen much more clearly than blue or green lenses. Just as important, the color of the glasses will definitely affect your overall mood. We sometimes say 'looking at the world through rose-tinted glasses' to indicate a feeling of optimism and joy and we know that very dark gray or blue lenses will make us feel 'cool' and detached. The point is that the glasses you choose need to be adapted to the sort of things you'll mostly be viewing, to the general contexts in which you'll be wearing them, and to the type of feeling you'd like to have when you put them on.

An aesthetic theory functions in much the same way with regard to art objects. First, it helps us encounter certain things as 'artworks' that we might otherwise never have considered as 'art' at all (think of the way of seeing, very different from the traditional one associated with 'beautiful pictures', required to consider Marcel Duchamp's urinal or Andy Warhol's soup cans as artworks). Second, it enables us to perceive details as meaningful that we might otherwise have overlooked or failed to perceive (for instance, Jackson Pollock's drip-paintings as complex plays of deliberate planning and uncontrollable randomness). Finally, an aesthetic theory serves to 'color' our entire experience, including feelings and moods, as we encounter certain types of artworks. Like our sunglasses, we must choose our aesthetic theory to bring *what* we will be encountering into some sort of productive harmony with *how* we'll be experiencing it.

The music and art of Radiohead, like much of the art of the twentieth century, presents a direct challenge to prevailing aesthetic theories and invites us to try on 'new shades' when encountering it. In this essay, I suggest that you consider the quite recent (and, yes, now rather fashionable!) lenses of 'abject aesthetics' for approaching Radiohead's work. But this comes with a warning: for a while, you'll have to put aside the rather rose-colored psychedelic glasses of the 1960s and the dark reflector existentialist shades of the 1970s and 1980s. Looking at Radiohead through these new lenses, you'll discover few catchy tunes or straight-ahead rock beats, and no anthems to psychedelic or spiritual transcendence. Instead, you'll discover another world, one weirdly attractive, strangely unsettling, and yet maybe already somewhat familiar.

Meeting in the Abject

Have you ever wondered what the inside of your body really looks like? Why, sometimes when you look in the mirror in the morning, you can scarcely recognize the figure lurking there? Why, even though you know it will be upsetting, you can't resist looking at the scene of a bad accident? Why you have that intense but strange and unsettling feeling when you see a dead body, especially if it's someone you have known? Why things like feces, urine, semen, blood, and severed fingers or limbs automatically trigger a response of nausea or revulsion? Why we sometimes tend to avoid contact with homeless, physically deformed, or mentally ill persons? And, even further, why so many of these phenomena figure so prominently in the most ancient religious rituals as well as in a good deal of the most *avant-garde* art, not to mention popular culture? After all, most of these things are just as much 'natural' parts of our world as others which we encounter every day with little response at all; so why do we have such strange and extreme responses to these things and not most others?

The French philosopher, literary critic, and psychoanalyst Julia Kristeva wondered about all this too and, in 1980, proposed a new idea to help us understand them in her book, *The Powers of Horror: An Essay on Abjection.* The work itself ranged over such diverse topics as contemporary philosophy, psychoanalytic theory, the history of religions, and such important literary figures as Fyodor Dostoyevsky, James Joyce, Marcel Proust, Antonin Artaud, and Paul Céline. However, probably the single most important legacy of her work has been providing the basis for a new way of viewing and understanding certain developments in contemporary art, literature, and popular culture—something that has come to be called 'Abject Aesthetics'.

In a broad sense, 'the abject' has since become a new aesthetic category (a new 'set of lenses') to be added to such more traditional ones as 'the beautiful', 'the sublime', 'the political', 'the abstract', 'the surrealist', and 'the authentic'. Today, Abject Aesthetics is frequently employed to help understand such otherwise difficult and troubling works as Robert Mapplethorpe's graphic photos of the human body, Josef Beuys's dead rabbits and garbage sculptures, Damien Hirsch's segmented cattle encased in clear plastic blocks, and Chris Ofili's infamous 'Madonna' decorated with elephant feces. This category has also been used to understand tattooing, body piercing and mutilation, and the many alien, zombie, and slasher films of popular culture. Though never quite as extreme as these, the art of Radiohead offers another example that can perhaps only be fully seen and appreciated when viewed through the lenses of Abject Aesthetics.

I Wish I Was Special but I'm Abject

Kristeva introduces the idea of the 'abject' by contrasting it with the 'object'. Most earlier aesthetics presupposed an 'object', literally something 'projected in front' of a viewer and recognized by the viewer as possessing some (usually positive) properties. By contrast, the 'abject' is that which is 'cast down', 'put aside', rejected from even bare recognition. It is, of course, still 'there', it still exists, but it is excluded from the sphere of those 'objects' that are part of 'the world' of social discourse and interaction, like the 'abject poor or homeless' whom most of us learn early on to pass by and ignore or the bodily functions that all of us perform every day without ever mentioning them in 'polite company'.

"Creep" (still Radiohead's best known single) from their debut album *Pablo Honey* (1993) directly expresses this feeling of 'abjection', of being rejected or perhaps excreted from the world of 'the beautiful people'.

> You float like a feather
> In a beautiful world
> You're so fucking special,
> I wish I was special.
> . . . But I'm a creep, I'm a weirdo.

The song goes on to suggest that the real problem with 'creeps' is that, like the 'abject', they're usually not even noticed, that they fall outside any recognition of even being a person—to the 'beautiful people' they don't even exist!

You Have Turned Me into This

Kristeva suggests that part of the reason why certain things become 'abjected' is because they lack the clear contours and definite forms that we ordinarily expect 'objects' to have. For instance, a person or artwork tends to be judged as 'beautiful' because it conforms to some clear model or ideal of proportion, regularity, and symmetry. The abject, however, tends to be something fluid, irregular, chaotic, or shape-shifting—something that fails to fit into any of our usual categories. Thom's lyrics say this well when he sings, in "Bullet proof . . . I Wish I Was" (*The Bends*, 1995):

> Wax me, mould me
> Heat the pins and stab them in
> You have turned me into this

The expression of this sense of being formless, without clear definition, 'free-floating,' occurs often in Thom's lyrics, even in some of the latest work, such as "Nude" (*In Rainbows*, 2007):

> Now that you've found it, it's gone
> Now that you feel it, you don't
> You've gone off the rails

Pull/Pulk Abject Doors

Whereas 'objects' are usually assumed to be clearly delineated ('It's this, not that') and 'subjects' are clearly separate from their 'objects' ('I'm me, not any other thing'), the 'abject' always occupies borderline territory ('Both this and that' or 'Neither this nor that'). For instance, my severed finger is, in a strange way, both 'me' and 'no longer me'; the corpse of someone I know is both that person and not that person. Or, an android (as in 'Paranoid Android') is neither a human being nor a mere machine. Such phenomena break down the boundaries that we usually assume to define the world.

In the case of Radiohead, the best illustration of this 'borderline phenomenon' can be seen in their overall musical style and its dramatic changes. Their sonic work up to *OK Computer* happens in the 'border territory' between Thom's fragile and introspective vocals and Jonny's slashing, dissonant, and extroverted guitar commentary. Then, beginning with *Kid A* (2000), this 'both/and'—basically 'both hard rock and alternative'—seems to implode into something else entirely, 'neither rock nor alternative.'

Looking at their radical change of direction after *OK Computer* from this perspective may then help us understand something that has baffled their fans and critics alike. If Kristeva is right that the abject is always a borderline phenomenon, then we can think of the 'pre-' and 'post-*OK Computer*' work as two sides of the same coin, two different but complementary ways of exploring and negotiating boundaries. Either you can frame the boundary territory by two extremes (making it a 'both this and that') or you can collapse the extremes into something emerging from but different than either (making it a 'neither this nor that'). It might not even be too much of a stretch, then, to suggest that their last couple of albums (*Hail to the Thief,* 2003, and *In Rainbows,* 2007) began a sort-ing-out process where new contours and boundaries in their son-icscape have begun to emerge.

Where I End and You Begin

Kristeva explains that, in one way or another, the abject is con-nected with the body and its processes and immediate sensations, rather than external objects or ideas, since it is the body that forms that often amorphous region between 'where I stop and the world begins.'

You can't listen to Radiohead long without noticing how fre-quently Thom's lyrics employ physical, bodily references (rather than, for instance, psychological imagery or poetic metaphors). For example, in "Bones" (*The Bends,* 1995), he sings,

> I don't want to be crippled and cracked
> Shoulders, wrists, knees, and back
> Ground to dust and ash
> Crawling on all fours

On the same album, "My Iron Lung" has the lyrics,

> My brain says I'm receiving pain
> A lack of oxygen
> From my life support
> My iron lung

On another occasion ("Knives Out," *Amnesiac,* 2001), a whole song is devoted to death in a very physical sense: the corpse of a mouse "bloated and frozen" to be "put in the pot" and cooked up.

How to Disappear Completely

Kristeva, in her psychoanalytic mode, explains the connection between the abject and the body by referring to that earliest human state where the newborn organism, still literally on the boundary between life and death, has yet to establish any firm boundaries between its own body and that of its mother. All its experience consists solely of its amorphous bodily states as it encounters the uncertainty and trauma of the alternating presence and absence of the mother. Because the infant is as yet unable to speak or understand language, it lacks any words or concepts that would allow it to describe its situation or understand its meaning, so its prelinguistic world is nothing but the formless and ever-changing flux of its own bodily states.

Everything changes when the infant later learns to speak, understand, and communicate with others. It is at this point that the infant first becomes a 'subject' capable of distinguishing itself from other 'objects'. However, at a deeper psychic level, the memory of this original state is never entirely forgotten and continues occasionally to erupt into consciousness when something, usually connected with the body, is encountered. As Kristeva views it, the abject is encountered as a visceral, bodily reaction to certain things that remind us of that primordial, formless, fluid state that was suppressed and rejected when, thanks to language, we became a 'subject' in world of 'objects' that are meaningful for us.

Radiohead is definitely not a psychoanalytic collective, so we can't expect to find such themes articulated the way Kristeva does. However, she does make another important point which gives us a clue about where to look. If the linguistically articulated, social world is one of definition, clarity, and meaning, then the eruption of the abject in experience threatens the collapse of all meaning and distinction, a key symptom of which is the disruption and fragmentation of language.

A recurrent device of the art of Stanley Donwood, the band's constant graphic collaborator beginning with *The Bends*, provides a perfect illustration of this. The most memorable example is the artwork filling the inside jacket of *Kid A*. Scattered across it we can make out fragments of letters, words, and phrases that seem on the verge of sinking into the chaotic background from which they seem to have only temporarily emerged.

Radiohead's lyrics also rarely tell stories or follow any clear logic or set pattern. Instead, they often have a quality of visceral but precarious meaning: such images as "a pig, in a cage, on antibiotics" and 'a cat tied to a stick" (from "Fitter Happier," *OK Computer*) pack just such an immediate punch even before we have time to process them intellectually. At other times, some scene, insight, or feeling seems to hover before us only to recede from our grasp and then evaporate by the end of the song. Their openings often express or seem based upon some discernable verbal phrase, event, or feeling, but in the end it has either slipped away or is finally enveloped by the music itself, especially in the often extended concluding instrumentals in live performances.

To see what I mean here, try taking the opening lines or section of some of Radiohead's songs after *Pablo Honey* (which is still rather conventional in this respect) and juxtaposing them with the concluding section or phrases. Here's a couple of examples. The first pair is from "Black Star" (*The Bends*):

Opening:

> I get home from work and you're still standing in your dressing gown
> Well what am I to do
> I know all the things around your head and what they do to you

Concluding lines:

> What am I coming to?
> I'm going to melt down.

Or, try this pair from "Pyramid Song" (*Amnesiac*):

Opening:

> I jumped in the river and what did I see?
> Black-eyed angels swimming with me
> A moon full of stars and astral cars

Closing:

> There was nothing to fear and nothing to doubt [repeated several times]

The music of this song has no regular or easily discernable rhythm and presents a good example of the sonicscape finally enveloping the words of the song.

So what's happening here, where a song seems to present a relatively clear meaning or feeling which is never quite developed and becomes lost by the end? Seen through the lenses of abject aesthetics, we might say that the song enacts the passage from something 'objective' and communicable to its dissolution in the formless and fluid realm of the abject.

Not Another Brick in the Wall

So far, we've talked mostly about *what* these new lenses help us see; now we need to consider *how* they change the way we look at things. Again, like buying a new pair of shades, the best way to do this is by trying on and comparing several different ones. Two groups with whom Radiohead is often compared are the Beatles and Pink Floyd, so a brief look at their aesthetics should help us here. (You might check out some of the chapters in the volumes in the *Popular Culture and Philosophy* series dedicated to these groups as background for these comparisons.)

While the Beatles' body of work was so diverse that it probably traversed several different aesthetics, most of us will first think of their songs and albums exploring altered states of consciousness (psychedelia and transcendental meditation), especially *Sgt. Pepper's*, *Magical Mystery Tour*, and *Yellow Submarine*. No better symbol of the aesthetic of these works could be found than those rose-tinted glasses that John Lennon (and many of us as well!) often wore during this period. Taking their cue from (among others) the writings and teachings of Dr. Timothy Leary and the Maharishi Mahesh Yogi, the Beatles took us on tours of alternative worlds accessed through psychedelic drugs and transcendental meditation. In the face of the complex reality of a brutal and increasingly pointless war, the violent birth-pangs of the Civil Rights Movement, and all-too-frequent assassinations and political repression, they offered us an escape into more brightly hued, clearly outlined, and exhilarating worlds of our own 'inner space'.

If we were to sum up their operative aesthetic in this period in one word, it might be 'transcendence'. The basic point was that, however ugly and cruel 'reality' was and however resistant to change it might be, it was always possible to transcend this through the alteration of your own consciousness: "You better free your mind instead" as John Lennon told us. Of course, this vision of the world seen through rose-tinted glasses proved to be a utopian dream that, even for the Beatles, died pretty quickly, but it did leave a significant imprint on the history of rock as well as on our collective cultural memory of the 1960s.

While Pink Floyd's early work was clearly influenced by this 'aesthetic of transcendence', the recordings and performances for which they are most remembered, especially *The Dark Side of the Moon* and *The Wall*, signaled a dramatic change of aesthetic lenses. By the mid-1970s, the Beatles' escapist attempts at transcendence appeared increasingly naive and was replaced by powerful experiences of loss, loneliness, and alienation. Whereas the Beatles tried to take us 'somewhere else', Pink Floyd explored, instead, the hard realities of 'being where we are'. They represented this most memorably by an actual wall that they built in performance separating the band from its audience. Like their philosophical forerunners, the existentialists, their work is a virtual catalogue of the various ways that the individual is alienated from society, other individuals, and itself.

From the viewpoint of Pink Floyd's 'existentialist aesthetics', we're all wearing dark-tinted reflector shades. Echoing the existentialist philosopher Jean-Paul Sartre's famous claim that the gaze of other persons only reflects us back upon our own lonely and alienated condition ("Hell is other persons," as the line from his play *No Exit* reads), Pink Floyd presents us as enmeshed in a solid, walled-in world where the colors are mainly grey and the only responses are either angry protest or anxiety-ridden acceptance of our alienated condition.

Radiohead's abject shades are dramatically different than either of these. On the one hand, there is little hint of the possibility of transcendence in any of Radiohead's work. Like Pink Floyd, for Radiohead there's also 'no other place to be than where you are': there's no possibility of escape from yourself. But 'where we are' looks entirely different when seen through the abject lenses of Radiohead than through the existentialist shades of Pink Floyd.

For Pink Floyd's existentialist aesthetic, the major issue is that we, as potentially free, creative, and fulfilled individuals (roughly, what Sartre calls 'Beings-for-ourselves') continually find ourselves hemmed in, blocked, and hence alienated from an indifferent if not hostile world of objects and institutions ('Beings-in-themselves'). We are continually alienated from this world because, while we know 'for ourselves' what it would be like for our lives to be meaningful, the world of objects 'in itself' neither recognizes nor responds to any such meaning: at most, it merely reflects our own gaze and indifferently turns us back upon ourselves.

The abject aesthetic of Radiohead differs from this in several important ways. First, that there *are* any clear or stable meanings, whether of our lives, our world, or even language, always remains questionable. Meanings are fluid and just as we think we've gotten something into focus, it seems to dissolve before our eyes. If Radiohead's music often expresses a sense of anxiety sometimes resembling that of Pink Floyd, it is not that the meaning of my own life is continually challenged by an indifferent world, but that I can never quite succeed in bringing into focus what that meaning might be. Even more, because abject aesthetics emphasizes the importance of the body as itself a part of the world, there cannot be the firm boundaries between self and world ('Being-for-itself' and 'Being-in-itself') invoked by any existentialist aesthetic. In the more fluid, boundary-less aesthetic of Radiohead, it makes little sense to speak of some sort of existential alienation or revolt against an indifferent world, because I myself, as an embodied being, am part of the world and that world is, at least in part, the foundation for any meaning that I might encounter.

Rise and Shine It's On Again Off Again

If, for abject aesthetics, neither psychic transcendence nor existential revolt is an option, then should we conclude that, in Radiohead-world, everything is 'painted black', that it finally amounts to the dead end of nihilism? If so, why would anyone want to buy or even try on a pair of such opaque black lenses? My answer to this final question is to suggest that abject lenses are neither opaque nor necessarily dark after all. Rather, abject aesthetics represents one aspect of the broader movement of 'postmodernism', specifically that derived from the work of one of Julia Kristeva's teachers, the controversial psychoanalyst Jacques Lacan. Following this line of thought, we might say that there are two sides to the 'fluidity of meaning' at the heart of abject aesthetics. On the one hand, it can definitely be disconcerting, even traumatic, in places where it highlights boundaries crumbling and meaning collapsing and dissolving before our eyes. But there's another side to this, too: if boundaries are uncertain and meanings fluid, there's also the possibility of establishing new boundaries and constructing new meanings. In an important though not always sufficiently recognized sense, abject aesthetics (and more broadly 'postmodernism') is not *just* about 'deconstruction'—it also opens the possibility for 'reconstruction.'

I'd say that Radiohead's two latest albums, *Hail to the Thief* (2003) and *In Rainbows* (2007), are exactly this. In the first, a new, if vague-edged, political stance seems to emerge amidst a somewhat disjointed assemblage of musical devices and lyrical themes familiar from their earlier work. *In Rainbows*, though not as directly political as the last, seems to signal a new departure or, perhaps better, the end of one cycle and the beginning of another. As Thom asks on "15 Step" in the first line of the album, "How come I end up where I started?" There is both an emotional directness about this album that reminds us of their first album, *Pablo Honey*, but also a clarity of purpose more like *OK Computer* than anything else they've done to date. There's still plenty of the experimentation we've come to expect from the band (for example, complex rhythms and ample doses of electronica), but there's also a gentleness in Thom's voice and lyrics and a lyricism in Jonny's guitar work that we would hardly have expected.

So, what color are 'abject lenses'? First, I'd have to say that they're probably about a medium-gray tint: they register the world pretty much as it is, but with its colors a bit muted and blended together. Second, to strain my metaphor a bit, I'd go on to say that they are progressive trifocals. They reveal (depending on what part we're looking through) a world of fairly distinct and well-defined meanings when seen at a distance, but which blur and dissolve when we attempt to view them up close, in terms of our own immediate bodily experience. However, somewhere in between, there's a 'sweet spot' that takes some effort and practice to find, a sort of precarious mid-distant region of relative clarity where we realize that it's just the nature of forms and meanings both to dissolve and then reassemble themselves into new, perhaps unsuspected patterns.

While these shades will never show you a vibrant fantasy world, neither will they leave you isolated and alienated from the world, other persons, or yourself. What they (like Radiohead and, in fact, postmodernism itself) will do is require some effort on your part to find that 'sweet spot' where there's enough form and meaning to allow you to keep looking while remembering that these 'objects' are always precarious, that your focus will continually change. In the end, Radiohead shades may not be for you and I'm certainly not trying to sell you on them, but they're at least worth trying on for a while.

6.

Why Such Sad Songs?

Micah Lott

> For it is not easy to determine what the power of music is,
> or why one should take part in it.
>
> —Aristotle, *Politics*

> Why is it that a person should wish to experience suffering
> by watching grievous tragic events which he himself would
> not wish to endure? Nevertheless he wants to suffer the
> pain given by being a spectator of these sufferings, and the
> pain itself is his pleasure. What is this but amazing folly?
>
> —Augustine, Confessions

> Open up your skull, I'll be there.
>
> —"Climbing Up the Walls," *OK Computer*

"The Bends" begins with a burst of energy. Guitars, bass, and drums come in together, quickly followed by Thom Yorke's opening howl. The energy builds throughout the song, reaching its climax just before the song ends as Yorke cries out, "I wanna live, breathe, I wanna be a part of the human race." This is followed by the closing moments of quiet and calm, as Yorke repeats the opening lines: "where do we go from here, the words are coming out all weird, where are you now, when I need you?"

These dynamics result in a fantastically satisfying song. But if you listen to what Yorke's saying, the lyrics are anything but "happy" or "uplifting." He sings of people in desperation ("am I really sinking this low?"), in isolation ("we don't have any real friends"), or feeling abandoned ("where are you now, when I need you?"), even feeling less than human ("I wanna be a part of the human race").

Dark images such as these abound in Radiohead's music, which is why you would not reach for words like "cheerful" or "upbeat" to describe the band. The music is far from dull, but its energy is saturated with "negative" emotions like sadness, anger and fear. So you might ask, "Why would I want to listen to that? Why would I want to listen to music that makes me feel *bad*?" To someone who appreciates Radiohead, of course, these questions are missing the point, and they suggest that you are expecting the wrong thing from this music. Still, the questions point to a real puzzle about our enjoyment of Radiohead, and of "darker" forms of art in general: As a rule, we don't *like* to feel sad or lonely or depressed. So why do we like music (or books or movies) that evoke in us those same negative emotions? Why do we choose to experience in art the very feelings we avoid in real life?

OK Catharsis

Aristotle deals with a similar question in his analysis of tragedy. Tragedy, after all, is pretty gruesome. In Euripides's *Bacchae*, for example, Agave murders her son Pentheus and then carries his severed head to the stage. And of course there's Sophocles's Oedipus, who blinds himself after learning that he has killed his father and slept with his mother. Why would anyone watch this stuff? Wouldn't it be sick to *enjoy* watching it? This is the question Augustine wonders about in quotation at the beginning of this chapter.

But Aristotle insists that there's a reason we're drawn to tragedy, and why viewing tragedy has its own *proper pleasure*. This is not the kind of pleasure that is proper to comedy, nor some sadistic delight in the suffering of others. In fact, tragedy's pleasure doesn't make us feel "good" in any straightforward sense. On the contrary, Aristotle says, the real goal of tragedy is to evoke *pity* and *fear* in the audience. Now, to speak of the pleasure of pity and fear is almost oxymoronic. But the point of bringing about these emotions is to achieve a *catharsis* of them—a cleansing, a purification, a purging, or release. Catharsis is at the core of tragedy's appeal.

Radiohead often achieves a catharsis of negative emotions. Songs like "Karma Police" and "Exit Music" function as mini-tragedies: both lyrically and musically, they present images of human vulnerability and failure, snapshots of characters in the midst of breakdown and loss. And they present these images in a way that engages both our cognitive and affective capacities. We recognize in them something *true* about human life and human weakness. At the same time, we also *feel* the associated emotions—sadness, anger, and fear. And through our engagement with the songs we can achieve the kind of catharsis Aristotle is talking about, that strange but familiar gratification and pleasure of tragedy.

Exit Music for a Story

When Aristotle discusses tragedy he's thinking specifically of Greek theater. His official definition of a tragedy is this: "Tragedy, then, is a mimesis of an action; in language embellished by distinct forms in its sections; employing the mode of enactment, not narrative; and through pity and fear accomplishing the catharsis of such emotions."[1]

To call tragedy a "mimesis" is to say that it *represents* something. Whereas a painting represents its object in one way, and a novel in another, a tragic drama represents its subject matter by the actors' portrayal. A tragedy will of course have a cast of characters, but the soul of tragedy, Aristotle says, is its *plot*.

The components of a good tragic plot are: reversal, recognition, and suffering. These roughly amount to: 1) things go from good to bad for the characters 2) the characters come to learn something they didn't know and 3) the characters are then left to endure pain and loss.[2]

Given this definition of tragedy, it may seem like a comparison with the music of Radiohead is a non-starter. Most Radiohead songs don't have a "plot" in any obvious sense like "Don't Take your Guns to Town" or "Frankie and Johnny." However, we can recognize *characters* in many Radiohead songs, even if they are fragmentary or vague. And even if there's no obvious plot, the songs frequently sketch situations that suggest

1 Aristotle *Poetics* 6, translated by Stephen Halliwell (Harvard University Press, 1995).

2 Aristotle actually maintains that the reversal could go in the other direction, though that doesn't seem to be the paradigm case of tragedy for him, and in certainly isn't what we would call a "tragedy" today.

stories. For example, in "Fake Plastic Trees", we see a woman and a man (apparently a plastic surgeon) in the midst of personal exhaustion: "she lives with a broken man . . . who crumbles and burns"; "it wears her out"; "it wears him out." "Exit Music" features a scene of two young lovers rising early to escape from their parents: "wake from your sleep . . . today we escape." There's the threat of violence and a sense of desperation: "pack and get dressed . . . before your father wakes, before all hell breaks loose"; "breath, keep breathing, I can't do this alone."

Often the principle character in a Radiohead song is the narrator, as in "Exit Music" or "The Bends." Other times, as in "High and Dry," a character is spoken to in the second person: "drying up in conversation, you will be the one who cannot talk, all your insides fall to pieces, you just sit there wishing you could still make love". Or again in "15 Step": "You used to be alright. What happened? Did the cat get your tongue? Did your string come undone?"

To be sure, these are not full-blown plots or developed characters. But there are glimpses of individuals and their stories, snippets of human existence. Moreover, these characters are typically marked by the experiences of suffering and breakdown, confusion and loss. What confronts us in Radiohead's music is a version of what we encounter in tragedy: depictions of people in dire circumstances, scenes of struggle and failure, the disintegration of meaning, the onset of despair.

Emotion in Its Right Place

In a successful tragedy, scenes of reversal and misfortune evoke pity and fear in the audience. According to Aristotle, we experience pity at the character's sufferings because we see the characters as essentially decent people (not thoroughly corrupt) and because we see their sufferings as undeserved. In that way, our response to tragic suffering is different from the satisfaction we feel at the sufferings of a villain who, at the end of a story, finally receives his comeuppance. However, the sufferings of tragic characters are not *entirely* undeserved. For in a well-constructed tragedy, the suffering comes about through some error (*hamartia*) on the part of the character, such as Oedipus's arrogance and anger in killing Laius at the crossroads. Of course Oedipus does not know he is actually killing his *father*, but he errs nonetheless. The sufferings of tragedy are not random misfortunes, like traffic accidents or pianos falling from windows. Rather the sufferings arise from the character's own agency, with the result that the characters are *implicated* to some extent in their own downfalls. Or, as Radiohead puts it in "Just": "You do it to yourself. You and no one else."

Tragedy would not elicit emotion as it does if we did not *identify* in some way with the characters. We feel fear because we recognize the individuals portrayed as like us, and therefore we see in their misfortune something that might befall us. This does not mean that we see the characters as exactly like us, or that we are literally thinking of *ourselves*, instead of the story, when viewing tragedy (which would make us poor audience members!) But we do see the characters and their experiences as *relevant* to our own lives. Their fates could be ours.

For Radiohead—and pop music, generally—music allows a particularly intense form of identification: singing along. We can literally *deliver the lines* of the tragic characters, and to that extent *become* the characters in a more immediate, visceral way. This doesn't mean we're "pretending to be" those character or literally "play acting." But we are finding ourselves in these characters and recognizing our own lives in their stories. Think about what it's like to sing along to "Karma Police": "I've given all I can, its not enough"; "for a minute there, I lost myself, I lost myself". When you're immersed in the song and singing along, who is the "I" that you're singing about? Is it a character in a song, or yourself? If the song works, that line starts to blur. And that melding of ourselves with the characters is part of why we *feel* the way we do; by identifying with the speaker's situation we share in the associated emotions. "I lost myself . . .," indeed: the listener "loses himself" in the character, and the character in turn gives voice to precisely the experience of losing oneself—perhaps in sorrow, or anxiety, or in feeling the weightlessness of one's own existence.

Something like this happens inside the slow, meditative sadness of "How to Disappear Completely." Even if you're not literally singing along, it's hard to engage the song without identifying with Yorke as he sings, "I'm not here, this isn't happening." You can quickly get caught up in his mood, as you can (again) in

"Fake Plastic Trees," when at the emotional climax of the song shifts from the third to the first person. The music swells and the character speaks in his (or her) own voice: "My fake plastic love, I can't help the feeling I could blow through the ceiling . . . it wears me out, it wears me out, it wears me out, it wears me out." As the music grows quiet and Yorke's voice comes to the fore, we are invited to sing along, and to *feel along* as well: "If I could be who you wanted, if I could be who you wanted, all the time."

This Just Feels (and Sounds) Like Spinning Plates

So far we have focused on the lyrical content of Radiohead songs. We've said relatively little about the *music* itself. We've also emphasized tragedy's ability to evoke negative emotions in us, but have said little about how exactly *catharsis* works. Surprisingly, Aristotle himself doesn't discuss catharsis at length in the *Poetics* where he discusses tragedy. In his *Politics*, however, Aristotle discusses the role of music in education, and he notes that listening to music can be one source of catharsis.

Music, he says, is pleasurable to people of all ages and characters—it's something "naturally sweet" to human beings.[3] One way to describe this natural sweetness is to say that music conveys *energy* to us, and there is something pleasant about that energy. Here, then, is one clue for solving the opening puzzle: even if the lyrics of Radiohead songs are dark and "unhappy," those lyrics are combined with a music that is energetic and "naturally sweet." Music moves us, sometimes literally (think of dancing, or even unconscious foot-tapping). And whatever else may be involved in the listening experience, it feels good to be moved.

Aristotle also holds that music can mimic human character and emotion. Lyrics aside, rhythms and melodies *themselves* can represent anger, courage, temperance, and other experiences. Moreover, when we hear the music, our souls are changed to conform to the feelings it presents to us. As Aristotle says, "everyone

---

3 Aristotle *Politics*, lines 1340a3-5, 1340b16-17. Music also appeals to some of the other animals as well (and the majority of slaves!).

who listens to representations comes to have the corresponding emotions." The music itself *embodies* the emotions, and in so doing brings about the emotions in us. The music conforms us to its image.

Think of "Climbing up the Walls," probably the scariest song Radiohead has yet created. The music is saturated with fear and heavy, lumbering desperation. These emotions begin with the opening drums and distorted bass line alone, even before words are spoken. And as Yorke sings, even without knowing what is being said the sounds themselves grow slowly toward a frenzy and panic. It takes an act of will *not* to feel these emotions when they are so effectively embedded in the music.

Baby's Got the Purgation

But all this only brings us back to a version of our original question: even if music is "naturally sweet", why would anybody want to be so *scared* by music? Because it facilitates catharsis. Aristotle notes that some kinds of music induce an intense emotional reaction in the souls of certain people, which is then followed by calm. He compares it to a "medical treatment and a purifying purgation"—which is what 'catharsis' means. Music represents emotions and thereby stirs them up in the souls of the audience. This surge of emotion is then followed by a sense of relief. Thus we are purged, or cleansed, of the emotions. In this way, Aristotle says, "the purifying melodies provide a harmless enjoyment for people."

In *Radiohead* the catharsis is often rooted in musical *dynamics*— the back and forth of dissonance and resolution, the progressive buildup of tension, the climax of energy and the resulting sense of release. Like story-telling or sex, the energy builds. The plot thickens. The temperature rises. And finally things reach the point where, looking back, we can say they were headed all along. Then there's a breaking point, a pinnacle, a relaxation of tension and dispersal of energy. There is a trajectory to this that helps explain how catharsis works: we go "through" the emotions to the other side, experiencing them intensely in order to be released from them.

Sometimes the climax is an explosion, as in "The Bends" or "Climbing Up the Walls." In other songs it is more like a slow burn and fade away. For example in "Videotape" there is no crowning burst of energy. Still, there's a clear sense of rising energy as the piano repeats and percussive elements and droning background tones are introduced. And the song does realize a climax of sorts in its closing minute, though the feelings conveyed are more ache and longing, rather than fear or anger.

So we are a little closer to answering our puzzle: We are able to *enjoy* the "dark" emotions in *Radiohead* -rather than simply *endure* the—because we experience the emotions as part of a particular developmental process that allows us to be *released* from them in the experience of catharsis. However, in recognizing the importance of catharsis, it would be a mistake to suppose that what we are "going for" in listening to music is the calm that follows, as if the emotions were just a means to that end. Rather, what we enjoy is not just the calm at the end but the swell of emotion as well. In this respect, the "purging" we experience in listening to "Karma Police" is different from the relief we feel after vomiting. In that case, we have a good feeling once its over, but we hate the nauseous feeling that precedes it. Musical catharsis, on the other hand, is more like the catharsis of story-telling and sex—what precedes the climax and release catharsis is a "stirred up" state that is (somehow) enjoyable in its own right.

You Can't Be Bulletproof

In Book 9 of the *Poetics*, Aristotle contrasts history and poetry (which for Aristotle includes tragic drama). History, he says, deals with "the particular"—with what actual, particular people did and said. Tragedy, on the other hand, deals with "the universal"—not with actual events, but with the *kinds* of things that people do and say in various circumstances. The situations and plot developments in tragedy may be outrageous, but the way in which the characters respond should not be implausible or unmotivated. They need not be factually true, but they should be "true to life."

Because tragedy deals with the universal, Aristotle describes tragedy as more philosophical and more ethically serious than history. Because tragedy is "true to life," it's an occasion for reflection about general truths of the human condition. As classicist

James Redfield puts it, "fiction presents an unreal world which is about the real world."[4] Thus in tragedy we can *learn* something, not about the facts of history but about the way things go in human life. In particular, tragedy reminds us that human life is marked by deep and pervasive *vulnerability*. Even if we wish it every day and every hour along with Thom Yorke, we are not bulletproof.

Threats to our happiness come both from within and from without. We are prone to error, what Aristotle calls *hamartia*, in ways that undermine our own flourishing. We can be our own worst enemy. We may also fall victim to circumstances and systems that are external to us and outside of our control. Powerful gods may seek our downfall. Fate may conspire against us and our happiness. And as Redfield argues, the sufferings of tragic characters may traced to conflicting cultural pressures that bear down on them—the "contradictory internal logic" of the social world' they inhabit (p. 28). Thus in crafting his story, the tragic poet "imaginatively tests the limits of his culture's capacity to function" (p. 80). By depicting the fates of individuals, tragedy invites us to analyze the commitments and practices that make their errors and sufferings possible. In this way, art opens up naturally into social criticism and political philosophy.

Songs like "Fitter Happier" and "Electioneering" are among the first to spring to mind when thinking about Radiohead's social criticism. But the kind of reflection Redfield points to arises from less overtly "political" and more tragic songs like "Fake Plastic Trees" and the "The Bends." What is it about our culture that fosters such a sense of isolation? Is there something about our outlook that leads inevitably to such feelings of hopelessness? Is it something about our way of life that leads to the erosion of connectedness? In short, artistic depictions of *unhappiness* invite philosophic reflection on the nature of happiness. And tragedy challenges us to trace the connections between the fate of individuals and the culture in which they—or we—live.

4 James M. Redfield, *Nature and Culture in the Iliad* (Duke University Press, 1994), p. 59.

Where Tragedy Ends and
Community Begins

Through its "philosophical" dimension, tragedy engages our *rational* capacities. Its appeal for us is inseparable from the *understanding* that we gain in watching or listening. To say this is not to over-intellectualize the experience, as if philosophical thoughts were *going through our heads* when we witness a tragedy or hear a tragic song. The goal of tragedy is to evoke emotion and catharsis, not provoke the contemplation of propositions. But the emotions themselves are not just "raw feelings." Rather, internal to the emotions is a kind of *recognition*. In *feeling* those emotions we register an *understanding* of human life. And this understanding matters to us, because we too are human. As philosopher Stephen Halliwell says, tragedy revolves around "the exhibition of sufferings which stem from profound human fallibility, yet by engaging the understanding and the emotions in contemplation of these phenomena it succeeds in affording an experience which deeply fulfills and enhances the whole mind."[5]

One way to put this is to say that tragedy *resonates* with us. We are able to discern in a tragedy a sense of human life that has the ring of truth. Part of the enjoyment of hearing "The Bends" or "How to Disappear Completely" is what seems so accurate or insightful in them. They affirm something about the vision of human life and character that the song presents. It is as if part of us says, "Yes, things really are like *that*," whether the subject is the fragility of love and friendship, the persistence of personal insecurities, the recurrence of childhood fears, the inability to articulate oneself, or countless other difficult aspects of human life.

If we did not feel that life was marked by experiences of breakdown and failure, surely we would feel differently about Radiohead. They would seem strange or phony to us. Which is why someone with a thoroughly sunny disposition, who always views the world through rose-colored glasses, is not likely to fall in love with a song like "High and Dry" or "Climbing Up the Walls."

But songs like these, along with other "dark" forms of art, can help us come to terms with these hard truths of human life. We

---

5 Halliwell, Introduction to Aristotle's *Poetics*, p. 19.

are able to acknowledge the difficult realities, engage them emotionally, and in this way, get a better *handle* on our situation. We can achieve a measure of control, precisely by articulating how out-of-control we are. Moreover, we can feel *less alone* in confronting our own weakness.

There's another human voice here, a bit of humanity we can recognize. There's a community, however thin, that is created when one human being engages the art created by another. And in tragedy, that community gives voice to its fears and reflects on its common vulnerabilities.[6]

6 Thanks to Brandon Forbes for discussions of the ideas in this paper. Thanks to Radiohead for such good music. Thanks to Aristotle for such good books.

7.

"The Eraser": Start Making Sense

DAVID DARK

Cities, in Milgrim's experience, had a way of revealing themselves in the faces
of their inhabitants, and particularly on their way to work in the morning.
There was a sort of basic fuckedness index to be read, then,
in faces that hadn't yet encountered the reality
of whatever they were on their way to do

—William Gibson, *Spook Country*

it was fun and quick to do.
inevitably it is more beats & electronics.
but its songs.

—Thom Yorke, description of *The Eraser*

On the outskirts of every agony
sits some observant fellow who points.

—Virginia Woolf, *The Waves*

As well as evoking the satisfyingly stark chorus of *The Eraser*'s
most popular single, "Black Swan," the notion of a "basic fuckedness index," William Gibson's illuminating phrase, might also
speak to the scene portrayed on the album's enigmatic artwork
provided, as we've come to expect, by Stanley Donwood. Titled
"Gold Cnut," a trench-coated figure dwarfed by rising tides and
storm clouds seems to maintain, for at least a moment, a storm-
free clearing by bidding the darkness halt with a raised hand, a gesture of magical command. Whether the gesture is effective or
entirely futile is left to the viewer's interpretation.

Drawn from Donwood's "London Views" exhibit, the image
is based on an anecdote concerning the eleventh-century Viking
King of England, Canute the Great, who, it is alleged, once set his
throne on the sea-shore and commanded the rising waters to

accommodate his comfortably dry robes by keeping their distance. As the story goes, he got soaked. And his epiphany concerning the ocean's recalcitrance led him to renounce the power of kings (the very concept of kingship) as empty and worthless. To commemorate this moment of clarity, he placed his golden crown on a crucifix and never wore it again. We recall how chaos (most notably the humanly-cultivated kind) will have its way, despite the pretensions of presidents, prime ministers, high-profile politicos, and other self-professed professionals. And the human misery index, predictably on the rise by way of our plundering and profiteering, doesn't appear to be on hardly anybody's radar. No note-taking, no foresight, no body counts. Just press conferences, photo ops, and assurances concerning how deeply our elected leaders feel the electorate's pain. Thus far, we're on familiar ground. This is the economy according to Radiohead.

But the figure on the album cover doesn't look anything like a king. A wizard, perhaps, or a detective in the vein of the Phantom Stranger, John Constantine, William S. Burroughs, or a shaman-like Shakespeare's Prospero who may or may not have the power to hold off the forces of evil in a bozo nightmare. Even if it is a spoof or a self-deprecating image concerning the presumption of the artist (Thom Yorke) who dares to believe himself capable of creating a space in which to proffer a redeeming word amid the static and the noise of an age of "everything all of the time," the image is nevertheless a heartening one. It could be a broadside, fitting nicely among the annals of consciousness-raising (whether folksy, comic, or theatrical), a little like a nameless man with a briefcase standing in front of a tank. The bardic figure will hazard a sense-making word even if it's doomed to fail. A lyrical witness will try, yet again, to ring true and to let the chips fall where they may.

If I understand it, this question of what it might mean to be a true witness, a witness that speaks to the reigning perversities of the times, is at work throughout *The Eraser*. The album operates within the Radiohead style of music as a sort of early warning system, an ongoing experiment in crazy prevention, even as it has a more purposefully claustrophobic feel, the sound of one man making a record, a collection of meaning-making, amid the madness. While it sits awkwardly to the side of the Radiohead canon proper, a peculiar little sonic missive for which Yorke alone can conclusively vouch, *The Eraser* serves as an illuminating example of how musical composition and performance serve a witness bearing function even as it self-consciously lingers upon (and never quite abandons) the question, self-effacing though it is, of whether or not this witness can be made to yield any positive or redemptive end.

Intelligence Gathering

As interviews, Dead Air Space postings, and Yorke's dismissive characterizations of his own lyrical contribution to the band's productions indicate, this question manages to animate every aspect of Radiohead's creative process. What constitutes real profit, real development, and actual, discernible, sustainable progress in our doing, spending, and manufacturing? What's it all for? And in typical fashion, Yorke has noted that he often goes to work having already done the business of writing particular phrases out even as he waits expectantly for his bandmates to tell him what the words mean, proffering them sheepishly, not as a finished work, but as words that might yet be *made to work*. How might private exercises in expanding ones sphere of sanity like writing out on a napkin a description of a realization we don't know what to do with, raw facts that can hardly be contemplated without inducing paralysis, be corralled in the direction of something helpful, something worth recording and making public?

Yorke describes his arranging of the fruits of his intelligence gathering, occasionally undertaken in an Oxford pub, thusly:

> I sit there, on the way in, because it's a really nice little table. . . . And then I get out my scraps of paper and I line them up. I need to put them into my book because they're just scraps of paper, and I'm going to lose them unless I do it. So am I writing here? Probably. I don't know yet. I'm just collating information. This is a nice, relaxing thing to do, and it also keeps your mind tuned in to the whole thing. And you see things you didn't know.[1]

1 Quoted in "A Head for Figures?" by Jon Pareles in *The Scotsman* (December 22nd, 2007); http://news.scotsman.com/features/A-head-for-figures.3615062.jp

In a process that appears to parallel William Burroughs's cut-up method, Yorke's practice of "collating information" is a way of giving form and meaning to otherwise inarticulate and what can seem to be completely futile and hopeless thoughts. "You *see* things you didn't *know*," even if the arrangements of the various fragments have yet to yield a sufficiently lyrical sensibility.

Yorke won't even call it writing for sure just yet, and even upon the release of Radiohead's albums, he's been known to insist that "the lyrics are gibberish,"[2] as if their contribution content-wise to the music can only ever be minimal. With this in mind, the appearance of *The Eraser*, inserted between *Hail to the Thief* and *In Rainbows* by way of borrowing Nigel Godrich and a bit of surreptitiously recorded Johnny Greenwood piano chords (on the title track) only owned up to a year or so after the fact, is an especially bold move in the only paradoxically self-assured and counterintuitively confident, creative output of Thom Yorke. If the music of Radiohead is an emergency broadcast system, *The Eraser* is Yorke's own personal, unconventionally articulate signal flare.

In the every-living-moment activity of collating information, one can easily imagine how Yorke's thoughts could linger over one tragic story of science and war-making and a maddeningly inconclusive paper trail. These thoughts come together in "Harrowdown Hill," Yorke's response to the death, in July of 2003, of the scientist David Kelly, an employee of the UK Ministry of Defense and a UN weapons inspector in Iraq once nominated for the Nobel Peace Prize. Named after the wooded area a short distance from his house where his body was found, the song doesn't seek to answer the question it poses over whether his death was a result of suicide or assassination, but in a gesture of self-identification it considers the role of the 'intelligence gatherer' and the vocational crisis that can often come with a determined commitment to be, in word and deed, reality-based. Kelly's attempt to be faithful to his own job description was placed under duress and clearly compromised when, having been asked to proofread the Weapons of Mass Destruction dossier that would contribute to the popular justification for the 2003 invasion of Iraq, his dispute over the claim that Iraq was capable of firing

2 Quoted in Nick Kent "Happy Now?" *Mojo* (June 2001).

chemical and biological weapons within forty-five minutes of receiving an order to do so went largely unaddressed. When *The Observer* went to press with his observation (as an unnamed source later confirmed) that it would be impossible to manufacture biological weapons within the two mobile laboratories he photographed and examined on an official visit to Iraq in June of 2003, his determination to be true to what he knew to be the facts on the ground, expert witness that he was, was no longer politically expedient.

Within the space of a month, he entered the crosshairs of the Ministry of Defence and found himself in the media spotlight of a public relations disaster. On the day of his death, he received e-mails from supporters as well as superiors within the Ministry demanding further details concerning his conversations with journalists. In an email he wrote back to a journalist at the *New York Times*, he expressed appreciation for the supportive words and spoke of "many dark actors playing games."[3]

Sung primarily in the first person, "Harrowdown Hill" warns of the ways people are "dispensed with" when their witness to what they know to be true proves inconvenient to particular high-powered interests. Are the pressures placed by those in power on the truth-tellers, even accidental whistleblowers like David Kelly, murderous in effect if not intent, consigning human lives to the Orwellian memory hole along with what they knew to be true? Don't ask me, Thom Yorke asserts. Ask the Ministry. But most movingly, the chorus strikes a note of solidarity that is anthemic to the degree that it speaks for the millions of people, even further from the command console of war-making than David Kelly, who also sensed (or, like Kelly, *knew*) that the intelligence was cooked in the selling of the war: "We think the same things at the same time / We just can't do anything about it."

Yorke's determination to commemorate Kelly's expert witness is like the sounding of an alarm. Another extended footnote, if you like, to the one-word chorus of *In Rainbows*'s "House of Cards," that mantra any self-respecting Radiohead follower should have within arm's reach whenever taking in what is popularly called the news: "Denial!" Eulogizing David Kelly's life, especially

---

3 http://www.the-hutton-inquiry.org.uk/content/com/com_4_0076.pdf

in view of his costly decision to be true to the truth, conjures that space Radiohead is always creating, the space where we turn our attention and pay heed to all the ways other witnesses are kept out of the witness box of public awareness, all that crowns itself "global development," all that sees fit to file human life (individuals or entire civilian populations) under the term "inconvenient."

When "Harrowdown Hill" ends with a repeated "I feel me slipping in and out of consciousness," we're reminded that the work of ethical remembrance is an ongoing summons to vigilance, a vigilance we forsake at the risk of losing a witness to life, to what's there, to all that might yet be redeemed on behalf of the future. Bearing witness, in this sense, isn't offering proof or positing an argument. It's the practice of being present to the time, paying attention, paying heed, and keeping good faith by making a record of the moment, a witness to a witness like David Kelly.

Playing a Part versus Giving Voice

"Crushing truths," Albert Camus once observed, "perish from being acknowledged."[4] It's as if saying or singing aloud of what can hardly be discerned without a sense of despair might somehow let some air in. And with *The Eraser*, Yorke means to give voice both to the voiceless disenfranchised, those on the death-dealing end of brutal economies, *and* his own ambivalence over the fact that a rock music celebrity would actually have a go at doing such a thing. If the ridiculousness of it all feels indefensible, this is exactly the redeeming risk of the poetic prerogative, that gesture that requires no self-justification. The lyric is its own credential. As Jacques Derrida observes, "A poem always runs the risk of being meaningless, and would be nothing without this risk of being meaningless, and would be nothing without this risk."[5]

This word on the poetic witness evokes a strength made perfect in weakness, the risk of being misread, badly used, or misinterpreted that, we might say, characterizes all speech but which is

4 Albert Camus, The *Myth of Sisyphus and Other Essays* (Knopf, 1969), p. 122.

5 Jacques Derrida, *Writing and Difference* (University of Chicago Press, 1978), p. 74.

especially necessary in the delivery and the reception of what comes to be called poetry. Poetry, as the poet W.H. Auden reminds us, unlike lawyers, guns, and money, doesn't *make* anything happen (or supply its own interpretation). It just survives in the valley of its saying—powerless, in its way, even maybe just powerless enough to change everything. As Yorke put it to David Fricke of *Rolling Stone* in an account of the seeming incoherence at work in the music of *Amnesiac*: "It's sort of bearing witness to things."

And in this way, the song that we might do well to view as a grid or a representative posture for the entirety of *The Eraser* is "Analyze." The labor of establishing and maintaining a sense of orientation in the workaday world, whether in an office cubicle, between military checkpoints, or sitting in a pub collating information, of making sense of what one takes to be the "facts on the ground," will often yield the debilitating realization that one is still only "playing a part" in some death-dealing mechanism or another, that even our most artful resistance will often get co-opted within marketing formulae or somebody else's not-so-edifying talking points. The sense we hope to make of things, Yorke intones over a hypnotic loop, might only be a *self*-fulfilling prophecy. Just as a solo project might only be a self-serving ego trip. But there's something ennobling in the lamentation of pilgrimages gone wrong, the confession that there doesn't appear to be enough hours in the day to achieve the work of seeing and thinking properly, something liturgical (liturgy as "the work of the people") in speaking of the absence of longed-for coherence, making a note of how it brings you down.

No spark, no light, no time to analyze, Yorke sings, as if he's operating out of some long-lost ascetic tradition, mourning the loss of good order. The song also strangely evokes the vocal stylings of *tajwid* (an Arabic term meaning "to render beautiful") in which the Qur'an is recited in broadcasts reaching mosques and taxi cabs throughout the Middle East. Giving voice to the sense that there's no time or space to make sense might make a way where there is no way. It's the positive work of mourning we find in the elegiac tradition. Or as Yorke names this lyrical impulse, "the whole point of creating music for me is to give voice to things that aren't normally given voice to, and a lot of those things are extremely negative. Personally speaking, I have to remain positive otherwise I'd go fucking crazy."[6]

As an instance of speaking out of an existential crisis, giving voice to an angst that seems beyond available powers of description, "Analyze" seems to channel an almost mystical sensibility, not in the sense that the song in any way banks on a miracle, but rather by doing the work that the album as a whole seems to do, that seemingly ineffective poetic act that undertakes the "transformation of data into metaphor,"[7] in Robert Stepto's phrase, making words work against crushing realities, attempting exorcism, conjuring a space for analysis, redemption, and fresh articulations of what's going on.

Against Self-Legitimation

In my employment of religious language to describe *The Eraser*, I don't mean to imply, within the work, a subtle adherence to any particular tradition of avowedly religious confession. But I would like to characterize the concerns of the album as ineluctably religious insofar as the songs bring, in an undeniable way, a profoundly ethical dimension to the quotidian dimensions the listener is already in, an emerging sense of responsibility animated by the demands of being (as well as receiving) a witness. This is the realm of concern that any sense of religiosity worthy of the name will name, a sense of the ultimate that challenges the status quo. Derrida names the concern most provocatively: "Religion is responsibility or it is nothing at all."[8] It is an investment in mindfulness.

This scruple, the unbearable lightness of actually paying attention and listening for the voices of other people, is at work in every act of witness, self-described religious or otherwise. In any case, it will keep such high-sounding words (true, just, responsibility, religion) in the Derridean sense, *under erasure*, because the question of its faithfulness has to be constantly deferred. It can't legit-

---

6 http://www.pitchforkmedia.com/article/feature/37863-interview-thom-yorke

7 Robert B. Stepto, *From Behind the Veil: A Study of Afro-American Narrative* (Univeristy of Illinois Press, 1991), p. 53.

8 Jacques Derrida, *The Gift of Death* (University of Chicago Press, 1995), p. 2.

imate itself. The good witness won't name itself as such, because so much *remains to be seen*. Like philosophy, the work of witness is always before us and always only underway, a work that's never exactly done. Like poetry, it can't be a choice or decision so much as it's a verdict, a verdict to be rendered on the strength of someone else's listening and attentive testimony. The question of its ethical coherence, the resonance of a witness, whether in a body of work or a single piece, in the deepest sense, won't be decided, for instance, by institutions, units sold, mercantile trends, or philosophy departments. It will be decided by a future that impinges upon our present even now, a future whose criteria for just witness, the witness that did justice to and for the events and contexts of its own time, might differ radically from our own.

The music might prove to be a hit, as the saying goes, in the short run, but did it bear meaningful, redeeming witness? Was it good? Poetry, after all, is the news that stays news. The work that illuminates and, over time, goes on illuminating. The classic that *says something* and never stops saying it.

Yorke recalls sitting in a car in Japan, stalled like myriad others in traffic around the world, emitting exhaust uselessly and harmfully and thinking, "A million engines in neutral." Committing the phrase to paper (later collated within "And It Rained All Night") doesn't change the fact that Yorke, like the rest of us, has been routinized into submission to a death-dealing system for organizing the movement of people and product in our worlds, but it's a start. It can be one of a series of small feats of attentiveness which, as movements go, have a way of adding up. The words, the lines, and the songs expand the possibility of resistance to the thought patterns, the failures of imagination, the obstructions to seeing what's in front of us that pre-empt the possibility of knowing what's going on, what devastation we're so easily corralled into funding by way of our seeming inability to pay adequate attention. Perhaps there's more than one way to get from point A to point B. Maybe the work can get done without moving at all. It might be that lyrics prove to be the unacknowledged legislation of new worlds on the way, better cultural forms, better economies, better ways of being a rock band.

Yorke views the state of global carbon emissions and the denial of the long-term consequences of any number of standard operating procedures (backed by people and governments ostensibly generated by their consent) in product manufacture, war-making, and cutthroat trade laws as an ongoing assault on human dignity now and a brutal squandering away of an inhabitable environment for generations to come. In view of this, the question of how to be a responsible historical consciousness, how to live a life of non-indifference, to think and live as if the lives of other people matter, the question of bearing witness to things in some sense haunts all things Radiohead. They mean to unsettle and somehow subvert the "self-legitimating imagination of the 'happy few.'"[9] The work of unsettling, we understand, is also self-administered; not only via the creative discourse within the band but in a dialectic, lyrically channeled, within Yorke's own imagination.

Profanity Prayers

Radiohead don't allow themselves an ironic detachment from their complicated vocation decrying the young-blood-sucking methods of mainstream popular culture while serving as a best-selling fixture within that culture. And *The Eraser* serves to make this dialectic disarmingly transparent. This tension is perhaps most intensely evident within "Black Swan," a song which appeared, appropriately enough, as a theme song in Richard Linklater's film adaptation of Philip K. Dick's *A Scanner Darkly*. "The basic fuckedness index," will not be denied. It will in fact be asserted in an Ecclesiastes-like mantra. Real live humans are everywhere "crushed like biscuit crumbs," reduced to bitumen like the dinosaurs, and the dead horses we see and feel with every step cannot be kick-started. Best to cross oneself and move swiftly on. The future will be what it will be, but in the meantime, Yorke is giving voice and bringing a word of relentlessly self-conscious dread pop that even problematizes itself, the opposite, we might say, of a self-legitimating imagination. The *you* and the *I* are poetically collapsed, and the listener is engaged. A mirror is being held up to the all-pervading dysfunction of our moment.

   This is the sound of one man tinkering with words and samples, music and melancholy within a computer program, a man at

9 Pierre Bourdieu, *Distinction: A Social Critique of the Judgment of Taste* (Harvard University Press, 1984), p. 31.

least a little scandalized that his inchoate meditations can be made to feel catchy. Or as Maurice Blanchot observes, "It seems comical and miserable that in order to manifest itself, dread, which opens and closes the sky, needs the activity of a man sitting at his table writing and forming letters on a piece of paper."[10] In Yorke's case, this sense of the surreal is only heightened by the strange fact of its commercial viability.

For better and worse, what Joni Mitchell called that star-maker machinery at work behind, around, and through the popular songs will foist upon an already overwhelmed and exhausted popular imagination one more poor, existing individual after another, enveloped as they are in an array of sad distractions. This is the sensibility of "Skip Divided" in which the celebrity stalker and the celebrity that is the object of the stalker's manufactured affections (that whipped-up frenzy of insanity-enabling that is the "successful" ad campaign of all manner of best-selling commodities) are no longer distinguishable from one another. The speaker resides within a kind of marketing malfunction, awaiting a clear signal for landing, and blinded by the daylight of what he or she believed to have been a big connection within a dubious relationship of escalating codependency. In the wake of a transmogrification that leaves the speaker a creature formed and sustained by "electric veins," the voice craves the number and location it forsook as it now wanders, phantom-like, without proper documentation or permissions secured, a voice neither lost exactly nor meaningfully found in the transaction of units sold in movement that might be merely mercantile.

This is the context of no context so powerfully described by George W.S. Trow, that "space for mirages of pseudo-intimacy" within which "celebrities dance"[11] and the nameless millions enter into a waste of perfectly good emotion like a mob in search of a revolution, millions trapped alone in their target-marketed, tailor-made, informational echo chambers.

---

10 Maurice Blanchot, "From Dread to Language," in *The Gaze of Orpheus and Other Literary Essays*, p. 6.

11 George W.S. Trow, *Within the Context of No Context* (Little, Brown, 1981), p. 19.

Like the album's title track, "Skip Divided" generates (or is generated out of) some very dark questions concerning the relationship of the audience to the artist and vice versa. What's being cultivated between these parties? Is it an unchecked and escalating dysfunction (the very dysfunction Radiohead means to militantly witness against)? Can the star-maker machinery be rehabilitated or salvaged through a more meaningful and mindful relationship? In typical fashion, Yorke brings these issues to the table of testimony ("collating information") without presuming to answer them. To tell the story, to give voice to the spirits, is not to explain these issues away. The music lights it all up, that ambiguous radiation that could be a blessing or curse. The nebulous genre Beck calls profanity prayers. The preferred mode of transport for sea sick sailors on ships of noise.

Don't Turn Away

As we give our attention to *The Eraser*, we sense that Yorke is pitching his vocational tent in the thick of this hi-tech dysfunction as he attempts a distinctly human word across a space in which death alone, it would seem, has complete dominion. As Yorke sees it, the deathliness doesn't honor the supposed boundaries (the marketing categories) of "politics," "entertainment," and "religion," and neither should we. Keeping the one safely sequestered from the other within our fields of perception is, in fact, the strategy whereby the forces of darkness suck young blood, literally *and* metaphorically, from a witless populace, and an artful resistance demands a constant refusal of all such compartmentalizations conveniently arranged by what we might name, to write it out largely in a variation of Eisenhower's famous phrase, a military industrial *entertainment* complex.

By Yorke's lights, the evil that would take David Kelly out one way or another, that erases little women and little men without bothering with body counts, is a palpable social reality beyond any one person's control, a Faustian economy that isn't overly ruffled by protest recordings that sell well. The difficulties of staging a resistance to such evil, of staring into the abyss without becoming what one beholds, appears to be the subject matter of "Atoms for Peace" in which the line, "So many the lies," becomes a playful, sing-songy chant, as if an overwhelming consciousness of ubiquitous evil has to be cast aside at least a few hours of each day to look after children and to wash a few dishes. "Quite a personal song, really," Yorke once remarked. "Trying to correlate my life with choosing to do this, and choosing to get over the fear which is a constant thing I have. Being a rock star, you're supposed to have super-über-confidence all the time. And I don't . . . It was my missus telling me to get it together basically."[12]

Getting it together, like thinking things through, like trying to make sense by collating what information we have might best be undertaken in a spirit of earnest nonchalance that means to keep its own witness, conscientiously under erasure; worth doing certainly, but not so self-seriously that it takes its toll on all other relationships. There is the fearful alertness of the poet that is a necessity for anyone having a go at lyrical sense-making or crazy prevention, but it requires a light hand. It isn't to be held on too tightly as work, this farming of a verse. Is it writing? Is it analysis? Does such self-consciousness undermine the possibility of right witness?

Here again, Derrida's word on his own words, in the deliberately marginalized piece "Circonfession," is especially helpful:

> Commotion of writing, give in only to it, do not make oneself interesting by promised avowal or refused secret, so no literature if literature, the institution of 'saying everything', breathes to the hope of seeing the other confess and thereby you, yourself, confess yourself, admit yourself, you my fall, in an effusion of recognition. . . .[13]

This word on a self-denying, self-referential "commotion of writing" that hopes to work its way out of its own solipsism by way of non-mastery (the scribbling that might occasion confessions by confessing itself first and foremost) is reminiscent of the endlessly reminiscent work that is "Cymbal Rush." One can try to

12 Craig McLean, "All Messed Up,"
http://observer.guardian.co.uk/omm/story/0,,1795948,00.html.

13 Jacques Derrida, "Circumfession," in *Jacques Derrida* (University of Chicago Press, 1993), p. 210.

save oneself ("your little voice") to the exclusion of everything and everyone, and lose all sense of soul, all in the name of not being numbered among "the losers" for whom there is no room and who are being (and will be) turned away forever.

"Don't turn away," Yorke pleads amid the sound of synthetic beats increasing in volume. And it brings to mind George Orwell's vision of the future—the vision of a torturer whispered to the tortured actually—in which it is authoritatively observed that the end of human history is a black boot pressed on a human face forever. "Don't turn away," is the last spoken expression as Yorke's crooning is eventually cut off by the beeps and beats that began the song. The spoken plea was done with even before we heard it. Words are always received, as it were, under erasure, their echo abiding insofar as we give them heed again, always vulnerable to being disregarded and ignored, their meaning depending on the receiver more than the sender. Every word, as the poet Robert Hass reminds us, is an elegy to what it signifies.

Ideology and Idolatry

To return for a moment to the question of genres, boundaries, and compartmentalizations, the terms we use to affirm (or to withhold affirmation from) the witness of other people, living or dead, as they come to us, I'd like to locate *The Eraser* within a mystic strand of the traditions called religious very broadly conceived. All our attempts at witness (sending *and* receiving) are acts of faith, a collating of what information we have with a strong sense of our own finitude, our own humanness. And we do less harm the more we keep this awareness in mind, maintaining a constant vigilance against our tendency to reify our favored abstractions. When we keep a vigil of this sort, we begin to get a sense of the Derridean view of religion, of pilgrims (everyone a pilgrim) moving through and moving by abstractions and (hopefully) seeking out more redemptive ones: "Should one save oneself by abstraction or save oneself from abstraction? Where is salvation, safety?"[14] I think of *The Eraser* as an experiment—an offering—in robustly, self-conscious abstraction, the knowingly finite, inescapably social work of folk traditions, the traditions we sometimes call religion.

14 Jacques Derrida, "Faith and Knowledge: The Two Sources of 'Religion' at the Limits of Reason Alone," in *Religion*, edited by Jacques Derrida and Gianni Vattimo (Stanford University Press, 1998), p. 1.

Derrida speaks of religion as our "clearest and most obscure" word, a touchstone of ethical alchemy, an arsenal of word and image out of which we sense an ethical summons, a river of song we do well to call sacred, even as we should probably employ the term with a sort of mandatory agnosticism if only for, in the deepest sense, *religious* reasons:

> We act as though we had some common sense of what 'religion' means through the languages we believe (how much belief already, to this moment, to this very day!) we know how to speak. We believe in the minimal trustworthiness of this word . . . nothing is less pre-assured . . . and the entire question of religion comes down, perhaps, to this lack of assurance. (p. 3)

As Derrida pitches it (and as I mean to argue as well), religion isn't best understood primarily as a collection of beliefs held by backward people with fear and trembling for most of human history (religion as brainwash). It is rather, among other things, a scriptorium of beleaguered witness, a record of collated information, both fragmentary and sometimes systematic, with which we may feel compelled to reckon as it somehow, across history, reckons with us, an inheritance, if you like, of difficult wisdom. Without wishing to contaminate its legacy with what could be taken to be a most poisonous form of bad press (Religious Rock) I locate *The Eraser* along this continuum, a work of witness to the possibility of witness, a witness that holds *as sacred* the witness of others, a grammar of grace, earthbound *and* ethereal. I imagine Bono of U2 had a similar affirmation in mind when he recently referred to Radiohead as "a sacred talent."[15]

Sacred, I would say, not merely because the music inspires feelings of otherworldliness or transcendence or a haunting sense of the holy in the otherwise merely everyday, but sacred in the way that the music of *The Eraser* questions everything, problematizing the given. It interrogates the ideological as well as the idolatrous (two words for brainwash) in the way it speaks truth to power, its relentless lyricism of protest. It isn't *merely* lyrical in the sense that it could be regarded as irrelevant to other more reality-based concerns, because the lyrical precedes the analytical as well as whatev-

er we call the philosophical. We might try to distinguish between
the witness of mystic traditions (institutionally sanctioned or otherwise) and political concerns but this, again, does justice to neither. It's politics all the way down. As the scholar of Buddhist traditions, Richard King, has observed: "The very fact that 'the mystical' is seen as irrelevant to issues of social and political authority
itself reflects contemporary, secularized notions of and attitudes
toward power. The separation of the mystical from the political is
itself a political decision!"[16]

There Are No Unrelated Phenomena

Against the rationale of myriad forms of officialdom whose discourse would carefully separate issue of business, "the economy,"
security, and the government in such a way as to pre-empt meaningful critique of the status quo, *The Eraser* speaks out of a world
where everything is connected to everything else. It is out of this
sacred *an*-archy that the poetic, as well as the prophetic, speaks. We
can call this space religion or literature or philosophy or the folk
tradition of truth-telling, the wisdom tradition of the folks, by the
folks, and for the folks.

As practitioners and partakers of the tradition understand,
such folk will have their work cut out for them. So much energy
and so many resources are devoted to broadcasting disinformation
which insists that *this* has nothing to do with *that*, that events are
unrelated to other events, and that some dots should never be connected. This is why collation of information, like the transformation of data into metaphor has always been an act of communal
resistance, dangerous news for the powers that be, subversive
meaning-making in the shadow of reigning mythologies. Within
this space I mean to celebrate and describe, Yorke and his fellow
artisans produce their alternative broadcasts. In this space, there
are no unrelated phenomena. Sacred music has always said as
much.

While *The Eraser* stands alone as a powerfully life-affirming
witness, I can't help but add that "Reckoner," played live by
Radiohead as early as 2000 and eventually appearing as a remark-

16 Richard King, *Orientalism and Religion: Postcolonial Theory, India, and
'The Mystic East'*

able Talk Talk-infused standout track on *In Rainbows*, is especially representative of the witness forecast throughout *The Eraser*. "Dedicated to *all* human beings," decrees the chorus. It's as if the voices working their way through Yorke's solo project land within a space of affirmation and infinite hospitality made known in an enduringly communal sound (of all of Radiohead's work, it's the one I most want to hear sung by a large crowd of people, it's as if it's made to be sung this way. As of this writing, it's the opening number on their set list). It calls the past and the future to the rescue of the present, and by performing a sort of vigil in anticipation of joy and justice to come, it realizes, in no small degree, something of that joy now. Not negating what *The Eraser* cultivates but enriching its life-giving witness.

Radiohead and the Music Industry. *(Rainbows and Arrows.)*

8.

Taking the Sting Out of Environmental Virtue Ethics

DANIEL MILSKY

> Time is running out for us
> But you just move the hands upon the clock
>
> —Thom Yorke, "The Clock"

The headlines are dire. The end of the world is near. Our planet is headed for environmental destruction. Like many, you feel a duty to repair the damage we have done—even as you head out the door, bottled water in hand, hop in the car, stop at the filling station, drive to Lollapalooza, and catch Radiohead live in Grant Park.

If you see the contradiction—if, say, while driving to the show, you wonder about the car, the bottled water, the long, hot shower you took last night, and the acres of trash and tons of pollution that went into making all this possible—you might panic at the thought of your own hypocrisy. That's what Radiohead seemed to do after they learned that their album *Hail to the Thief*—the CDs, the travelling of the band members, and especially the fans driving to the venues—put nearly eight tons of carbon dioxide into the atmosphere. That's roughly the amount 1,400 cars would emit in a year. To offset and reabsorb that amount, some fifty thousand trees would have to be planted and maintained for a hundred years (if there's that much time left).

The band's response, it turns out, was fairly progressive—not only environmentally, but also philosophically. For environmental ethics has lately become less preoccupied with specific environ-

101

mental problems (How risky is nuclear power?, say) and more interested in a virtue-centered approach. Rather than focusing on individual environmental problems, virtue ethicists focus on broader questions, like "How ought we to live?", "What constitutes human flourishing?" and "What are the relative roles of humans and their (non-human) environment in answering these questions?" An enormous benefit of this approach is the framing of environmental issues as essential to the good life, rather than some burden we must shoulder out of necessity. Radiohead has embraced a virtue-centered approach to environmental issues and actually addresses this relationship between humanity and nature. The band has in fact become a moral exemplar, a model for living more in harmony with nature and promoting human flourishing that we can all look up to. (And not just because "anyone can play guitar.")

Kid Akrasia

Radiohead and Yorke as a solo artist are not the first to engage political and environmental issues, of course. Classic protest songs like Bob Dylan's "Blowin' in the Wind" (1962), and Pete Seeger's "Where Have All the Flowers Gone?" (1962) established a tradition in modern pop music that extends through Eminem's "Mosh" or "White America" and Green Day's Grammy-winning album "American Idiot."

Specifically environmental issues were put on the map by Woody Guthrie, who dedicated an entire album to songs about the Columbia River (anchored by the song "Roll on Columbia!"), and have continued with songs like Ani DiFranco's "Animal" and Dar Williams' "What Do You Love More than Love." Radiohead's *Hail to the Thief* has some things to say about a certain American president, while Thom Yorke's *The Eraser* goes to the heart of current worries about global warming. The album is anxious, its lyrics are desperate, and the album cover artwork imagery of King Canute trying to hold back a giant wave is an obvious metaphor of our struggle to control something that is ". . . relentless, Invisible, Indefatigable, Indisputable, Undeniable" (as Yorke sings in "And It Rained All Night).

In order for these environmental messages to be taken seriously, though, we must believe that the artists behind them take them seriously as well. This points to a deeper moral question first addressed by Aristotle in his *Nicomachean Ethics* (Book 7, Chapter 3). It involves the idea of *akrasia* or weakness of will, a form of moral weakness. Those that fall victim to *akrasia* act in ways that contradict their better judgment. Simply put, one ought to act in accordance with reason or risk acting immorally. If I chose *a* over *b*, even though I'm convinced that *b* was the better thing to do all things considered then I've certainly engaged in puzzling, potentially immoral behavior.

Take the artist Sting, for example. Much has been made of his politics and his failure to adhere to his own message. In one interview, Sting and his wife Trudie Styler were confronted by a journalist charging that he and his wife have a carbon footprint nearly thirty times greater than the average Britain. Sting said, "I'm a musician; I have a huge carbon footprint." Apparently, he is also friendly to less than environmentally responsible business ventures. In 1995, he accepted a reported £500,000 to advertise the Seagaia golf complex in Japan, where developers had flattened miles of historic pine forests to build a luxury leisure resort. More recently, he blessed an advertisement for a gas-guzzling Jaguar that used his hit "Desert Rose" as its backing track. Sting was reportedly paid a six-figure licensing fee. Even more recently, in January 2008, The Police were named "the dirtiest band in the world" in a survey of the eco-friendly credentials of live acts sponsored by the UK music magazine *NME*. Their concerts leave the largest carbon footprint in the world, mostly due to their choice of venues and the transportational requirements involved.

Given Sting's commitment to rainforests and other environmental causes, we may be witnessing a clear case of one choosing *a* over *b*. Let *a* = actions that increase his carbon footprint and *b* = actions that reduce his carbon footprint. If he is truly committed to what he preaches then it would seem he would be convinced by the superiority of choosing *b*. Since Sting acknowledges the incompatibility of his actions with his beliefs, he is either unable or unwilling to act in accordance with his beliefs. But certainly he is able, leaving us to conclude that he must unwilling and hence *akratic* (weak willed) in Aristotle's sense.

The point is not that Sting's actions necessarily undermine the legitimacy of his environmental message. The *ad hominem* fallacy forces us to distinguish between the person and his or her views.

Sting has shed much light on the plight of the South American rainforest and his Rainforest Foundation has raised millions of dollars for rainforest preservation. His *akrasia* has nothing to do with the logical or factual validity of his beliefs and message. But it does highlight our own (and Radiohead's) similar struggles to find an environmentally virtuous way to think and live through these issues.

Wake Up (Morning Bell)

Radiohead's wake up call came in 2005, long after Yorke and Radiohead had become celebrity spokespersons for the Friends of the Earth's "The Big Ask" campaign. The campaign calls on seventeen countries as well as the European Union to sign up to legally binding, year-on-year targets for reducing carbon dioxide emissions. So it was natural for the public and the press to turn their eyes on the band's own carbon footprint. In May, the *Sunday Times* did just that by quoting Yorke saying, "The music industry is a spectacularly good example of fast turnover consumer culture. It is actually terrifying. Environmental considerations should be factored into the way the record companies operate." The paper enlisted the Edinburgh Centre for Carbon Management to perform a carbon and pollution audit on the band itself, and produced the bad news about the *Hail to the Thief* album and tour.

Radiohead's response was quite different to Sting's. In the same 2008 report that named Sting and the Police the dirtiest band in the world, Radiohead was named the *cleanest*. So what changed in the three years since the *Sunday Times* article? The band began to make a serious attempt to avoid *akrasia*. They took steps to make sure they were no longer ignorant of the effects of their actions, and consciously decided to act in accordance with their beliefs and their reason. First, they commissioned their own report on the band's carbon footprint, hiring Best Foot Forward Ltd, an environmental consulting firm, to produce a carbon audit. In July of 2007 the company released "The Ecological Footprint and Carbon Audit of Radiohead North American Tours, 2003 and 2006." The results were rather sobering.

Ecological footprint and carbon output reports typically measure the tonnage of CO_2 emissions and, in this case, the global hectares, to represent the amount of land required, on a global scale, to provide the resources and absorb the CO_2 associated with a particular activity. As it is for most rock band tours, the majority of the environmental impact comes from fans travelling to and from the performance venues. This stands to reason since the 2003 Amphitheater tour drew nearly a quarter of a million fans and the 2006 theater tour drew approximately seventy thousand. Most of those attending the shows arrived in high-emission US cars. Of the bands touring impact, nearly sixty percent (theater tour) and forty percent (amphitheater) was a result of travel and energy use. International travel accounted for another thirty-four to forty percent of the impact.

Other ecological costs came from shipping and trucking equipment via air and truck freight. Air freight from the UK to the US accounted for twenty tons of CO_2 to the east coast and twenty-six tons of CO_2 to the west coast. The trucks carrying equipment accounted for sixty-two tons CO_2 (2006) and seventy-three tons of CO_2 (2003). And then there's beer. Estimated at approximately two bottles per fan, this accounted for fifty tons, while the bottles and plastic glasses accounted for another sixteen (for the theater tour) and about 160 (for the amphitheater tour). Food was estimated at 215 tons of CO_2 impact. The total combined impact from both tours was approximately 11,368 tons of CO_2 with an ecological footprint of 4,557 global hectares.

Fitter Happier Emitting
Carbon Dioxide in Moderation

Faced with loads of information and public interest demanding some sort of reform, Yorke and the band had some thinking to do. In a recent interview with David Byrne (of Talking Heads fame) in *Wired* magazine, Yorke pointed to the ecological contradiction they were dealing with:

> YORKE: . . . at the moment we make money principally from touring. Which is hard for me to reconcile because I don't like all the energy consumption, the travel. It's an ecological disaster, traveling, touring.

BYRNE: Well, there are the biodiesel buses and all that.

YORKE: Yeah, it depends where you get your biodiesel from. There are ways to minimize it. We did one of those carbon footprint things recently where they assessed the last period of touring we did and tried to work out where the biggest problems were. And it was obviously everybody traveling to the shows.

BYRNE: Oh, you mean the audience?

YORKE: Yeah. Especially in the US. Everybody drives. So how the hell are we going to address that? The idea is that we play in municipal places with some transport system alternative to cars. And we minimize flying equipment, shipping everything. *We* can't be shipped though. (*Wired*, 2007).

This was no greenwash.[1] Yorke and Co. sincerely sought ways to reconcile their environmental and musical goals and values, to tour in ways that would leave the smallest possible carbon footprint.

The first thing the band needed to address was fan travel. The Best Foot Forward report identified it as the single biggest contributor to the band's carbon footprint. The first major decision was to select venues in major cities that offered the greatest access to public transportation. In December of 2007, the band hired an eco-coordinator who crafted a hit list of practical requirements for venue selection:

1. Give car poolers preferential parking and make sure fans know about it.

---

1 Greenwashing is the attempt by a company, an industry, a government, a politician or even a non-government organization to appear environmentally virtuous by creating a pro-environmental image, selling a product or a policy, after being embroiled in controversy.

2. Use low-energy light bulbs in all areas.

3. Purchase green power or power from renewable sources from electricity provider.

4. Use reusable cups rather than disposable ones.

5. Use recycled paper for all office stationary, tickets, posters, flyers and napkins.

6. Use compostable recycled paper crockery and wooden cutlery (not plastic).

7. Install recycling points for all cans and bottles.

Car pooling and composting showed the most immediate promise, with an average of twelve percent reduction on the total number of cars used, and an average of one thousand spots taken each night in the car pooling lot. Compostable food waste from the venue backstage kitchens has been collected and used by venue grounds keepers and local gardening clubs.

It's difficult to control the audience, to force them to bike, walk or take public transport, as Yorke told David Byrne. But that does not reduce the importance factors that remain within the band's control. They have stopped air freight, opting instead for sea shipping, which produces a much smaller carbon footprint. And in a move to save fuel, they've outfitted all of their tour trucks with Auxiliary Power Units (APUs). These are small generators mounted on the side of truck cabs that can be powered by alternative fuel sources to prevent the truckers from idling their engines to run the air conditioning.

Other measures to reduce energy consumption and waste involve the actual performance and staging of the band. The lighting and visuals designer for the band has introduced LED lighting systems which use far less energy than heat-generating incandescent lights and can therefore be powered by alternative power sources. Currently the band charges large batteries with electricity thereby avoiding running large fuel-consuming generators. The crew is currently looking into charging these batteries with solar and wind systems and perhaps even hydrogen in the near future.

Radiohead is so committed to the cause that, in an interview with John Elliott, Yorke said: "You have a certain amount of credit you can cash in with your celebrity and I'm cashing the rest of my chips in with this" (*Sunday Times*, May 29th, 2005). He has been deeply disturbed by the current global climate crisis and blogged on the Radiohead website:

> THIS IS WHAT I AM DOING NOW. This is big shit. This is the big ask. About climate change the stuff that wakes me up at 4 am in a sweat, . . . is that normal? I worry too much, apparently. . . . THOMx.

Yorke was so moved by the crisis that he dedicated his solo record (*The Eraser*) to addressing global climate change. He told the *Los Angeles Times* his inspiration for the album came from British environmentalist Jonathan Porrit, who dismissed any efforts of government to stop global warming—"saying that their gestures were like King Canute trying to stop the tide," Yorke recalled. "And that just went 'kaching' in my head. It's not political, really, but that's exactly what I feel is happening. We're all King Canutes, holding our hands out, saying, 'It'll go away. I can make it stop.' No, you can't" (*Los Angeles Times*, June 28th, 2006).

This Is Really Happening (So Do Something)

Radiohead's contribution to environmental ethics begins with their music, some of which serves as a warning, a narrative about the current state of our environment. Lyrics like those from "Idioteque," "The Clock," and "And It Rained All Night" articulate a sense of internal conflict and moral despair. The songs focus our attention on a morally important question, namely, the human, anthropogenic origins of global climate change. Like other compelling environmental narratives, like Thoreau's *Walden* or Aldo Leopold's *A Sand County Almanac*, they ask us to deeply consider humanity's impact upon the land and the environment. If we are convinced by the principles and reasons articulated by these narratives then we are obligated to act accordingly or risk, once again, *akrasia.*

But Radiohead also serves as a model for an environmental virtue ethic. The band's commitment to Friends of the Earth is a commitment to a virtue based ethic insofar as the organization links environmental problems and human flourishing. If we are to flourish as people, this ethic holds, then we must fight environmental injustice and repair our damaged ecosystem. Adhering to environmental virtues such as simplicity, recycling, sustainability and the reduction of our carbon footprints are not only important for our survival—they allow us to flourish. In the band's commitment to these environmental virtues, they changed course. They altered their behavior and took steps to live lives and make music in ways that are consistent with reason and, remain consequently, morally virtuous.

Of course Radiohead is not going to save the universe. We must all act together to promote these environmental virtues. But for those starting down a more environmentally sound life, or those having difficulty with the follow-through, music like Radiohead's can be inspiring.

So when you're on your way to Lollapalooza and "Idioteque" starts playing from the *Kid A* in the CD player:

> We're not scaremongering
> This is really happening
> Happening

You may catch a glimpse of *akrasia.* Turn the car around and take it back into the garage, hop on your bike, and head down to Lollapalooza, BPA-free bottle in hand. In terms of environmental virtue ethics, you will have put everything in its right place.

9.

We (Capitalists) Suck Young Blood

Joseph Tate

For the greater part of his life, the German philosopher Karl Marx (1818–1883) lived in London. One evening, feeling a bit overly nationalistic after a pub crawl—one beer each at the eighteen pubs between Oxford Street and Hampstead down London's Tottenham Court Road—Marx is reported to have harassed a group of patrons at the last stop. Marx proclaimed: "No country but Germany . . . could have produced such masters as Beethoven, Mozart, Handel and Haydn; snobbish, cant-ridden England was fit only for philistines." After igniting the ire of locals at the pub, Marx, with drinking companions in tow, fled into the night and threw paving stones at streetlights.

This anecdote, remembered by Wilhelm Liebknecht, one of the evening's co-conspirators, gives us a glimpse of a human Marx. There's likely little rhyme or reason to what prompted a Marx who was three sheets to the wind to trot out musical composers as the height of German achievement. Marx not only cherished the names of his countries' great composers but mentioned them instead of other Germans—like Hegel, a major philosophical influence on Marx, or Goethe, one of the country's greatest writers—who'd left the most obvious marks on his written work.

In conjunction with the work of Radiohead, if we can imagine a metaphorically "Nude" Marx—yet with wild hair and beard remaining for dramatic effect (he consciously cultivated the beard, letters reveal)—then we can rearrange the puzzle of his philosophy so at least some of the jigsaw pieces fall into place. Marx's philosophy might be best summed up by a sentence from a work that pre-dates the multi-volume, oversized monument known as *Capital*: "Men make their own history, but not of their own free will; not under circumstances they themselves have chosen but under the given and inherited circumstances with which they are directly confronted." This sentence, in some ways, captures what's been dubbed "dialectical materialism," the name later given to Marx's philosophical outlook. But we don't need to name Marx's philosophy to understand the core of it: people exist in tension between what they would make of the world and what the world would make of them. This gets at what Thom Yorke and other members of Radiohead has seen as the problem for much of their lives as artist: they have stood in tension between what they would make of themselves and what their record company would make of them.

Bringing Radiohead together with bushy-haired Marx might seem like sucking the band's blood. Marx never imagined digital distribution and he wrote nothing systematic on music. Plus, many of us come to Marx with too many presuppositions. For this essay, at least, set aside what you might know about Marx. I'd rather that we not, in Radiohead's words from "Nude," "get any big ideas." Toss out the quotes from *The Communist Manifesto* or any ingrained ideas about Communism or Marxism that you have encountered. Marx would ask the same. He once heard a group call themselves Marxist and said, "I at least am not a Marxist." Approaching Marx without preconceptions is difficult or maybe impossible—approaching a "Nude" Marx is maybe, as the Radiohead song says, "not going to happen." But the Marx we rarely hear about was human. And he loved music.

Six Fluffy Wee Rabbits

Thom Yorke is troubled by making money. Gauging how the rest of Radiohead relates to money is harder. Interviewers tend to hound the other band members with less bark and bite, but when questions directed at Yorke tend toward record contracts or celebrity, his responses give away a singular unease. There's wry misdirection: "It's all for the cash!" Or over-direct anger: "we did not ask for a load of cash from our old record label EMI to re-sign. that is a L I E . . . We are extremely upset that this crap is being spread about." Or meandering lecture:

> . . . it's tempting to have someone say to you, "You will never have to worry about money ever again," but no matter how much money someone gives you—what, you're not going to spend it? You're not going to find stupid ways to get rid of it? Of course you are. It's like building roads and expecting there to be less traffic.

He misdirects. He gets angry about it during interviews—even in Radiohead-produced parodies. But he can't laugh about it.

In late 2004 the band released *The Most Gigantic Lying Mouth of All Time* (or as fans refer to it, *TMGLMOAT*), an eclectic DVD, originally planned as part of a Radiohead TV channel that never materialized. It is almost two hours long and contains music videos directed by the likes of Sophie Muller, video shorts contributed by fans (such as an instructional video on how to create a chickenbomb), and odd interludes. During a comic interview titled "My showbiz life: THOM YORKE OUT OF RADIOHEAD," Yorke is asked all the uncomfortable questions he's asked regularly. Before the questions begin, Yorke clarifies for the off-screen interviewer that, "This is the stupidest thing you've ever done."

The questions delve into Yorke's celebrity status and his relationship to money. Yorke admits he accepted "a Russian egg" from "some big fish at Microsoft" and confesses to using his celebrity to get free petrol. But when asked: "What's the most money you've blown in a single day?" he lets go an embarrassed baritone "ew" followed by a quick edit to an "uh." Yorke then stares for a long four-seconds into the camera with a pasted-on, uncomfortable grin and answers: "Six fluffy wee rabbits." Watching Yorke become uncomfortable is discomforting. Ew, uh, and paused fake grin add up to: next question, please. The mock-interviewer says as much, and moves on.

TMGLMOAT was released not long after 2003's *Hail to the Thief*, the band's last album under contract with EMI. After touring to promote the album for nearly ten months, Radiohead took a year off. When the hiatus ended in 2005, the band started *Dead Air Space*, a blog (http://radiohead.com/deadairspace/), but, at first, there was no news about a renewed or new record contract. Fans and the press itched for an update. In August 2005, Yorke broke the silence with a sarcastic post and his trademark misspellings:

> we have no record conntract.
> as such.
> any offers?..what we would like is th e old EMI back again, the nice genteel arms manufacturers who treated music a nice side project who werent to bothered about the shareholders. ah well not much chance of that.

The same day the short post appeared, it was deleted, only to survive as a quotation scattered around the internet in various other blogs.

Yorke sings on *The Eraser*, his 2006 solo album, that "The more you try to erase me / The more that I appear," lines that ring true in this case: deleting the blog post caused it to loom that much larger, especially looking back after the "pay what you want, no really" release of *In Rainbows*. It's clichéd by now to say Radiohead's digital distribution of the album took the music business, music critics, other musicians, fans, and the press—the world—by surprise and even angered some (Nicky Wire of the Manic Street Preachers declared that it "demeans music"). Yet people who've closely followed Radiohead's career expected a tectonic shift. They didn't know how or when, but the *why* was scrawled across nearly every page of Radiohead's biography.

We Want Sweet Meats

Yorke's unease about money and music started after signing Radiohead's first record contract on December 21st, 1991. *Pablo Honey*'s success stressed Yorke and the band more than it elated them. Plus, their first album's tour took a toll. Night-after-night performances at times caused Yorke to lose his voice. At one point during the tour while getting off a bus in San Francisco, Yorke fell to the ground, exhausted and collapsing from back pain. At corporate congratulatory get-togethers, he would sit in an aggressive sulk. The record contract was an albatross. If they made it to a second album, Yorke joked, it would be titled *Unit*, as in "unit shifter," the music industry's term for a single that helps sell albums.[1] As Yorke would sing ten years later, the recording industry wanted the sweet meat, and by signing the contract and agreeing to whatever it demanded, Yorke must have felt he was using a pen dipped in his own young blood, a theme explored by the vampiric *Hail to the Thief* song "We Suck Young Blood (Your Time is Up.)."

The song verges on the over-obvious. The viscous, ill-timed handclaps and Yorke's glacially slow delivery of the lyrics make it powerfully creepy:

> Are you hungry?
> Are you sick?
> Are you begging for a break?
> Are you sweet?
> Are you fresh?
> Are you strung up by the wrists?
> We want the young blood

Before the album was released the song was at the center of a fake advertising campaign. In April 2003, posters appeared around Los Angeles and London advertising: "Hungry? Sick? Begging for a break? Sweet? Fresh? Would you do anything? We suck young blood. We want sweet meats." If you fit the criteria you could call 1-866-868-4433, or 1-866-tot-hief. Someone, Yorke said in an interview, took it seriously: "Someone I heard on the radio completely missed the point, or maybe they didn't. They kind of thought we were running some kind of Radiohead talent show. Just genius—that would have been perfect but sadly not." Yorke rarely explicates the band's songs, but this time he did: "It's all very tied up with Hollywood and the constant desire to stay young, fleece people, suck their energy . . . It's not really about the music

---

1 Radiohead wasn't the only band feeling pressured. It's no coincidence that the same year Yorke agonized over the band becoming little more than a source of unit shifters Nirvana released *In Utero,* a platinum album with the song "Radio Friendly Unit Shifter."

business as such, definitely much more about the glamorous world of Hollywood."

Radiohead had recorded *Hail to the Thief* in a several-weeks blitz in Los Angeles so Hollywood culture might well have been on his mind. But a version of the song had been circulating around Radiohead's repertoire since at least 2001, when Colin Greenwood said the song was about "these multiplatinum artists hooking up with the latest French disco producer to do their new record." Whether pointed at Hollywood or French disco producers, the target is likely what Yorke said it wasn't: the music business as such, and how it exploits the very musicians it needs to succeed.

We Suck Young Blood

Marx would have liked Yorke's comparison of a business, or a capitalist culture like Hollywood, to blood-sucking vampires. He made it too. Once a worker signs over their labor via a contract to a profit-making, capitalist enterprise, Marx wrote (quoting his long time colleague Friedrich Engels), the worker is stuck and "the vampire will not let go 'while there remains a single muscle, sinew or drop of blood to be exploited'." On another occasion he wrote: "Capital is dead labour which, vampire-like, lives only by sucking living labour, and lives the more, the more labor it sucks."

A capitalist—the business owner who lives off the work of others—is an undead, parasite that relies on the worker's vitality. Marx was haunted not just by the image but the reality of the workers exploited at times to the point of crippling physical ailments. Capitalism was "wasting not only flesh and blood, but also nerves and brains." Capitalism wants the sweet meats, the young blood and Yorke could feel it breathing at his neck.

When it came to digital sales, Yorke knew the vampire was not about to let go. Everyone made money off Radiohead's music, except for Radiohead. Yorke explained in a *Wired Magazine* interview with David Byrne:

> In terms of digital income, we've made more money out of this record [In Rainbows] than out of all the other Radiohead albums put together, forever—in terms of anything on the Net. And that's nuts. It's partly due to the fact that EMI wasn't giving us any money for digital sales. All the contracts signed in a certain era have none of that stuff.

Yorke, uncharacteristically, wants his fair share, but you can't fault him. What he saw happening was the vampires sucking his blood, living off it for the sake of the blood itself and not for the music. And for digital sales, contracts tipped the scales in favor of the music industry which then became the proverbial blood-sucking vampires. How a company can take what you make and profit at your expense bothered Marx as much as it does Yorke.

Thom Yorke tried articulating this tension between what Radiohead would want to make of themselves and what their record company would make of them in 1997's *Meeting People Is Easy*. Even though making music had brought them money, he feared money would dictate what music they made. It's a lengthy quote and he has trouble wording just what the problem is, but his attempt is worth reading in full:

> It's like a supply and demand thing. It's like: "Well, this is what they want me to do, you know, this is what they want to hear, so I'll do more of this. Because this is great and they love me," and that can be the demise of so many recording artists. You know, because you suddenly, suddenly people start giving you cash as well, suddenly you've got money and you get used to this lifestyle and you don't want to take any risks because they've got you by the balls. You don't want to take any risks because like, why, you know you've got all this baggage you're carrying around with you everywhere. And you can't let go. You know you've got all these things you've bought or you're attached to, or, you know, if you start spending all this money.

Just after this interview, the documentary continues with shots of Radiohead in the studio attempting to record new tracks. The shots are revealing but boring because they show a Radiohead afraid to take risks: the music industry has them, as Yorke says, by the balls.

The last song we see performed live before the credits role is an early version of "Nude," the third song on *In Rainbows*, a song then untitled. Seconds later, Grant Gee, the director, cuts to Yorke joking with an MTV reporter that he'd like to call the song, "Your Home Is at Risk if You Do Not Keep Up Repayment," but he's not sure if the title's "catchy enough." Yorke's deadpan-dark humor doesn't spark a giggle in the room, but the risk the title alludes to is exactly the sort of risk Yorke fears losing. As he said, once you're given money for what you do, you feel you need to keep doing what you do or risk losing what you have. The fear money engenders makes one afraid to take risks, and "that's how they get you," that's how the record companies crack your little soul, as Yorke sings on *Amnesiac*.

Crack Your Little Soul

2001's *Amnesiac* was overshadowed by *Kid A*. Though recorded during the same sessions, the band insisted *Amnesiac* was not a b-sides album, despite being labeled as such. One song on *Amnesiac* best gives voice to Yorke's suspicion and fears surrounding money. The song twists and turns between self-help axioms ("Be constructive / With yer blues") and suggestive but masked aggression ("There are weapons we can use"). It ends, however, with the song's speaker comparing himself and an undefined "we" to currency, and the comparison isn't pretty:

> We are the dollars and cents and the pounds and pence and the mark and the yen, the yen
> we're going to crack your little souls

The song is as strange as anything Radiohead has done: we can't hear Yorke's quiet voice well, yet he's most clear when singing the admonishing lyrics, "Won't you quiet down." Musically it moves at a disturbing pace, building slowly then breaking down with anything but relief.

Yorke's lyrics do, even if he might deny it, express concerns that intersect with comments he has made during interviews. If we could exchange Yorke's lyrics for any passage of Marx's it might be this one: Capitalists, those who accumulate wealth in order to accumulate more wealth, can

> distort the worker into a fragment of a man, they degrade him to the level of a machine, they destroy the actual content of his labour by turning it into a torment; they alienate from him the intellectual potentialities of the labour process . . . they transform him his lifetime into working time, and drag his wife and child beneath the juggernaut of capital.

About to be free of a record contract, and staring across the record business's wasteland, Radiohead was angry and confused. Money had been cracking their souls. But they found a way out of the torment with their next album by freeing themselves from money altogether: the album was more or less free. Whether or not this changed the music business, it helped turn a spotlight on not just how the music business has exploited musicians, but on how creative talent risks being exploited. This was the ultimate focus of Marx's philosophy, a focus that changed much philosophy after it. Early in his career he stated: "The philosophers have only interpreted the world; the point is to change it." With Radiohead's departure into contract-free territory, the vampire was getting a stake through its heart and, as Yorke said on the band's blog, "We made the sign of the cross and walked away."

But some complain that Radiohead's change of music business models helped few artists beside themselves. Sales from the album, while unknown (guesses pin sales somewhere in the multi-millions), make clear that pay-what-you-want was a smart business move. But by taking over the enterprise of selling their own music, you can ask, isn't Radiohead just becoming the money-making capitalists they despise, removing the middle man to make even more money? But this misses a crucial point Marx emphasized: Radiohead's move does not accumulate wealth for wealth's sake. What they're doing, by wresting the method of distribution from the hands of the record business, is removing the capitalist middle-man, the business in the middle that does little more than make money from album sales for the sake of making money at the artists' expense.

Still, you might object, Radiohead were hardly being what Marx called "immiserated," rendered miserable by the circumstances of their employment. Liking their former record contracts or not, they're millionaires. They've done well by capitalism. But doing well in this way does not mean they succumbed to capitalism and became accumulators of wealth for wealth's sake. In fact, their new distribution method would hardly be a blow to capitalism if capitalism hadn't brought Radiohead to world-wide prominence. Capitalism, then, enables Radiohead to more widely circulate their critique of music business methods than they could ever do otherwise. As other philosophers have argued, capitalism's products will be its own downfall. Capitalism wants rapid and wide distribution of goods: but what if the goods being rapidly and widely distributed make consumers think twice about capitalism itself? Capitalist interests made Radiohead an international phenomena, and capitalism gave Radiohead a platform from which to help remove exploitation from the capitalist equation.

C-M-C Music Factory

Marx, it's no surprise, had an equation that helps make sense of Radiohead's move to remove the middle-man: C-M-C. Economic transactions that don't exploit, Marx said, can be represented as C-M-C. "C" is commodities and "M" is money. A person exchanges C, sells a commodity, for M, for money. That money, in turn, can be used to buy C, or commodities. I sell the product of my work for money and use that money to buy the product of someone else's work: C-M-C. Capitalism works differently—more like, M-C-M. A capitalist uses money to buy commodities and the capitalist sells those commodities for money.

There's nothing inherently wrong with this formula, but it can get perverted into what Marx represented as M-C-M*. The M* represented transactions that sold commodities for more than they were worth only for the accumulation of M*, money above and beyond what's reasonable. This surplus is then passed back into the M-C-M* transaction, and on and on, at the expense of those providing the capitalist the necessary Cs, or commodities. Also, a capitalist, perhaps above all, is one that takes the work of another and uses it for M-C-M*. The worker providing the C never gets their rightful due. That's the cycle Radiohead felt trapped in.[2]

Radiohead's move, then, was toward C-M-C. Yorke told BBC Radio 4 that "the big infrastructure of the music business has not addressed the way artists communicate directly with their fans. In fact, they seem to basically get in the way. Not only do they get in the way, but they take all the cash." The music business was oper-

2 Marx began detailing this formula some time around 1844 in his *Economic and Philosophical Manuscripts*, but these remained unpublished until 1932. The formula gets detailed treatment beginning in Volume 1, Chapter 3 of *Capital*.

ating under the sign of M-C-M? and Radiohead switched to C-M-C: they made a record that you could buy with, or without, money and that money the band can use to live, not just turn into wealth to make money, but to make more music. Whatever one might say about the money made, *In Rainbows* gave the music business a different economic model where there's no capitalist in the middle stringing Radiohead up by the wrists.

Freed this way, Radiohead made what might be their most human-sounding album. Jon Pareles wrote for the *New York Times* that much of the album "comes across as fingers on strings and sticks on drums." Going back to fingers and sticks on instruments while going forward with a new way to get their work to fans may be Radiohead's biggest triumph in years. With *In Rainbows*, digital distribution ends up hardly as disembodied as it has been accused of being. The band has done several live performances released online, performances in which you can see their fingers on strings and drums. And you can see a Thom Yorke that would be out of place in *Meeting People Is Easy*: he's visibly happy.

Radiohead took its name from a Talking Heads song titled, as one might guess, "Radio Head." David Byrne sang on one of the band's songs, "Found a Job," that "if your work isn't what you love, then something isn't right." It isn't far-fetched to argue that the band found something right. The band's freedom from contracts enlivened its work, freeing that work from the capitalistic vampires that suck out the creative marrow. To borrow from Marx, their working lives have been reverted to lifetimes, where work is enjoyment. The kind of enjoyment, let's say, that one might find reveling drunk and throwing paving stones at streetlights.

10.

Everybody Hates Rainbows

D.E. WITTKOWER

"The Culture Industry." Does that phrase make you as uncomfortable as it makes me? Culture shouldn't be an industry; it should be something natural and organic. Culture is our communal history and legacy; the context in which we learn and grow, and to which we may contribute. In the past, our culture might have consisted of the stories we learned as children, the songs we all sang together, perhaps traditional clothing or dances. In some sense, it's hard to imagine today.

Our culture, to whatever extent we have a culture, might still consist of stories (Disney), songs (the *Jeopardy!* theme), clothing (Prada), and dances (The Electric Slide). But these elements are integrated within the marketplace, and, if not produced out of an explicit profit motive, they are at least taken up into a system of economic control and exploitation.

It's a strange thing to consider that an element of culture as basic as, for example, the song "Happy Birthday to You," has an owner. I'm not making this up. It'll be under copyright until the year 2030. That's why big chain restaurants don't sing it—they'd have to pay royalties. Oh, and who owns it? Half the rights are held by AOL Time-Warner. The other half is owned by the estate of Patty Hill Smith (died 1946) who wrote a different song (in

123

1893) which "Happy Birthday" was based on. Consult Snopes if ye doubt.

When Theodor Adorno and Max Horkheimer came up with the phrase, "the Culture Industry," they used it to describe how profit-motivated capitalist production had fundamentally changed the role that art played in our lives. Instead of offering an alternative to the very limited view of the world offered by our lives as economic actors, industrially-produced music and film helps to integrate us even further into the cycle of mindless production to support mindless consumption. "Amusement under late capitalism," they wrote in 1944, "is the prolongation of work."

Since then, of course, many things have changed. The movie studios have had to open up to indie films and alternative entertainment options, and the whole game will undoubtedly change even more in a couple years when the YouTube generation takes over. The monolithic system of record labels, radio stations, and payola has been broken, and, while a great many cultural choices are still in the hands of a very few huge corporations, finding alternate media outlets is becoming easier and easier. Despite this, Adorno and Horkheimer's fundamental point is as relevant as ever: as long as cultural products are industrial goods, they will be basically inhuman and dehumanizing. They wrote then that "personality scarcely signifies anything more than shining white teeth and freedom from body odor and emotions." As long as we continue to confuse self-identity with brand-recognition, even something as personal as our experience of music will suffer from a fundamental disconnect.

But alternate, less industrialized ways of making and enjoying music are becoming more prominent, and, even though Adorno and Horkheimer might not have been too hopeful about what this might mean, I think it might offer us a way towards a healthier relationship with art. Let me tell you why.

House of Cards

With digital media, it's become possible to encounter music in many different forms and contexts. From streaming media and MySpace to leaks and BitTorrent, the context of record label-based centralized sales distribution is being torn down at every front. The days when it made sense to think about music as an object for sale (an "album"), just like an apple or a pair of pants, are long gone, and the RIAA's ad campaigns will never bring them back.

We post songs on our Facebook pages, we share tracks with our iPods and Zunes,[1] and, yes, we illegally download. In a way, musical recordings are becoming more like what they used to be—one of a number of different ways that different forms of music and performance enter our lives. Regardless, the CD is becoming an increasingly unimportant site for us to encounter and enjoy music.

There has always been a kind of basic tension here, though. Music is expressive, and the idea of transforming something fundamentally *communicative* into a *commodity* for sale has always been a bit of a house of cards. For example, consider what's happened in print publications. There's a similar tension there between information as commodity and as communication, and with the new opportunities for self-publication and open access, a great deal of the material which used to be bought and sold is now downloaded or accessed online. Think of all the books that Wikipedia—for better or worse—has replaced in the life of the average student!

And even within a purely market-mediated experience of music, the fan has always encountered music as an expression and a communication—from the fan-perspective, music as a commodity has always been only a necessary evil and an unwelcome precondition. In musical subcultures, economic factors are usually viewed as directly hostile to what listeners perceive as the "real" value of music. Otherwise, the charge of having "sold out" wouldn't make any sense—after all, shouldn't we be happy that musicians who we like will be able to enjoy a larger following?

Once there was a glimmer of hope that this evil would no longer be necessary, listeners, unsurprisingly, rushed to embrace these alternate, de-commodified modes of listening to and enjoying music. At the turn of the century, the sudden freedom from

1 Sorry to use an obscure term here. "Zune" is a word that was used for a short time in late 2006 to early 2007 in the United States—it referred to an object that was able to wirelessly share songs. It is suspected that some of these may actually exist in the hands of consumers, although studies have been inconclusive. Some believe that one can be seen in frame 351 of the so-called Patterson-Gimlin film.

economic constrictions opened our desktops and playlists to a virtually limitless world of new and exciting sounds, and although things have certainly changed since those heady days of Napster—and most music fans today continue to regard commodification as a necessary evil—still, the public perception of the role of economics in music has been permanently altered. I think there's something to be said for comparing the current digital rights management (DRM) efforts to trying to get the toothpaste back in the tube, but that's a discussion for another day. Whether or not the effort to close down filesharing is doomed, it is clear at least that there is now a real desire on the part of fans to think about music as something other than just another object for sale in the marketplace.

Jigsaw Falling into Place

Rightly or wrongly, there's a strong public perception that labels pass on stunningly little of music profits to musicians. But what's the alternative model? Should bands treat their recorded music as little other than advertisements for performances, and should we start to think of music as a service rather than a product? Should we go back to a patronage model, where shares of an album are sponsored by fans? Are online ad-based revenues enough to keep bands going? Could they use an up-sale model, where additional content or access can be purchased? Perhaps a shareware model will work, where a great many fans might choose to donate just a few dollars, or where long-tailing can support a project just on a relatively few dedicated hard-core fans.

These models have been tried by different artists, such as Jonathan Coulton, Trent Reznor, and Maria Schneider. These models have succeeded, but this success has been limited to relatively small and loyal fan bases, and these models remain unfamiliar and strange to the majority of listeners. To succeed on a large scale—large enough of a scale to offer an alternative business model attractive to a wide variety of musicians—they would need a familiar public face and a prominent success story. With *In Rainbows*, the shattered and fragmented system of music distribution and acquisition began to look, to some, like a jigsaw puzzle falling into place. Radiohead, a highly regarded band with a very strong international following, was adopting a DRM-free, pay-what-you-feel downloadable distribution model! They would show that it can be done; that this is, at least in one prominent case, a viable business model.

The fit, for the fan, was a very natural one. Instead of paying for the object on the basis of the costs incurred—or perhaps just the industry-standard pricing model—you would pay for your own perceived use-value that the product delivered. What could be more fair from a consumer perspective? Of course, the problems were numerous. Most notably, you were asked to pay upon download, *before* listening to the album and determining its value to you. But still, this was a hopeful sign that real change might be on its way.

To the industry, of course, this looked like a dangerous betrayal. If it succeeded, this would only feed the perception that labels are unnecessary intermediaries, and would cover over the supposed necessity of paying all the producers, executives, marketing people, lawyers, and so on. Legitimating a user-consumer-centered sales model further undermined the basic business model of the industry. At the same time, the fact that Radiohead reverted back to a traditional sales model rather than seeing the experiment through made this respect for and legitimation of listener-centered pricing into a mere gimmick to increase hype. So, in the end, it didn't really make anybody happy. Trent Reznor, for example, called it "insincere" and a "marketing gimmick," while—on the other side of the issue—James Blunt suggested that the pay-what-you-feel approach would "devalue" music, saying "I've got to pay a band and a producer and a mixer."

The labels have grounds for complaint—after all, they are playing in accordance with the rules. (Of course, they helped make up those rules through lobbying Congress, but they are the rules.) Furthermore, they did spend a good deal of money producing and marketing music that they have a legal basis to expect to be able to sell. Just because it's free to download doesn't mean it was free to make, and they have a legitimate expectation to be able to recoup their costs. The bigger issue, of course, is whether the business model is sustainable in the digital age, and whether it is exploitative and undeserving of protection or preservation.

So, how do we adjudicate between these different claims—that music is a commercial product to be bought and sold, and that it is communication and should be free, and artists should be supported in some other way? Who deserves what here, and are the established property rights to be respected and preserved?

Reckoner

In political philosophy and in applied ethics, we regularly deal with the question of how to justly distribute limited resources. Probably the most famous and influential philosophical perspective on distributive justice is that of the American philosopher John Rawls.

Rawls's 1971 book, *A Theory of Justice*, really changed the conversation going on in political philosophy. He put forth an ideal of 'justice as fairness': he wanted to construct an ideal of justice appropriate for liberal democracies; one which would not be dependent on any particular ideas of right and wrong, or of the nature of the "good life." He claimed that, if we were able to ignore our own self-interested assumptions, based on the part of society in which we find ourselves and what we stand to gain or lose, we would all agree to distribute limited resources such as economic and political opportunity approximately as follows:

1. Everybody gets a robust set of basic rights and freedoms; as great as can be given alike to everybody, and

2. Whatever inequality there is should benefit the least among us.

How does he get to these principles? Let's start with his claim that we all basically agree on the egalitarian principle that we should all, ideally, have the same rights and opportunities as each other, and nobody should enjoy special benefits or favors. But if we were to, for example, all enjoy the same *income* no matter what we did, then we'd all be worse off! We wouldn't feel we were rewarded for our efforts, and we wouldn't be motivated to achieve greater things, and our entire economy and society would stagnate and suffer.

So, even on an egalitarian basis, inequality is good, at least to some extent. But to what extent? There's a classic problem in utilitarian theories of distributive justice—it has a number of different forms, but one of them is this: imagine a group of four people in a room. They have a pleasant conversation for an hour, resulting in, say, ten *hedons*, or arbitrary units of happiness (just assume we can measure that, okay?) per person, for a net gain of forty hedons. Okay, now imagine that they're sadists. If three of them torture the fourth, we get, say, a gain of a hundred hedons each for the three torturers, and a loss of two hundred hedons for the fourth poor fellow, for a net gain of 100 hedons. So, if we use a pretty basic (and silly) interpretation of utilitarianism's basic claim that the right action is the one that results in the greatest overall happiness, then it seems that the utilitarian would have to prefer that the sadists torture the fourth fellow.

Now, that's not fair to the utilitarian position, and Rawls knows better than to use such a simplistic example, but it does demonstrate his point: we need to take into consideration the importance, not just of net gain of benefit, but of how that gain is distributed among persons. So, he says, we should allow inequality to increase *only* until it comes at the expense of anybody within the society. So, that rules out the sadist circumstance, and the four are left just having a pleasant conversation. In which, presumably, they politely avoid talking about how much they'd like to put the screws to the fourth fellow.

That's the basic idea. Having a fair system of distributive justice would guarantee a basic set of benefits to everybody, and would only allow as much inequality as is still for the best for everybody. In the abstract, this sounds pretty uncontroversial. But what would this mean in practice? Let's look at the question of distribution of wealth.

If some of us have wealth holdings, for example, of around $190,000, and others of around $5,500, then it is hard to see how even roughly similar kinds of opportunities for education, competition in the marketplace, or success in general could be enjoyed throughout our society. Those are, however, the median holdings of the uppermost and lowest quintiles of our population (as of 2002, sorted by income).[2] So those two very disparate and unequal

2 US Census Bureau data, taken from "Net Worth and the Assets of Households: 2002," available at http://www.census.gov/prod/2008pubs/p70-115.pdf.

groups represent forty percent of our society—the rest of us are in the middle somewhere. Furthermore, this inequality has a clearly racial component: the median net worth of non-Hispanic White households is $87,056, while that of Black householders is $5,446.

Even if you think that explicit racism and bigotry is widespread in the US today, this still doesn't seem like enough to explain this inequality. Instead, we need to say this: the rich tend to get richer, and the poor tend to stay poor. So, if we want the kind of real freedom of opportunity that would allow the legacy of racist disenfranchisement to even out, in time, we need to narrow the gap between rich and poor. Rawls's perspective would clearly call for a redistribution of wealth through something like a progressive income tax, or some other way of lessening the advantage of those born wealthy, and providing expanded opportunities for those born poor.

Up on the Ladder

The predictable response is that it would be unjust to treat wealthy individuals differently in order to benefit others in society. Surely, after all, a basic principle of justice is that like cases should be treated in a like manner, so how can you justify taxing people at different rates? Don't we have basic property rights? If I obtained my holdings without force or fraud, how can the government be justified in taking a disproportionate share of them? With regard to the racial inequality, rich Whites, placed high up on our ladder by the accidents of birth and family might ask: I didn't enslave anybody, why should I have to pay for the crimes of dead people who happen to share my skin color?

There is clearly something to be said for this response. This comes into even sharper relief when we look at the example of affirmative action. From a larger perspective, we see systematic disadvantages in the market. While this takes many forms, perhaps the most dramatic is the cycle of poverty in Black America, where those from impoverished backgrounds are less likely to have the same educational and economic opportunities, leaving them with little time and energy to raise their own children, who grow up in depressed areas with underfunded public schools. At the same time, from the smaller, local perspective, the employer might ask, "why should I hire the person I think is less qualified just because he shares a skin color with a group of people who tend to suffer from disadvantages?" The White job applicant might ask, "why should I be disadvantaged just because of my skin color?"

There are many arguments on both sides here, and very good points have been made about, for example, how 'reverse discrimination' is not wrong in the way that racial discrimination is wrong, or how our rights in the marketplace are all based on having a healthy marketplace, so economic redistribution or affirmative action are justifiable because they are necessary for there to be a healthy marketplace. These may be right, but they cover over an important point: if we respect universal basic property rights, then the wealthy are right to complain of unequal treatment; and if we think skin color should be irrelevant, then acting on the basis of whiteness is wrong too.

In my view, the problem isn't that one side is clearly fair and the clearly unfair—the problem is that the *world* isn't fair. If we pay attention to the social problems, we violate individual rights and fail to respect those who happen to be advantaged. If we pay attention to individual rights, we allow people to remain in the cycle of poverty, and we allow racial and economic disparities to widen. Either way, we fail to respect what seem to be serious claims about what is just and unjust. Personally, I'd rather work towards social justice, even if it means failing to properly respect individual rights, because the way in which the wealthy and privileged suffer is inconsequential compared to the way in which the poor and disadvantaged suffer. To put it a bit overdramatically, I'd rather disrespect property rights than have people live without enough food or safe housing. It's not a simple matter, and both sides deserve to be taken seriously, but that doesn't mean that there isn't a right choice.

Go Slowly

Now, what would Rawls say about *Rainbows*? It's a very different case, of course, but I think we can see a few places where Rawls's discussion of distributive justice helps us think about how *In Rainbows* might help us go slowly towards finding a good solution here.

Can we give everybody the right to listen to music as they please, and to download and share music as they see fit? In other words, to have the right to enjoy music as a part of our *culture*, rather than as part of an industry?

Let's look back at Rawls's first principle. Rawls thinks we should all hold whatever liberties can be given alike to everybody. Back when only a big record label would be able to support, develop, and promote artists, we, arguably, couldn't all hold this right, because it interfered with the centralized machinery necessary to create that music. Back then, it very well might have made sense to say that it was dangerous and harmful to undermine the standard album-as-consumer-good model. Now, though, many other models are viable, and we can't claim that it's irresponsible to suggest to fans that the relationship between listening to artists and supporting artists is negotiable, and might take various different forms. We might want to say instead that we all now ought to have the right to listen, to rip, to share, and to burn.

Where does that leave the artist? Well, it leaves the artist looking for new ways to support herself. Is that fair to the artist? Maybe it doesn't seem like it is, but, on Rawls's view, we can't justify limiting the freedom of others unless it benefits them in the end, and the old model of restricting listeners just isn't a necessary limit anymore. Models like those that *Rainbows* point us towards can allow artists to survive and support themselves without doing so at the expense of fans' free relationship to music.

I say the same thing here as I said above about affirmative action. Is this fair to everybody? No, probably not—but, hey, it turns out the world isn't fair, and that just means we need to figure out which claims about fairness are more important. And, in my view, having a free relationship to music, and to culture in general, is more important than ensuring that musicians can keep making money in the way they have been. Musicians made a living before the DRM-restricted download, before the CD, before the tape, the 8-track, and before vinyl as well. What we stand to lose is not music, or the possibility of making a living as a musician— what we stand to lose is only the narrowly commodified relationship to music that has been in place for the last few decades or so. And good riddance, I say.

Labels certainly don't need to wither and die either. When the way that we think about rights changes, this can certainly force some people with legitimate claims into unfortunate positions. For example, after the Emancipation Proclamation, I'm sure there were a good deal of Southern plantation owners who were upset about the way that their business model had been undermined. And why not?—they were conducting business on the basis of what had been the law. But rights are more important than profits, and the farmers who lost their slave labor adapted or went under.

As our thoughts about the rights of listeners change, labels need to adapt to the new environment. They need to start to think of their business as providing services rather than products. They, in the end, are in the business of finding, developing, and promoting musical talent and creativity. As artists find new ways to support themselves, labels—no longer the only show in town, so to speak—will have to find new ways to provide valuable services to musicians. The current movement towards "360 deals"—contracts which give labels a cut of concert, licensing, and other revenues—might allow labels to remain profitable even as listeners are increasingly unwilling to think of music as an object to be bought and sold. They will only have to start thinking of themselves as service providers rather than gatekeepers, and to offer better, fairer deals to artists in order to remain relevant.

All in all, *Rainbows* suggests the possibility of a different future for music—a future with new rules and perhaps with fewer profits, but certainly with more freedom. Maybe there's no pot of gold at the end of it, but over this rainbow, at least some of our dreams might come true.

Music is part of our cultural heritage, and part of our social interaction. The song which we sing along with is one which we should be free to share, perform, and remix. Every song is an expression, and a part of a conversation, and nobody should have the rights to tell us what we can and cannot do with words and sounds dear to us, and which speak to our hearts.

Yet, music is an industry, and managers, employees, and stockholders have made investments of time and money, within an established legal regime, which they have a legitimate expectation to be able to recover. Songs are commodities in our society, and music given away undermines the viability of the system.

So, where do we go from here? We must go slowly; we must find new ways of supporting artists, and we must oppose legislation that cuts us off from our culture and that supports labels to the detriment of artists. If we can find a clear path forward, together, our culture may be ours again.

Radiohead's Existential Politics. *(First Against the Wall.)*

11.

Nietzsche, Nihilism, and "Hail to the Thief"

DEVON LOUGHEED

> We're rotten fruit, we're damaged goods.
> What the hell, we've got nothing more to lose.
>
> —"Backdrifts," *Hail to the Thief*

An eruption occurs one minute and fifty-three seconds into "2 + 2 = 5," the first track on Radiohead's *Hail to the Thief*. In some ways, it's simply the culmination of a classic rock'n'roll meme: the quiet-to-loud buildup and release of tension that Radiohead has employed before, perhaps most famously on "Paranoid Android."

Yet there's a greater significance in this first moment of intensity on *Hail to the Thief* than in any comparable explosions on *OK Computer*. It serves as a wake-up call to the desolate, passionless, self-contemptuous characters (we could call them "the lukewarm") of *OK Computer*, *Kid A*, and *Amnesiac*. The lyrics of these albums expose the suffering of a nihilistic life that denies the objective existence of "right" and "wrong." The overwhelming sense of loneliness and isolation that saturates those three albums can be seen as a consequence of a loss of all morality. Read this way, these albums represent the existential nausea of a paranoid android who has discovered that the "truth" of moral claims are relative to each separate individual. To the inhabitants of the despondent psychic landscapes of these earlier three albums, Thom issues a rallying cry: "You have not been paying attention."

Beginning with this critical exhortation, *Hail to the Thief* can be seen as a sharp break from the band's previous efforts, acting gainst nihilist apathy towards life. Instead of a certain political apathy found in earlier albums, the lyrics on *Hail to the Thief* take on a prescriptive and distinctly normative quality, endorsing and rejecting different moral judgments. Thus, the pig in the cage, the paranoid android, and the self-professed "reasonable man" are encouraged to transcend their inhuman surroundings and, as Thom sings on "Sail to the Moon," "know right from wrong."

Yorke is not the only one concerned with the degeneracy and domination of human life in a post-industrial, acutely modern era. The German philosopher Friedrich Nietzsche (1844–1900) sees the potential nihilistic consequences of a loss of belief in morality. He warns about the "death of God", by which he means a loss of belief in objective morality. The nihilistic consequence is that "our existence (action, suffering, willing, feeling) has no meaning."[1] Still, Nietzsche urges humanity to overcome the stagnation of nihilism by transforming *ourselves* into godlike beings.[2] His critique of nihilistic self-indulgence and "saying no" to life and his new mission for humanity—to say yes to life and achieve greatness—are complex and not easily summarized. But the parallels between Nietzsche's project and Radiohead's lyrical switch allow us to understand Nietzsche's philosophy better by looking at it through *Hail to the Thief.*

The Lukewarm

The bleak landscapes of *OK Computer, Kid A,* and *Amnesiac* are a stage upon which characters play out lonely, stagnating existences. Living among the endless cycles of "transport, motorways and tramlines, starting and then stopping, taking off and landing" described in "Let Down," these characters exemplify the dangerous mediocrity of what Nietzsche calls *der letzte Mensch,* or the "Last Humans."[3] They are passive, conformist, non-responsive, and content simply to avoid danger. They say NO to life. Like

1 Friedrich Nietzsche, *The Will to Power* (Random House, 1967), section 585.

2 Friedrich Nietzsche, *The Gay Science* (Random House, 1974), section 125.

3 Friedrich Nietzsche, *Thus Spoke Zarathustra*, in The Portable Nietzsche (Viking, 1954), Prologue, section 5. The direct translation is "Last Man," but my use of the gender-neutral term is not too problematic.

paranoid androids, they wander around reminding themselves that "ambition makes you look pretty ugly."

As an example of one of these Last Humans, the exhausted protagonist of "No Surprises" begs for his life of "a heart that's full up like a landfill, a job that slowly kills you, bruises that won't heal" to continue uninterrupted. "Bring down the government?" he asks rhetorically, answering that he would rather "take a quiet life, a handshake, some carbon monoxide." The obsessive-compulsive narrator of "Everything in Its Right Place" mindlessly repeats the titular mantra over and over while a sampled, incorrect echo suggests just the opposite. The rejection of life is clear in "How to Disappear Completely" with the claim that "I'm not here, this isn't happening. I'm not here. I'm not here." The "nervous messed up marionette floating around on a prison ship" described in "Optimistic" is utterly helpless and dependent on both puppet master and ship's captain.

Sometimes the most exemplary (and thus, pitiful) thoughts of Last Humans are also those that are fragmentary, broken off from a more complete character. One can see this in the fragile call for help of "Release me" in "Morning Bell" or the lukewarm optimism of "I Might Be Wrong" ("I used to think there was no future left at all!"), an empty cheerfulness that is undermined when the new future is revealed to be suicide over a waterfall. The realization in "True Love Waits" that "I'm not living. I'm just killing time." or of the "local man" of "Climbing Up The Walls" who has "the loneliest feeling" further reveals the broken nature of the Last Humans. In "National Anthem," Radiohead reveals that if anything is going to unite these passive, spiteful characters, it is the acknowledgment that "Everyone has got the fear."

Let Me Hear Both Sides

Nietzsche knows why these characters have ended up here—and why these lyrics strike nihilistic chords with so many listeners. During Nietzsche's lifetime, he saw the idea of God-given morality lose popularity among the elite, and anticipated the gradual diffusion of this crisis of faith throughout humanity.[4] According to

4 Friedrich Nietzsche, *Human, All Too Human* (Cambridge University Press, 1986), Book I, section 243; *The Gay Science*, p. 343; *Thus Spoke Zarathustra*, Book IV, section 6.

him, humans have used "God" to fool ourselves into believing that moral judgments exist objectively. On this line of thinking, "right" and "wrong" and "good" and "evil" are not arbitrary, socially-constructed concepts, but rather, can be found in nature and/or religion and outside of humanity. But Nietzsche famously says that "God is dead." We start to realize that there are as many logically contradicting "truths" in the world as there are people: "there are various eyes . . . and as a result there are various truths, and as a result there is no truth." Each individual has his or her own perspective and personal "truths." Without the myth of God prejudicing us towards certain actions as "right" or against others as "wrong," existence itself becomes subjective, and we potentially experience a nihilistic crisis. If truths of right and wrong as we commonly conceive them are an illusion, how are we to make moral judgments at all?

This is precisely the confused, amoral wasteland projected by *OK Computer*, *Kid A*, and *Amnesiac*. Thus, the homonym is significant when Thom sings in "Subterranean Homesick Alien" of the "weird creatures / who lock up their spirits." After the death of God and spiritually-based existence, people fail to take advantage of life's opportunities and end up acting maliciously towards others out of a feeling of lonely resentment. We see this played out by the protagonists of "Karma Police," who demand the arrest and punishment—a moral claim—of others for selfish reasons. They do not enjoy those who they see as talking in maths or buzzing like a fridge. The hopeful politician on the campaign trail in "Electioneering" acknowledges the subjectivity of moralities, but with a slick talking-head-on-a-stick smile, promises that a compromise is possible: "When I go forwards you go backwards, and somewhere we will meet."

Perhaps the reason that the protagonist of "Everything in Its Right Place" is "sucking a lemon" (making a sour face) is that he is holding onto an outdated belief in objective morality in a world whose other inhabitants have largely acknowledged the death of God. "There are two colors in my head," he says, in reference to black and white, right and wrong. Any resistance he finds in logically contradicting truths provokes the fingers-in-the-ears response of "What? What was that you tried to say?" Somewhat differently, the frantic lyrics of "Idioteque" depict an acknowledgment of good-versus-evil moral questions ("Let me hear both sides") that inevitably give way to the self-interested, decadent decision to "Take the money and run." The leading character of "Optimistic," on the other hand, realizes his saturation in hateful, isolated, nihilistic resentment: "The big fish eat the little ones. Not my problem, give me some," he says, before adding sarcastically, "I'd really like to help you, man." "Knives Out" presents this scowling mockery of sincerity, as well: "Look into my eyes, it's the only way you'll know I'm telling the truth." But the most biting example, perhaps, is "Paranoid Android," in which "God loves his children . . . yeah . . ." These characters reveal the list of moral tropes in "Life In a Glass House" (don't throw stones, you should turn the other cheek) to be stunningly ironic. After the death of God and the descent into passive nihilism, these social niceties are very nearly the *only* things we think about doing.

The true Nietzschean dilemma of these Last Humans is *not*, however, that they create a world of self-interested active competition. Instead, filled with resentment, they become passive and lifeless. Inside their heads, they make hateful promises: "When I am king, you will be first against the wall / with your opinion which is of no consequence at all." The tragedy is that they can never become king. Trapped in a nihilistic inward rage, saying no to life, these Last Humans will never take risks or seek greatness.

Pull the Last Humans Out of the Aircrash

Yet this doesn't have to be the way. Admittedly, most of the Last Humans are stagnant, consuming narcotic after narcotic to try and make life tolerable. Yet, to balance every protagonist like the sad singer of "Motion Picture Soundtrack" ("red wine and sleeping pills help me get back to your arms / cheap sex and sad films help me get where I belong") is a glimmer of hope for Nietzsche's alternative. Nietzsche wants us to overcome the intractable conditions and surroundings of our lives, fully develop our talents, and affirm life by saying "Yes" rather than "No" to its challenges.[5] This will be an extremely difficult task within the amoral wasteland of the paranoid android, the purported "reasonable man", and the

5 Friedrich Nietzsche, *The Will to Power*, pp. 22-23.

ɔn antibiotics. Pathways to higher living are treacher-
ɛms such a major shift in morality would be irre-
us, the protagonist of "Lucky" foreshadows
ɪswer to the Last Humans: "Its gonna be a glorious
day . . . I'm your superhero. We are standing on the edge." The
Übermensch, or "Over Human," stands on the edge of conventional morality, ready to pull the remains of the Last Humans out of
the aircrash and refashion them into free beings with a new moral
code.[6]

Hail to the Over Humans

All this changes with *Hail to the Thief,* which breaks sharply from
this moral landscape. The characters here are no longer content
to waste away in the passive nihilism of the Last Humans. Instead,
they embrace the challenge of saying yes to life, standing on the
edge, and take that next step as Over Humans. The pig in the cage,
the paranoid android, and the reasonable man must act on the prerogative of the new Over Humans: to create a new and improved
system of values. While the old "myth of God" system of moral
values was a reaction against life, this new system of morality
should be life-affirming and creative. The message is pointedly
anti-authority and anarchistic: it is immoral for individuals (especially those who, "have not been paying attention") to impinge on
the freedom of action of others.

The various protagonists of *Hail to the Thief* strive to become
Over Humans in a truly Nietzschean sense. They risk self-destruc-
tion in hopes of realizing transcendence by embracing the
processes of life even when they are painful, lonely, messy, and
harsh.[7] Denying the ability of the "dreamers" who are not connected enough to the world to "put the world to rights", the protagonist of "2 + 2 = 5" claims rights to that position, shouting
"Don't question my authority or put me in the box!" In "Sit
Down, Stand Up," Thom acknowledges the dangers of attempting to transcend conventional morality ("Walk into the jaws of
hell") while at the same time warning the nihilistic puppeteers and

---

6 This term is sometimes confusingly mistranslated as "Superman."

prison ship captains that the Over Humans "can wipe you out any-time." "Backdrifts" is a rejoinder to the nihilistic autopilot of "No Surprises": "We're rotten fruit, we're damaged goods / What the hell, we've got nothing more to lose." This character is even closer to the point of schism than the protagonist in "Lucky"—he is not just standing on the edge, he is "hanging off a branch" and "teetering on a breaker." The rallying cry in "Go to Sleep" of "We don't really want the monster taking over . . . we don't want the loonies taking over" sounds like an exchange between potential Over Humans on the topic of Last Humans. Although tackling passive nihilism sometimes feels like "walking out in a force ten gale" (described in the appropriately titled "Scatterbrain"), the message of *Hail to the Thief* is clear: in contrast to the previous three albums, there is now, as "The Gloaming" iterates, a "genie let out of the bottle." This is truly the gloaming, the dusk, the twilight, the sun setting on the nihilistic life of the Last Humans.

Where the Over Humans Begin

For Nietzsche, the strong-willed, contradictory, plural-perspective-seeking individuals who are to become the Over Humans must protect themselves from becoming infected with the nihilistic sickness of society.[8] This may require a physical or emotional separateness like the one described in "Where I End and You Begin" where there is a "gap in between where I end and you begin," because "I am up in the clouds, and I can't come down . . . I can watch and can't take part." Watching, but not taking part, provides the critical distance. From an external position, unaffected by nihilistic sickness, we are able to resolve the amoral conundrum: while truths may not be objective, this shouldn't stop us from seeing that there are better and worse answers. So, the moral realization in "The Gloaming" of "murderers, you're murderers" is legitimately based on the judgment that "we are not the same as you." Similarly, this difference between the Last Humans and the Over Humans is emphasized in the decision in "I Will" and "Go to Sleep" to privilege the life of children over the life of their parents: "Lay me down in a bunker, I won't let this happen to my chil-

8 Friedrich Nietzsche, *On the Genealogy of Morality*, pp. 59, 87.

dren" and "[hurt] someone's son or someone's daughter? over my dead body!" "Right" and "wrong" may not exist as objective fact, but following both Nietzsche and *Hail to the Thief*, this does not necessarily mean the death of *all* morality.

Part of this privileged outer position is accomplished not through rejecting but *embracing* human impulses as fledgling sources of transcendence. So, while the Last Human of "Motion Picture Soundtrack" relies on sleeping pills and alcohol to escape to an illusory, dreamlike sexual encounter, the "mongrel cat" of "Myxomatosis" has "been where he liked, slept with who he likes." The one has already given up on existence ("I will see you in the next life") while the other has, as a result of his embrace of his basic drives, stepped off the edge, let go of the branch, and teetered over the edge of the breaker. He's understandably shaken—"But now I don't know why I feel so tongue-tied . . . so skinned alive." Given the amount of twitching and salivating going on for the duration of the song, I must admit some pessimism about the mongrel cat's potential for transcendence. What's significant, however, is that because of his embracing and subsequent critical examination of his animal instincts, his thoughts are possibly not as "misguided" or "naive" as he claims.

Luckily for the mongrel cat and the rest of our strugglers against stagnation, Nietzsche provides a thought experiment that acts as a check on the desirability of their actions: the idea of "eternal recurrence." He demands that we strive for a life filled with enough passion, vigor, panache, and vehemence that we would want to relive it perpetually, forever and ever.[9] Thus, the ironic ark-imagery in "Sail to the Moon" forces listeners to think about what they'd do differently the hypothetical 'next time around': "Maybe you'll be president, but [this time] know right from wrong." Here, right and wrong are not determined objectively by God, but rather, by an individual who maintains a critical distance from nihilistic sickness, embraces her basic instincts, and says YES to life as if she must live it eternally.

9 *The Gay Science*, sections 285 and 341; *Thus Spoke Zarathustra* Book III, sections 2, 14-16.

Brush the Cobwebs from the
Let the Genie Out from the b⌐

Nietzsche outlines a political program for the Over Humans to transcend life as a pig in a cage on antibiotics and transform into a genie let out from the bottle. His critics, however, suggest that he underestimates the potential of common people, arguing that the self-creation of a few fantastic, truly glorious Over Humans is not the most desirable response to nihilistic passivity. Instead, we should all work to slowly but continuously move humankind past its generationally-achieved degree of self-perfection. So, my generation should try and be "better" than our parents, and our kids should try and be "better" than us, and so on and so on until the threat of nihilistic stagnation is erased. In truth, perhaps we are not as badly off (just yet) as the empty, vapid, wandering vessels of *OK Computer*, *Kid A*, and *Amnesiac*. Not many of us *truly* want a life of no surprises, and many *do* seem discontented to simply sit back and let the government rule over us.

There does, however, seem to be a certain amount of "big fish eat the little ones, not my problem, give me some," "take the money and run," and "your opinion is of no consequence at all" in today's post-industrial, capitalist, increasingly globalizing world. We are surrounded by the emptiest of feelings, and mustn't look hard to see disappointed people clinging on to bottles. Nietzsche wants us to fundamentally challenge an existence that proclaims "I'm not living / I'm just killing time." *OK Computer*, *Kid A*, and *Amnesiac* foreshadow the overwhelmingly lonely and isolated nihilistic existence that Nietzsche predicts awaits us if we do not challenge this way of thinking and living. *Hail to the Thief* moves in the direction of Nietzsche's project for humanity: to stave of the nihilistic consequences of the death of God, say yes to life, and transcend humankind itself. For the protagonists of *Hail to the Thief*, as for us, taking up this challenge comes with great risk, but is an obligation undertaken on behalf of all humankind.

What are our chances of success? Here, a pessimist might point to "15 Step," the opening track of *In Rainbows*: "How come I end up where I started? How come I end up where I went wrong?" Yet even this seeming step back can be seen through the lens of Nietzsche's idea of the eternal recurrence as a necessary part of the process of becoming an Over Human. The sheer drop that awaits may lock most into inaction, but for those of us that choose to take fifteen steps, it is a moment which underlines the importance and moral significance not of *successful* transcendence, but rather, its *pursuit*.

12.

The Real Politics in Radiohead

Jérôme Melançon

Songs tell us more than we realize. In its lyrics and musical structure, Radiohead's "Exit Music (For a Film)" reveals a meaning that
goes beyond what we might hear at first. The title immediately
refers to its inspiration: Baz Luhrmann's movie *Romeo + Juliet*, to
which Radiohead was asked to contribute. This fact helps to flesh
out the story of love and anger told in the lyrics. The song appears
even more clearly as a new version of the story in light of what
Thom Yorke said in an interview: "The song is written for two
people who should run away before all the bad stuff starts. A personal song."[1]

Yet this interpretation isn't satisfying. It's not enough to follow
Shakespeare's story, or even to focus on the moment when Claire
Dane's Juliet holds her gun to her head, which Yorke tells us
inspired the song. Radiohead's take on *Romeo and Juliet* leaves out a
major feature of the song, in which—if we listen to the music and
lyrics together—suggests another meaning. The first part of "Exit

---

1 I took all the background information about Radiohead's songs from long-
time fansite Green Plastic Radiohead (http://www.greenplastic.com/).
Most pages in the "Lyrics" section of the site have details from interviews.

Music" tells the story from Romeo's point of view (or Juliet's, but we can start from the fact that a man is singing). He speaks to someone about the sadness of their lives, their plan to escape and his need for them to act together. When he sings, "there's such a chill," he's foreshadowing an ending that's not so different from the classic tragedy.

Following this mention of the "chill," and after a long rise in its dynamics, the song topples over. The drums and bass kick in forcefully, distorted, and the tone of everything changes. Up until this point, we had a subject, Thom/Romeo, speaking to a defined character, Juliet, with whom he is running away, presumably from her father. But these lines—"and you can laugh a spineless laugh / we hope your rules and wisdom choke you"—couldn't possibly be addressed to Juliet. She's supposed to keep them warm, to keep them together. There's a reversal, as the "me and you" of the first part turn against the "you" of the second part: they become a "we" who together hope that "you" choke and "are one in ever-lasting peace."

Whether they're in peace because they *did* run away or because they followed the more tragic path of Romeo and Juliet, one thing remains. These two run away together, they form a "we," they speak as one—and they speak *against* this "you," the father, and everything he represents. With the distortion in the bass and with the force of the words "we hope that you choke" repeated at the end of the song, this rejection is violent. It's no longer just a matter of running away: it a denunciation of the rules and the wisdom of the other, this "you," that stands in the way of their peace. It's from the height that make "them" or "him" able to impose rules and wisdom on others that this spineless laugh is possible—there's no courage, no merit involved, and only a rejection of authority. If those in authority have caused the escape or the death of our characters, then the rules are broken and the wisdom is annihilated—they amount to nothing, they are meaningless.

"Exit Music" tells us more than the story that inspired it. Asking about this "you" and what becomes of the "we" in the context of the song's musical dynamics led us to a new way of hearing the song, away from the traditional story of *Romeo and Juliet*. It leads us away from asking "what is the song *about*" and toward asking instead "what does this song tell us?" We can do the same with its album, *OK Computer*, especially given its lyrical continuities with "Exit Music." We can push even further Radiohead's discography and interrogate what else Radiohead has to say about "we," "you," and the rules and wisdom of others.

This One's Optimistic

One of the main features of the story of Romeo and Juliet is longing. It appears lyrically in "Exit Music" in lines like "sing us a song to keep us warm" and musically in the quiet spaciousness of the first half of the song. In contrast, the second part of the song reinterprets this longing into a source of revolt and confrontation. At the origin of this revolt, there's a desire for something better than the life put in place by the rules and wisdom of others, the longing to be together, and a yearning for warmth instead of the chill that's coming over them. Yorke's delivery evokes despair and hope simultaneously: the story may end in death or it may lead to escape, but either way the revolt is still worth pursuing.

This paradox, where we try to attain things we know will have very little probability of actually achieving, was explored by the French thinker Albert Camus in his book *The Myth of Sisyphus*, published in 1940. In Greek mythology, Sisyphus was punished for showing contempt for death through his attempts at living passionately. Because of this rebellion, he was condemned by the gods to roll a giant rock uphill until he reached the top. And each time he finished, the rock would roll back down, forcing him to start again. This work was *meant* to be useless—that was his punishment.

Camus thought that Sisyphus was most interesting at the moment when, from the top of his mountain, he saw his rock, far at the bottom, finally stop rolling, and paused before heading back down to start over: by actively deciding to try again, by becoming conscious of the absurdity of his attempts, he overcomes his condition. Like the options evidenced in Yorke's delivery in "Exit Music," Sisyphus can walk down his mountain in despair, or he can do it in joy. By accepting his futile efforts as his only reality, he becomes master of the destiny that was forced on him, and his continual uphill struggle becomes enough to make him happy.

Absurdity is a state of mind, a malaise we feel when we face the world: it has to do with the feeling that maybe *it just isn't worth it*. The question Camus raises in *The Myth of Sisyphus* is whether or not life is worth living: for him, the first problem of philosophy is suicide. Some people choose death because life isn't worth living; others put themselves in danger and are killed for the ideas that they have decided make life worth living.

We don't have to go as far as Camus, but we can see how the story of Sisyphus frames his question about the meaning of life. We haven't chosen to live in the first place; our existence is imposed on us, just as Sisyphus's punishment is imposed on him. In the end, it won't amount to very much. Why bother, then?—*this* is the feeling of absurdity. Why go through the motions of getting through our days, of pushing our rock up a mountain, when we know we'll just have to do it all over again, that tomorrow's only going to bring the same suffering? One answer is this: because maybe that's not *all* there is. There is a happiness we can claim through absurdity by deciding to make our situation, whether good or bad, into our own.

What You'll Get when You Mess with Us

This theme of the absurd is present throughout Radiohead's work. What they ask at the very beginning of *OK Computer* is whether or not it's worth trying to change our situation. "Airbag" tells us about surviving an accident and being born again—this time, with a mission. This near-death experience makes Yorke turn back toward others, toward his past. But it also reverberates throughout the album as the temptation to simply let go in face of the absurdity of any effort.

Two images in *OK Computer* illustrate the absurdity and the malaise of despair that plague us. The first image is the android, desiring rest from voices in his head he can't even understand. In "Fitter Happier," the computerized voice of the android lists the characteristics of his life in a monotone that dissipates in the directionless music that accompanies him. This list of rules, sounding at first like a wise and reasonable road to happiness, includes hints of the temptation to despair. There's fondness, but there's no love, no chance of escape as the voice drones on. The android is concerned but powerless, even though he's "an empowered and informed member of society." Finally, he compares himself, in all his health and productivity, to "a pig in a cage on antibiotics." And he does it without emotion. *This* android is exactly who he's supposed to be.

Yet this is not the voice that dominates the album. Besides the android's voice, a human voice emerges to sing about an alien, about the wish to be someone else, something completely other than the human being he's supposed to be. This wish comes from the experience of feeling like an android, of being uptight, of being locked from understanding himself, unable to communicate with others. Seeing the world from an alien's perspective would allow him to be at peace with this distance. Having the experience of seeing the meaning of life from the point of view of outsider, he could even be happy with being ignored or shut away.

In fact, he does see humans as aliens do. He sees others like bugs in the ground, "starting and then stopping." He sees their emptiness, their disappointment. Yet even then there's hope, because as a bug he sees himself grow wings (just as he saw himself abducted, just as the android sees himself king). He longs to be hysterical and useless, because being useful and serious—as he's trying to be and as it is being asked of him—is the problem in the first place. Trying to see *every*thing—as an alien might—would overwhelm his sense and make him blind to *any*thing.

"Karma Police" talks about others—Yorke in an interview alludes to "bosses"—who buzz like fridges, who don't quite sing in tune with him, and who don't even try. He gives them all he can, he does all he can, but that's not enough to get him off the hook. More and more will be asked of him despite his objections. It's not who he is that matters to those who threaten him if he "messes with us."

There's a tension between these two images and roles, the android he's trying to be in order to conform to the rules of society, and the alien he wishes he was. This same tension also takes place on the level of relationships, as in the fear of divorce that emerges in *Kid A* and *Amnesiac*. The narrator is the one, at first, asking to be released, leaving everything and admitting that the kids will be "cut in half." But there are things that are kept quiet, that aren't said outright, that are barely audible to us in the last part of "Morning Bell." Fighting, divorcing and metaphorically cutting the kids in half—all of it could be prevented if only if these things could be understood. But it's his fault he's not being understood as he's already out the door "walking walking walking." As the song progresses, we see that "clothes are on the lawn with the furniture," completely exposing the conflict within the home to the world, despite the efforts to keep up appearances: "the lights are on but nobody's home." With such painful revelations "Morning Bell" arrives at the conclusion that all that can be done is a request for release.

Kid A closes with "Motion Picture Soundtrack" and we can see Thom/Romeo trying to get back to Juliet's arms. He asks for her help despite that fact that he thinks she might be crazy. He wants to stop using the wine, sleeping pills, cheap sex, and sad movies that distance himself from her. Those are all lies that he's being fed, but his dreams remain. He'll see her in the next life and they will reunite once all these lies have vanished.

The closing track of *Amnesiac* is thematically similar: Thom/Romeo is in trouble with his only friend, the one he's afraid to fight with, because he's afraid of losing her. He can't even just talk to her, even though she's trying to help by papering over the windows of their glass house. There's an ominous presence listening and watching them, keeping them from really communicating—like the father from "Exit Music" with his rules and wisdom and all the others in *OK Computer* that tell him what to be. Even as she's trying to hide what's going on by covering the windows, she puts on a smile to keep up appearances. And as *they* feel the difficulty of their situation, *they* (and not just him anymore) are in no mood to turn the other cheek. They "are hungry for a lynching."

Why It Really Hurts

Why then, if any attempt is bound to fail, if there are always obstacles (others and their devices) and the temptation to go too far (cutting the kids in half, calling for a lynching), why should he even try to be something else? Why should they even try to make it work? The answer is on the other side of the coin: there's more than the absurdity of their situation, which is described by the rules that are being forced on them and by their lack of understanding. Alongside this feeling of absurdity there is a tension, just like in "Exit Music." Here, Thom Yorke or Romeo is speaking for himself in relation to others, and particularly with Juliet. But there, as soon as he becomes aware of those who would impose their rules and wisdom onto him, he turns against them and starts speaking for a "we," which sometimes includes a particular other, and sometimes includes a larger group of people.

In other words, as soon as he realizes that his condition is not inescapable, but is imposed on him by people he can pinpoint, and more importantly that he can change this condition, he revolts against them. It's only then that he can overcome the hesitation expressed in "No Surprises": there's the unhappiness, the job that kills him, the traces of the past that haunt him, and all of it is blamed on the government, who don't speak for us because they disregard all this suffering. And so instead of taking down the government, he leaves things as they are—since there really are no surprises, there's no need for alarms.

There's a deeper reason why he has no time for the government, even for the head of state who calls for him by name. It's the suspicion that nothing good would come out of interacting with them and that "luck could change" for the worse. In fact, he's on a roll already. He doesn't say that *he's* standing on the edge, but that *we* are. We're standing there together, where we only have each other. He's our superhero *and* he needs our help. He needs to be "killed" with love, as it has happened before, to make his day glorious, to pull him out of the air crash, of the lake, of everything bad that can happen.

Those who are excluded, against whom he's revolting, are heads on sticks. They have no depth, no reality, no self. They're ventriloquists who hide something—shadows at the end of his bed, menacing because they have no reality. They're marionettes, who are being handled by someone else (presumably the ventriloquists). They are flies and vultures, or big fish waiting to eat him—carnivores waiting to take their knives out. There is the "Gucci little piggy," but also the little piggies from the nursery rhyme who are also pigs from *Animal Farm* feeding the other animals to keep them content and to maintain their own privileges.

In interviews, Thom Yorke has spoken of businessmen (about "Knives Out") and bosses (about "Karma Police"). Those "others" who make up the rules also appear as cannibals in "Dollars and Cents": they will crack your soul but not your head, they'll make you as empty as they are, forcing you to live in a "cloud cuckoo land" instead of the sky of moon and stars of your fantasies;

they'll make you put on a show, and feed you to the lions regard-less—or worse yet, they'll let your bodies float in a muddy river instead of the river leading to the moon. In all these cases, there is an appeal to the "us" or "we" that stand opposed to the others. His revolt and his attack against those who impose their rules and wisdom always imply that there are others like him, others he calls; as soon as these others appear. The "I" is always collective. Even in the songs dealing with the difficulties of the relationship, set against these others there appears a "we."

We Are Born Again

Compare the architecture of Yorke's revolt to that of Albert Camus's. In Camus's novel *The Plague,* the characters adopt differ-ent attitudes to what seems like an incurable and unstoppable event. Some despair while others act together in the hope of over-coming the disease. By acting, the ones who hope achieve a hap-piness, similar to Sisyphus. Where *The Myth of Sisyphus* dealt with suicide, *The Rebel* deals with murder—and there's a lot to be found in this book about the horrors of the twentiethth century.[2] Just as Radiohead's paranoid android doesn't put anyone against the wall, Camus's rebel doesn't agree that murder is ever justified: only life allows for the happiness that comes from our confrontation with the world, and it must be allowed for everyone to enjoy it. If we ask, as Camus does and as Radiohead do, to live life according to our own rules and wisdom, we can't refuse others the same. Absurdity is not an end in itself, as Radiohead's songs show. It is instead a starting point. As we struggle to decide whether to accept our condition and or dream of an impossible one, it can also lead us to something else.

Our feeling that our situation is absurd and that we can only keep going as androids or in dreaming of becoming aliens can lead us to shout violently that our life is absurd (even though we might not do it literally). As soon as we become conscious of this

---

2 *The Myth of Sisyphus* was first published in 1942; *The Plague,* in 1947; *The Rebel,* in 1951. Camus was born in Algeria and was thus a French citi-zen, he moved to Paris just before World War Two. The fact that he won the Nobel Prize for literature in 1957 doesn't take anything away from the force of his ideas and the vividness of his novels.

absurdity, we have watered the seeds of revolt. Radiohead, as we've seen, give us specific reasons for nurturing this revolt, specific words to shout. Revolt is born out of a lack of understanding as well as a lack of reason or justice. Because it wants to transform the world, revolt gives us hope for the creation of something new. In revolt, therefore, we're also saying yes to something, to our right to something better. We defend something from ourselves, we affirm that something in us is worth being defended and respected. We affirm our values and we appeal to others to take them on. Of course, there are pitfalls and dangers, which Camus's book explores; but there are also great potentialities.

Camus updates Descartes in this way: "I revolt, therefore *we* are." As soon as we feel that others will listen to us because they share our situation or because they are able to understand it, we identify our destinies with each other's. We affirm that the value we are defending is also a value for everyone else and we join those others who can understand us and agree with us. Revolt and solidarity depend on each other: solidarity is the justification of the revolt that was its origin—and so a revolt is only true when it recognizes even for those whom it opposes what it claims for itself. The suffering of absurdity is no longer individual; it becomes shared as a feeling and as a task. The ultimate value that revolt defends is what we share with everyone else.

Sing Us a Song

Revolt is also a creation that allows us to listen to Radiohead differently yet again. We can follow their lyrics and look at what they tell us, but we can also listen to their "shout" (as Camus said) and we can find a meaning in the act of their expression, *together* with what they're saying. By doing so, we're taking their songs as part of another whole. It's no longer the series of songs in a series of albums: instead, we're listening to the whole that is the singing of the song, with everything it entails as far as performing, recording and distributing go. The whole is made up of the interdependence and the entwining of what is expressed and how it is expressed: we can't separate content and form.

Let's keep Camus as a guide for now to see the close relationship between revolt and art: both seek a unity, both refuse the world because of what is missing in it and because of what it is. Because of their inability to find unity in the world, both start from reality to create something else. They fabricate a closed universe: songs begin and end harmoniously, after having given us an arranged melody, while nothing does in the world. Music, like painting, sculpture or literature, stops the world at a certain moment or gives us a specific part of it, and takes away its indeterminacy. Art, like revolt, both refuses and consents: Radiohead refuse what is ugly and unjust, but they can't affirm that *everything* in the world is ugly or unjust: they have to start with something. And those parts they keep in the universe they are creating shows us what they're consenting to, what they're trying to shine a light on, what they want to show us in a different light. They correct the world, they fix it, based on their capacities (in language and music) and on what they find in reality—and this correction is their style. Through it, as they are artists and as they are revolted, they give a new law to the world. Through the style deployed in their creative efforts, they make the world over with the slight deformation that is proper to both art and revolt. They force reality, expanding the meaning of certain parts while caricaturing others.

Somewhere We Will Meet

But to understand what Radiohead are doing, we have to go beyond the idea of creation, toward the idea of expression as articulated by Maurice Merleau-Ponty, who wrote—and died—at around the same time as Albert Camus (although the two had very little to do with one another: to put it mildly, they detested each other).[3] Merleau-Ponty is helpful in showing us that Radiohead go beyond revolt. They're acting socially and politically by recording their songs and singing the words they sing. Revolt and art go together. Just by playing their songs, Radiohead infuse values into our societies, values that can end up changing them. We can hardly doubt, especially given the overtly political meaning of *Hail to*

---

3 At a party thrown in Saint-Germain-des-Prés during the late 1940s, after Merleau-Ponty had published a book about Communism, Camus took him aside and started to yell at him. Merleau-Ponty was friends with many Communists; Camus was very much an anti-Communist. Apparently Merleau-Ponty tried to argue back calmly, but they appeared almost to come to blows. Sartre separated them and Camus headed home. Neither

the Thief for example, that they have the intention of showing us our world differently, so that we may share their revolt and the values they suggest. And already, long before they make any overtly political statements, their songs are political. They open new possibilities and they'll remain examples in the future—for those who'll hear them and for those who'll pick up a guitar. And we know how anyone can do that.

Merleau-Ponty suggests that what we expect of artists and of politicians is for them to lead us toward values that we'll afterwards recognize as being our own, that they express what we've always felt and wanted to say without even knowing it. This is because they show us their values together with the roots of these values—the roots of their need to communicate them that spring out of their experience. As artists, their creations are attempts at showing us their world. But they're not expressing thoughts that are clear, for those thoughts would have already been said. Instead, Radiohead try, time and again, to express muddled, uncertain things which *still* need to be expressed and to find a certain form on their records. And they do it on different levels: lyrically, there are thoughts about dysfunctional relationships or domination in society. Musically, Radiohead do it through songs like "How to Disappear Completely" where the detached, airy mood expresses a frame of mind or a kind of day we have. The very engaged "Electioneering" tells us how frantic the band feels with its harsh, scattered guitar lines. It's the finished song that proves that there was something to express in the first place, that there was something important in the original "malaise," which Merleau-Ponty calls a "fever." The number of songs and ideas that lead nowhere are proof enough that sometimes there really wasn't much, if anything, in the "fever." And sometimes, as with "Big Ideas" (which was finally recorded and released on *In Rainbows* as "Nude") it can take many, many years for it to finally *be said* and make sense.

ever really discussed the other in their books or articles; Camus saw himself as a writer (and made his living that way), Merleau-Ponty, as a philosopher (he was a sort of official philosopher of France from 1952 on, when he was appointed to teach at the Collège de France). Camus died in 1960, in a car crash, at 47; Merleau-Ponty died in 1961, at 53.

In Merleau-Ponty's terms, Radiohead have come back to the mute and solitary background of experience on which culture is constructed. They throw their songs toward us like the first human beings speaking their first words without knowing if they'll be anything more than a shout. They play their songs without knowing if they will detach themselves from the flux of their individual lives and experience in which they have been born and lived. With this experience, they can present—whether to themselves in the future, to the others who coexist with them, or even to unknown others in the future—the independent existence of an identifiable meaning which they can claim as an expression of their own life.

Many artists create and express ideas in ways like this in the hope that they will awaken in us experiences that will give root to the idea of change and revolt in our own experiences. The meanings *they* flesh out in their songs, from *their* lives and *their* experiences, give to *our* experiences and to *our* lives a shape and a meaning that wasn't there before we heard them. And if this is possible at all, it is because they pull us toward them, they show us how *they* experience, hear and see the world, they make us hear and see it in a bit more of a similar manner. Ultimately, their songs make the world a bit more common between them and us—and between us, you and I, who are listening to the music.

Merleau-Ponty describes how the lasting expressions and actions of artists and politicians shape us, more than they try to please us: as their public, we don't pre-exist to their songs or actions, we're not waiting for them. It's their work, their actions and their songs that call and summon us to them, that create a public around them. They shock us into listening to them. They try to grab a hold of us. They shape us so that they can live with us.

Merleau-Ponty calls this an "action of culture": through their songs, artists like Radiohead find a place in other people's lives. They confront their lives to ours and they show our lives to each other to let us see how alike they are (and in what essential ways they are different). They create a sort of universal life that we can all share. Their words and music, because of the meanings they have for us as we come in contact with them, pull us into a common universe with them and with the others who are listening and will potentially listen to them. Why else would we push the music we love on others?

How to Misunderstand Politi
Completely

Once we start to compare art and politics as Merleau-Ponty does, "political" action becomes something other than passing laws and getting elected. The popular debate about whether *Hail to the Thief* is "political" for instance—something most listeners assumed, but which Yorke and others emphatically denied (at least at first)—refers to a traditional understanding of politics. Instead, Radiohead are political in all their albums as they unveil the world to us and show it in a new way. This unveiling is completely different from the "action of governing." The unveiling goes beyond government and beyond the state, although it does try to influence government and cannot take place without it.[4]

What Radiohead say about politics shows a certain understanding that in a sense, they're not that different from those they criticize—an understanding, too, that they're not just appealing to those like them who feel that things are uneven and that only certain people get to dictate their rules, but even to those "others" as well. Take "Electioneering," for instance. There's a menace here: when they go forward, when they advance, we go backward, we recoil. And if we take the chorus in a different direction, when they get what they want, when they gain, we lose something, we go backwards. But that's what Radiohead do in their interviews: they try to sell us their albums and their concert tickets, they're trying to get our vote, our money. When "electioneering," when trying to sell something, they must say the right things.

For Radiohead to say "somewhere we will meet" may sound ironic, since they're speaking as if they were themselves politicians and diminishing their distance with what they do. But there's still quite a distance in the song's second verse: nothing in Radiohead's actions compares to the violence of riot shields and of cattle prods, or to the complete lack of control that's implied in "voodoo economics" and in structures like the IMF. "Somewhere we will meet" may therefore be an admission that we *will* find a

---

4 Merleau-Ponty develops this idea in *The Adventures of the Dialectic*. He wasn't talking about music at all; but then again, he wrote in 1955 and he only liked classical music—and not even the weird kind.

compromise with the "others"—and that we do in fact, meet, somewhere, with the people that deal in economics and the IMF, with those ventriloquists with their heads on sticks, with those unknown shadows at the end of our beds.

An overtly political meaning is also present in "The National Anthem," if only because of its title. Thom Yorke's voice here is so deformed that it finds its place among the other instruments, it's layered like them and it takes part in their general confusion. And so the music here becomes most important. On one hand, the bass takes the lead, repeating the same melody over the course of most of the song and giving it its unity. On the other hand, the song features horns, like most national anthems, but horns that are in complete discord and that give an illusion of chaos. They highlight the menace in the booming, distorted bass line: if "everyone is so near" it's because "*it's* holding on" and "everyone has got the fear." The question, What is it that's holding on?, has two meanings: *what* is it that's holding on? and, second, what does holding on mean?. If something is holding on, if we're faced with a lasting overall menace, and if everyone is also holding on, then, out of discord, of conflict and confrontation, a certain harmony (musical and, figuratively, social) will emerge.

Radiohead's revolt is creative because it's an appeal and a call to others in whose lives their expressions find root and who may revolt together with them and turn things around. In sharing their music, they are not only acting artistically, but also politically. They aim for something positive, they want to shape us and bring us together by singing about us. For listening to Radiohead cannot simply be a passive activity; it is also hearing their call. We may choose to ignore it call and reduce their music to a commodity, to music we can buy and enjoy (which of course it is, in part). Or we may find ourselves in agreement with their expression of our lives, and from there, we can choose to hear their call, to try to go beyond what's presented to us as impossible and out of our reach, and move toward an acceptance of absurdity and the creation of rules and wisdom that are our own.

13.

The Impossible Utopias in "Hail to the Thief"

Sean Burt

If, in the summer of 2003, you had heard a few details about the forthcoming Radiohead album, the one that was said to be a more accessible return from the electronic experimentation of *Kid A* and *Amnesiac* to guitar-based rock, you likely wouldn't have been surprised to open *Rolling Stone* and read Thom Yorke saying this about the genesis of the album:

> It was a formative moment—one evening on the radio, way before we were doing the record. The BBC was running stories about how the Florida vote had been rigged and how Bush was being called a thief. That line threw a switch in my head. I couldn't get away from it. And the light—I was driving that evening with the radio on—that was particularly weird. I had this tremendous feeling of foreboding, quite indescribable, really. To me, all the feelings on the record stem from that moment. (David Fricke, "Bitter Prophet," June 26th, 2003)

Surely, with a title like *Hail to the Thief*, this new record would be Radiohead's attempt to send a broad political message, a protest against an American regime that only weeks before celebrated its "mission accomplished" of enforcing its will across the globe.

161

And that "tremendous feeling of foreboding," Yorke's explanation
of "the gloaming" (a poetic term for the darkest period of the
night, along with the name of a track on and the alternate title of
Hail to the Thief), must have referred to the rapid expansion of military and surveillance powers in Bush's America and Blair's UK.

But, at the very same time, other band members explicitly
denied that *Hail to the Thief* is a direct response to current politics.
Jonny Greenwood, for one, stated that, "We'd never name a record
after one political event like Bush's election. The record's bigger
than that." Yorke, too, stepped back, saying that *Hail to the Thief* is
"trying to express . . . the absurdity of everything. Not just a single Administration." And he continues from another source that
"the whole thing about it being political is a bit far-fetched. I keep
reading stuff about how this album is all about politics and anti-
America . . . just because of the title and one or two quotes I
gave."

Some of the band's defensive tone here is no doubt due to the
current unfashionableness of political music, a contemporary
trend also reflected in some of the critical reception of the record,
such as Ethan Brown's review in *New York* magazine. Brown, who
frets that "the album promises a lefty monotone," celebrates the
album's many musical (that is, specifically not lyrical) joys and
writes:

> Radiohead obsessives won't hear the album this way: Like the
> devotees of eighties bands like the Smiths and the Cure, they'll
> devour the lyric sheet for *Hail to the Thief* as though it were
> Hammurabi's code. But for everyone else, *Hail to the Thief* will
> likely be listened to with the lights out and the speakers turned
> up loud. It's not going to start the revolution—great art never
> does. (Ethan Brown, "Radioheadline," *New York*, June 9th,
> 2003)

I'll admit to the charge of sweaty obsessiveness. Just note, though,
how Brown portrays a political interpretation of *Hail to the Thief* as
not only ineffective but profoundly embarrassing. Making a political record, in Brown's opinion, is no more noble than drowning
in melodramatic goth angst. And indeed, straightforward protest
music these days seems quaint and uncool (think "aging hippies"),
a relic of past politics and past musical trends and tastes. The flip

side of "great art never starts the revolution" is that bad art is that which attempts to. More importantly, protest music in contemporary American culture seems ineffective and, even worse, easily co-opted by brand-oriented multinational capitalism (here, the use by Nike of Minor Threat's album cover or the bombastic career trajectory of U2 comes to mind).

White People for Peace

Yet despite all their distancing comments concerning the political nature of *Hail to the Thief*, members of Radiohead have often aligned themselves with left-leaning anti-global capitalism causes such as Naomi Klein's 'No Logo' movement. This does not somehow subvert what members of the band have said about *Hail to the Thief*'s politics, but it does open up a space for us to think of *Hail to the Thief* as somehow concerned with the problems inherent in a political use of art. If the heyday of protest music has justifiably passed, then new strategies that recognize the inefficacy of politics in music must be seen as a part of the responsibility of socially conscious bands.

One such strategy very different from Radiohead's can be found in Against Me!'s song "White People for Peace," from their 2007 album *New Wave*. The chorus goes, "the people sang protest songs in response to military aggression, / protest songs to try to stop the soldier's gun . . . / but the battle raged on." This song recognizes the ultimate inefficacy of political music while at the same time functioning very much like a protest song (the verses illustrate the senselessness of war and the venal motivations that drive it). "White People for Peace" clearly is a politically charged song but at the same time seeks to step back from the protest so as to be a "meta" comment on protest music. In other words, it wants to have it both ways, telling the listener that yes, we can protest the war, while at the same time being a knowing statement about protest music. This ironic stance implies a real lament for the loss of pop music's political power, or at least the idea of its power. It also, however, creates a self-congratulatory link between artist and audience. The listener of a song like "White People for Peace" is in on the joke and belongs to a selective group that is able to maintain its critical distance.

Hail to the Thief has no interest in ironic self-congratulation. It gives us a darkly authoritarian world, projecting the listener head-first into a repressive regime straight out of George Orwell's *Nineteen Eighty-Four*. This blurs the lines between the observing would-be critic of that world and the helpless person actually submerged within it. The very opening line of the first track ("2+2 = 5"), "Are you such a dreamer, to put the world to rights?" scoffs disaffectedly, like the ironic meta-protester, at the prospect of political idealism. But, in a chilling turn, the narrator immediately answers his own question by demurring, "I'll stay home forever, where two and two always makes five." This opening couplet suggests that political paralysis is borne not of critical, knowing distance, but of the dominant political ideology, neatly internalized. The militaristic imagery in the commands of the next track, "Sit Down Stand Up," and the repetition of "payin' attention" in "2+2 = 5," envision a repressive system imposing its will on the populace. As the chanting of "Sit Down Stand Up" warns: "Walk into the jaws of hell. Anytime. Anytime. We can wipe you out."

Hail to the Thief implies that a truly totalitarian society is one in which the control that the powers that be impose on the citizenry reaches into the home, into the family, and even into the mind. Instead of the "having-it-both-ways" irony of "White People for Peace," Radiohead seems to want to have it neither way: effective protest music is not possible, but neither is a disavowal of engagement. We are in this world, we are a part of it, and critical distance is not an option. We are not in on the joke so much as the joke is on us.

The Sky Is Falling In

So *Hail to the Thief* has much to say about political consciousness, after all. But this political commentary actually comes with a surprise. Despite its opening references to authoritarian control, *Hail to the Thief* can actually be seen as a form of genuine utopian thought—as a counterpoint to the Orwellian dystopia that seems to be the easy interpretation.

But let there be no doubt about it: this record is bleak. It sketches out a fictional world dominated by fear and maintained through mind control. Several science fiction or horror elements form a minor, though repeated, motif. From the echoes of *Nineteen Eighty-Four* in "2 + 2 = 5," to the monsters in "We Suck Young Blood" and "Wolf at the Door," to the ill-defined plague in "Myxomatosis," to the reference to *Gulliver's Travels* in "Go to Sleep" ("We don't want to wake the monster / 'tiptoe round tie him down'"), the story worlds of the songs in *Hail to the Thief* evoke dark, uncanny places.

More insidious than boogeymen at the threshold, however, are the repeated implications that effective resistance is impossible. This theme is first found in "2 + 2 = 5" and reintroduced in "Go to Sleep (Little Man Being Erased)." This begins with some kind of anticipated conflict: "Something big is gonna happen," which receives the response "over my dead body." Resistance quickly dissipates as the narrator capitulates ("I'm gonna go to sleep / let this wash all over me"). The concept of not being in full control of one's will is also perhaps hinted at in the black humor of "We Suck Young Blood," which begins with a shuffling zombie-like handclap rhythm, and it continues into "Myxomatosis"—about which Yorke once said, "This song is actually about mind control. I'm sure you've experienced situations where you've had your ideas edited or rewritten when they didn't conveniently fit into someone's else's agenda" (Chuck Klosterman, "Fitter Happier: Radiohead Return," *Spin*, June 2003).

By the last track, "A Wolf at the Door," the independent self has almost completely withered away. Over an incongruously stately waltz line, Yorke's skipping half-rap creates a deeply claustrophobic scenario that explicitly rejects the possibility of resistance. In the face of a nameless threat, the narrator mutters "Get the eggs / get the flan in the face," a phrase evoking the comedic protest tactic used by some anti-globalization groups serving pie to the faces of powerful political and economic figures. Soft dessert weapons, however, pale in comparison to the threats posed in the chorus ("I keep the wolf at the door but he calls me up / calls me on the phone tells me all the ways that he's gonna mess me up / steal all my children if I don't pay the ransom / and I'll never see them again if I squeal to the cops"). Toward the end, even this nominal protest is dropped as the narrator retreats into a fearful shell, abdicating any role in resistance ("Someone else is gonna come and clean it up / Born and raised for the job / someone always does").

The miasma of hopelessness that covers *Hail to the Thief* is probably best epitomized in "The Gloaming", the song that Yorke himself—"the light"—takes to be the album's thematic core. The scratchy, trance-like beat captures that sense of foreboding, of a "genie let out of the bottle, it is now the witching hour." While the gloomy atmosphere of this track stands for *Hail to the Thief* as a whole, it also presupposes an objective distance unusual for the record. In contrast to the refrain of mind control throughout the record, whereby the narrators are either incorporated by the controlling regime, or cower in fear to it, here the narrator is able to cast him or herself against it. "We are not the same as you" resists assimilation. "Your alarms, they should be ringing" puts the narrator in the post of the sentinel warning against what is taking place.

Don't Get Any Big Ideas—They're Not Gonna Happen

The nearly relentless desperation found throughout *Hail to the Thief* is not the end of the story. Something about this project is deeply utopian. Not, of course, in its planning, but in its dedication to imagining a different world, even a world that is repressive. How does imagining a dystopia have utopian connotations? Recent writers on the idea of utopia can help us expand our concepts of utopian thought beyond the realm of pie-in-the-sky plans and crackpot schemes that we usually attribute to utopian thinkers and help us see the connection between utopia and the dismal world of *Hail to the Thief.*

To Ernst Bloch, the mid-twentieth-century German philosopher, the concept of utopia should not be limited to the confines of a proscribed literary genre (such as works by Thomas More or William Morris). Rather, the act of imagining a different, better world is a fundamental human desire found throughout all kinds of communication, literature, and arts (including music). Bloch's massive, three-volume *The Principle of Hope* (Blackwell, 1986) is an attempt to collect the entire range of manifestations of this utopian impulse, from its most rudimentary forms in daydreams to more elaborate, meticulous plans.

A whole range of phenomena is found in *The Principle of Hope*, but there is a basic two-part division. Bloch articulates both a basic utopian impulse, or "abstract utopia" and the thought behind more rigorous, planned utopias, or "concrete utopia."[1] Abstract utopias are essential to utopian desire, for Bloch, even if they do not attain the complexity of utopian world-creation. Abstract utopian thought tends to be negative, to critique the current order of the world (wishing that, somehow, things could be different). Bloch finds abstract utopia ultimately lacking because it, unlike concrete utopia, is fleeting and not accompanied by a real will to change things and thus is susceptible to the feeling of nostalgia for former times. The underdeveloped impulse of abstract utopia instead finds its fulfillment in concrete utopian plans, which implies an informed commitment to change.

Bloch wrote *The Principle of Hope* during his brief stay in the United States in the 1950s, but he was a committed Marxist, an East German citizen, and a vocal supporter of the Soviet Union at a time when Soviet communism still held out hope for some as a site of potential social perfection. For us in the western world post-1989 (and post-1984), the promise of the effective and well-planned utopia has justifiably faded. Now, the term "utopian," when it does not suggest impractical, crackpot ideas, evokes something sinister, even horrifying. Most often, the notion of utopia can be seen as shorthand for totalitarianism or for unintended consequences (in literature *Nineteen Eighty-Four*, *V for Vendetta*, *The Handmaid's Tale*; from history think of Stalinism, China's Cultural Revolution, ethnic cleansings in the Balkans and Rwanda, "a land without a people for a people without a land" in Palestine). In other words, the gigantic blind spots of the utopias of the second half of the twentieth century seem to have ruined concrete utopianism, leaving those of us stuck in the twenty-first century with much less optimism for the future.

Nevertheless, the American literary critic Fredric Jameson has recently taken on the problem of utopia. In *Archaeologies of the Future* (Verso, 2005) he argues that the role of utopian thought in our post-concrete utopia world lies in the simple act of contem-

---

1 See Ruth Levitas, "Educated Hope: Ernst Bloch on Abstract and Concrete Utopia," in *Not Yet: Reconsidering Ernst Bloch*, edited by J.O. Daniel and T. Moylan (Verso, 1997).

plating the future. Recent history and literature teaches us that "all our images of Utopia, all possible images of Utopia, will always be ideological and distorted by a point of view which cannot be corrected or even accounted for" (p. 171). Concrete utopias, in other words, will necessarily be utopias for only some, and likely repressive for others.

Yet, the future still is of desperate importance, especially when we live in a world in which "there is no alternative to capitalism," to borrow a slogan from Margaret Thatcher. The complete dominance of global capitalism and exclusion of other possible sociopolitical systems produces, in Jameson's words, a "future prepared by the elimination of historicity, its neutralization by way of progress and technological evolution" (p. 228). This regime, even in its social-democratic (or Democratic) forms—and in fact contemporary global capitalism seems quite impervious to political changes in individual nations—removes hope for a different future. It guarantees that the future will be pretty much like the present, even if changeable through small, incremental reforms. As many partisans of the political Left (at least some of the members of Radiohead included) recognize, global capitalism has produced a world that is far from ideal. The prospects of an eternal present and a "colonized" future show that utopia still has a part to play. It enables us to imagine a disruption from the present, to think that, yes, the world is one way now, but it always hasn't been this way; in fact, it has been radically different and therefore it could (and will) be in the future, even if we cannot now quite conceive how it could be so.

The inchoate utopian impulse (Bloch's "abstract" utopia), accordingly, takes on the lead role of utopian thought in Jameson's framework. It becomes the demand to "concentrate on the break itself: a meditation on the impossible, on the unrealizable in its own right" (p. 232). In this way, dystopias are as essential as utopias for visualizing the possibility of a reality utterly different from our own. Even, in other words, when dystopias are meant to teach us some particular negative lesson about our own times, formally (or, simply by existing as a story about another world) they also tell us that historical disruption is at least imaginable. It's not that utopia's possible, but that it's necessary.

Back to the Future

The significance of this for *Hail to the Thief* is that dystopia and utopia are two sides of the same coin. The act of imagining a different world, even one as totalizing and repressive as *Hail to the Thief*'s, itself derives from the impulse toward "abstract utopia." Even more, while the dominant mood on the album is dark and pessimistic, *Hail to the Thief* also reveals more direct hints of the yearning for a better world. It is not just about the relentlessness of an authoritarian vision, but also about the glimpses of hope that are real precisely because they are fleeting. Consider "Sail to the Moon (Brush the Cobwebs Out of the Sky)." Coming on the heels of the two claustrophobic tracks that open *Hail to the Thief*, this song balances the gloom and offers a glimmer of redemption. The main title evokes the archetypical space journey, hearkening back to the novels by nineteenth-century science-fiction pioneer Jules Verne (such as *From the Earth to the Moon* and *Around the Moon*). If the moon stands in for a place of imagination and promise, the elliptical lyrics that open the song ("I sucked the moon / I spoke too soon / And how much did it cost?") seem to take back some of the relentless pessimism of "2 + 2 = 5" and "Sit Down Stand Up". Yet, any possibility of escape remains only tentative and distant: "maybe you'll / be president / but know right from wrong / or in the Flood you'll build an Ark / and sail us to the moon."

"Sail to the Moon" is hardly a concrete plan for a new society. But it does offer an uncertain hope for something different—not a castle in the sky, but a clearing away of the cobwebs. The bleakness still remains, but it lurks in the background as a glimmer of moonlight appears. But the next track slams the door on this brief glimpse of hope, dispelling this daydream as quickly as it arrived. "Backdrifts (Honeymoon is Over)" is a dystopian retreat. Its narrator hesitating in the face of the unknown, "backsliding" and announcing "this far but no further." Even more, if the sky and moon of "Sail to the Moon" stand in for possibility and change, the subsequent song, "Where I End and You Begin (The Sky Is Falling In)" dramatically closes off the possibility of connecting that dream world with our own situation: "I am up in the clouds / And I can't come down". This is a variety of hope, but only one that floats in the abstract, unable at this time to find purchase in concrete reality.

Since hope won't stick, we're left desperate and searching for refuge and comfortable familiarity, even if that means resting in the safe arms of Big Brother. In "I Will," Yorke sings "I will lay me down / in a bunker underground. / I won't let this happen to my children." This notion of retreat seems to be driven in large part by fear, a fear also replete in the breathless paranoia of "Wolf at the Door." In that song, the thing that the narrator wishes to protect is, quite literally, the space of the family, identified as a stereotypical suburban domesticity, found in lines like "Stepford wives, who are we to complain?" or "Investments and dealers / cold wives and mistresses / cold wives and Sunday papers." However, the obviously ideological content of phrases like "Stepford wives" remind us that, in the dystopian world of *Hail to the Thief*, even the most intimate areas of life—the family and even the mind—are not safe from the forces outside. "A Wolf at the Door" in this way brings *Hail to the Thief* full circle: the inability to keep the wolves at bay, even from the insulated home is a reiteration of "I'll stay home forever / where two and two always makes five" in "2 + 2 = 5." Dreamers imagine future hopes, but then backslide. Individuals consider resistance but are either assimilated or hole up in bunkers and wait.

Hope at the Door

But hope also bides its time. The unmistakably pessimistic conclusion to *Hail to the Thief* does not seem to lead to a total abdication of the impulse toward utopia. While "A Wolf at the Door" most certainly depicts the intimate sphere as a house of straw, "I Will" refuses to completely renounce resistance. The narrator of "I Will" perches in the bunker only to hold out in preparation for a renewed engagement. After the phrase, "I won't let this happen to my children," the song continues. "Meet the real world coming out of my shell / with white elephants / sitting ducks. / I will rise up." "I Will" and the album as a whole both keep the future open, if not as a likelihood, then at least as a topic of discussion. Utopia, even in its twisted form of dystopia, is still always an exercise in hope. Even if concrete utopias are not possible now, the imagination must keep going for the day when they might become possible again.

If *Hail to the Thief* resembles Jameson's concept of utopian thinking as a contemplation of a future (even a horrifying one) that breaks away from the present, then this means that utopian thought must have a primarily negative, critical function (much as with Bloch's "abstract utopia"). Stopping short of concrete plans for utopia means, as Jameson writes, adherence to "the obligation for Utopia to remain an unrealizable fantasy" (p. 227). It becomes a necessary critique of the here and now, an insistence that whatever the future may look like, it will not be, and cannot be, like this. The horrifying and oppressive world of *Hail to the Thief* is built out of pieces drawn from the political situation of the twenty-first-century western world. The fragmentary critiques of contemporary politics like the album title and the hope for a president who will "know right from wrong" are unmistakable. Yet, the protestations by members of Radiohead that this album is not immediately political are important to remember as well (remember Yorke's "trying to express the absurdity of everything").

Hail to the Thief creates imaginative worlds that draw us out the situation of the present day. Even in a highly exaggerated manner, this, too, is an essential part of utopian thinking. As Jameson notes: "at best Utopia can serve the purpose of making us more aware of our mental and ideological imprisonment" (p. xiii). This is a doubly negative critique, a 'no' to the never-ending present of this world, but also a 'no' to concrete utopias. *Hail to the Thief* does not reach for some embarrassed, ironic distance from utopia. Rather, it offers a full recognition of the difficulty and, yes, impossibility of imagining a better world, along with an equally resolute refusal to let the impossible get in the way of the necessary. It brushes the cobwebs out from the sky.

14.

Where Power Ends and Violence Begins

BRANDON W. FORBES

> Power grows out of the barrel of a gun.
> —Mao Zedong

> Power is everywhere; not because it embraces everything,
> but because it comes from everywhere.
> —Michel Foucault

> Little babies' eyes
> —"I Will (No Man's Land)," *Hail to the Thief*

"All power tends to corrupt," goes the tired aphorism from Lord Acton, "and absolute power corrupts absolutely." One need only look to recent political history to see the seeming resonance of this statement, as the list of despots and dictators that haunt the twentiethth century, as well as the twenty-first, is long indeed.

Farther back, the political evils perpetrated by the aristocracies of the seventeenth and eighteenth centuries, the kings of the Middle Ages, and the tyrants of ancient civilization further confirm the evils of power when it is consolidated in the few, or worse, in the one. In our current political climate in the West, we associate such evils as torture, terror, and the existence of a dreaded secret police with totalitarian power—the ultimate form of absolute power, a power that crushes individual freedom, the fundamental principle of liberal democracy, through violence and terror. The many books and films about the problem of totalitarianism speak not just against the possible rise of absolute power in our governments, but also of our intense fear and anxiety about losing freedom and democracy to a violent power. The War on Terror's desperate co-opting of the Manichean rhetoric of the World War II/Cold-War era is one example of this fear's hold on contemporary America's national conscience. Its very name is another.

Radiohead seem especially attuned to this fear of the tie between violence and power. From *OK Computer* to *Hail to the Thief,* their records consistently portray a world rife with terror, despondency, and violence. Piggies squeal, bruises don't heal, and police arrest citizens for random crimes like offensive hairdos or annoying conversational habits. Knives come out, armies are taken out, and bodies float down muddy rivers. Little men are erased, young blood is effaced, and the feeling of being strangled, beaten, and skinned-alive is never far. Radiohead seem to live in a violent world.

This world not only sounds nightmarish, it looks it, too. Stanley Donwood's sleeve art, from *Kid A* and after, especially, depicts wide-eyed demonic creatures weeping, screaming, or perpetrating violent acts. The hidden booklet behind the CD tray on *Kid A* is especially disturbing. Creatures kick each other with razor-sharp feet, drip blood from their claws, and gather with machine guns and masks under the ironic headline "Glamorous." The cover of *Hail to the Thief,* which uses a painting of Donwood's called "Pacific Coast," further exemplifies the terror and anxiety found in these disturbing creatures. Utilizing blocks and blocks of text, the painting translates social anxiety into a wall of media-crazed buzz words like "Oil," "Fear," and "Security," all the while aping a map of Los Angeles. One can easily recall the alienated fear of Pink from *The Wall* here, as each block adds yet another moment to the individual's feeling of separation and powerlessness.

Yet Radiohead also present an optimism—of sorts, at least—in the face of power. They depict moments of resistance in which they rear a defiant head. The moving "I Will" from *Hail to the Thief* features a resilient Yorke promising to "rise up" in the face of overwhelming odds, promising not to let anything happen "to my children." *Amnesiac*'s "I Might Be Wrong," while channeling an anxiety that sees "no future left at all," still urges us to "think about the good times and never look back." And *Kid A*'s "Optimistic" offers the consolation that trying the best you can is good enough, even if one feels utterly powerless, like "nervous messed up marionettes floating around on a prison ship."

So Radiohead raise a variety of questions about violence, power, and resistance in our world. How are we to understand power and violence as political subjects? Does power always give birth to violence? Are power and violence even the same thing?

I Am Born Again

Immediately following World War II, political and social philosopher Hannah Arendt (1906–1975) penned a three-volume investigation into the origins of totalitarian power—the Communist and Nazi states. Covering the trial of Nazi criminal Adolf Eichmann for *The New Yorker*, Arendt coined the phrase "the banality of evil" and in her book *Eichmann in Jerusalem* suggested that the *bureaucratizing* of barbarism—the meetings, memos, uniforms, and schedules that Eichmann described during his trial—blunts the psychological power of violence, allowing normal people to facilitate horrific ends. Arendt's treatise *On Violence* and her earlier study of modern political subjectivity, *The Human Condition*, offer the best interrogation of the philosophical concepts of power and violence.

In *The Human Condition*, the philosophical concept of action is the fundamental element of politics. Action is made possible only by the "human condition of plurality," and allows humans to begin anew, to create new possibilities and break with the mistakes of the past.[1] Arendt calls the possibility to create the new in action "natality," in reference to the new beginning of human birth: "Action has the closest connection with the human condition of natality" because the newborn "possesses the capacity of beginning something anew, that is, of acting" (p. 9).

A few songs off of *OK Computer* get at Arendt's notion of natality. The hopefulness of the air crash survivor in "Lucky" channels this idea that new action or a new event can move social life in a different direction: "It's gonna be a glorious day! / I feel my luck could change." Similarly, after having emerged unscathed from a car crash on album opener "Airbag," Yorke proclaims: "I am born again." These near-death experiences create a space for the narrator in each song to realize his capacity to act again in society, just as if he was given a second chance at life. The power of these emotions is the power of "the new beginning inherent in birth" (p. 9), a power that presupposes a plurality of social actors.

This human plurality is not only the prerequisite of action and natality, but of power as well. Arendt says "power springs up

---

1 Hannah Arendt, *The Human Condition,* second edition (University of Chicago Press, 1998), p. 7.

between men when they act together and vanishes the moment they disperse" (p. 200). Power can only exist within community, within the human plurality that is the presupposition of politics. It cannot exist without both the support and existence of the populace. When the tyrant forces his subjects to kneel before him, his power is actualized by the kneeling itself, by the action of the populace, and not by a power that is independent of social relations.

This means that tyrannical power is essentially only the obedience of the people; it is not a thing or substance or supernatural power held by the tyrant or the dictator. As Arendt defines it in *On Violence*, power is "never the property of an individual," but is rather the ability of humanity "to act in concert."[2] In fact, when we use the phrase "in power," we are actually referring to a leader "being empowered by a certain number of people to act in their name" (p. 44). For Arendt, power is ultimately the social relation between political subjects that keeps any leader, dictator or democratically-elected president (even Supreme Court-installed president), for lack of a better term, in power.

They Do It to Yourself

In the infamous video for "Just," a man lies on the sidewalk, refusing to get up despite the protests and imploring requests of passers-by and police officers. He declares, via subtitles, that he cannot tell everyone why he is lying down on the street. When finally forcefully pressed, he breaks down and gives the reason for his bizarre action to those surrounding him. The subtitles cut out for this revelation, leaving the viewer in the dark as to what the man says. As the video ends, an aerial shot of the street now reveals that everyone is lying prostrate on the sidewalk alongside of the man.

Most react, I think, by supposing that the power here is in what the man says. After all, everyone is standing before he speaks his piece and then lying on the ground after they hear him. But Arendt would say power is not found in the man's words, but in everyone's reaction to those words. If the man had said something ridiculous like "I know aliens will swoop down and capture us

2 Hannah Arendt, *On Violence* (Harcourt Brace, 1970), p. 44.

unless we lie down right now," the spectators could easily have passed it off as lunacy and gone about their business. But the fact that everyone lies down in active response to these words makes them, even if they are supposedly nonsensical, incredibly powerful. For Arendt, it is in a plural action like social obedience where power finds its essence. The fact that the viewer of "Just" never knows what the man says, in fact, underscores Arendt's interpretation: power is not in singular word, but in plural deed.

How does this notion of power compare to Acton's aphorism? As our look at "Just" shows, Arendt might respond that it is not power *itself* that corrupts, since power is ultimately not a thing but a group action. It is rather that power allows the *possibility* of corruption in the political sphere. Arendt's definition of power is not pejorative; power is not necessarily bad or evil. Instead, power creates a space for good or bad political action —we don't know whether what the man said is good or bad, but we do know group action was taken, and therefore power was exercised. When it comes to a moral decision on power, then, it is up to the group, to the populace, to decide whether or not to obey, follow, and empower. If the people don't want the loonies taking over, as "Go to Sleep" opines, then they must not participate in empowering them. Or, in the visual language of "Just," they shouldn't lie down.

We Can Wipe You Out Anytime

But, if merely not participating in power relations immobilizes a dictator or a tyrant, why does Acton's aphorism ring so true historically? Power would never have the chance to enable corruption if the people never left the corrupt in power, so why have the people left, and continue to leave, the corrupt in power?

Arendt answers with one word: violence. "Under the conditions of human life," Arendt writes, "the only alternative to power is not strength—which is helpless against power—but force," an alternative enabled "by acquiring the means of violence" (*Human Condition*, p. 202). Violence is instrumental, using instruments like weapons to amplify the strength of a powerful individual. Weapons, therefore, cheat the definition of power and multiply the strength of an individual so that they may ape the effects of empowerment. Thus, one person with a machine gun can command obedience from a large group of people in just the way that a legitimately elected king or president commands attention and obedience upon entering a room. The instruments of violence, then, are a shortcut; an attempt to deliver the power that is found in group acquiescence by side-stepping the whole business of political approval in favor of cold, hard steel. In this sense, Arendt argues, "the extreme form of violence is One against All" (*On Violence*, p. 42).

The narrator of *Hail to the Thief*'s "Sit Down. Stand Up." seems to rely implicitly on the implements of violence. The repeated refrains of "sit down, stand up" and "walk into the jaws of hell" are hardly requests—they come from a place of command which we can only assume is backed by the menace of violence. Yorke's eerie delivery of the lines "We can wipe you out anytime" makes this threat explicit: unless you, the listener, do what you're told, you'll be erased. Faced with this situation, Mao Zedong's saying that "Power grows out of the barrel of a gun" seems to ring true.

But Arendt disagrees: "Power and violence are opposites; where the one rules absolutely, the other is absent" (*On Violence*, p. 56). But aren't Mao's gunmen and the narrator of "Sit Down. Stand Up." powerful in that they command obedience? It's true, Arendt says, that "out of the barrel of a gun grows the most effective command, resulting in the most instant and perfect obedience." But this obedience stems ultimately from the fear of violence and death, and not out of a plural political empowerment. In fact, Arendt states, "violence appears where power is in jeopardy" and "left to its own course it ends in power's disappearance." This is because "no government exclusively built on the means of violence has ever existed," as even extremely violent totalitarian regimes "need a power basis—the secret police and its net of informers" (p. 50). Even the most violent of governments must still have some form of political empowerment—somebody has to be doing the dirty work for the dictator and, as we have seen, that somebody's action is the essence of any political power.

Go and Tell the Thief that the Sky Is Falling In

Revolution is Arendt's example of how, though they are intertwined, power is separate from violence. In a revolutionary situation, the "superiority of government has always been absolute" when it comes to instruments of violence; tanks beat Molotov cocktails every time. But "this superiority lasts only as long as the power structure of the government is intact" (p. 48). Thus, "where commands are no longer obeyed, the means of violence are no use," and the question of obedience to command is dictated not by the means of violence but by the opinion of resistance "and the number of those who share it." When you and whose army end up joining the resistance, it is not long until power will shift hands.

But before that shift occurs, the temptation to violence is at its most extreme. As Arendt observes, "rule by sheer violence comes into play where power is being lost" (p. 53). No longer backed by the power of the people, violence, the means of destruction, becomes the determining end of government. It's no longer a means to an end guided by the power of the people invested in the ruling party or person—it's now only an extension of that ruling party or leader's desire, ironic as it may be, to keep hold of that very power which is slipping away. "The means of destruction," Arendt warns, "now determine the end—with the consequence that the end will be the destruction of all power."

Hail to the Thief's opening track, "2 + 2 = 5," can be read as a commentary on Arendt's interpretation of power and revolution. Yorke's lyrics seem to be a back and forth dialogue between a brain-washed, impotent citizen and a ruler who is asserting authority. The citizen is torn between wanting to stay home under sand-bagged safety and the comfort of a brain-washed world where "2 + 2 = 5" and the reality that she has "not been paying attention" to the political situation that has allowed the king to become a thief who boldly dares citizens to "question my authority." Yet the call of not paying attention can equally be applied to the king, who, though he has been swatting detractors like flies, like flies "the buggers keep coming back." As Arendt understands it, the king's violent attempts to dispel dissent will only create more dissenters, leading to a revolutionary situation. The mocking "ahhhh diddums" found at the end of the song's lyrics in the *Hail to the Thief* booklet, then, seem pointed at the king, and not the citizens. We can easily imagine the mocking sentiment of this childish phrase in this way: "You poor thing, your majesty, it seems the people are on to your thieving ways."

The Fear Is Holding On

Despite the mocking tone of the end of "2 + 2 = 5," the real political situation "where violence, having destroyed all power, does not abdicate but, on the contrary, remains in full control," is a reign of terror. Arendt sees "the use of terror to maintain domination" as the ultimate end result of power's abdication, and the logical result of a rule by violence. Terror is the final stage in violence's rampage—power is completely destroyed by the violence of terror. Citizens in this situation, as Yorke's unsettling melody on "Like Spinning Plates" relates, are being "ripped to shreds" while leaders "make pretty speeches."

Arendt thinks that, unlike merely tyrannical rule, the rule of terror is the true essence of totalitarianism, a government only realized by a situation in which everyone, even friends and supporters, becomes targets. Since everyone can become a target, even the secret police and those closest to a totalitarian leader, then "potentially every person one comes into contact with" can become an informer. Like the paranoid narrator of "Life in a Glass House," there's always the chance that "someone's listening in." Because the government has become afraid of all forms of power, even the power of its friends, then it "begins to devour its own children, when yesterday's executioner becomes today's victim."

The sweat meats and the young blood of all citizens become a feast for the totalitarian police state, where the national anthem might easily proclaim, like *Kid A*'s "National Anthem," that "everyone has got the fear." The totalitarian ruler, like Yorke in "Where I End and You Begin," might muse that where he ends and the other begins is actually the space in which the ruler will "eat you alive" so that "there'll be no more lies." This moment, where everyone becomes a target and where everyone is suspected of lying and plotting, is "the moment where power disappears entirely" (p. 55). When violence reaches its zenith, power has learned how to disappear completely.

Rising Up

On *The Bends*, album opener "Planet Telex" describes a situation in which an unnamed force eludes control: "You can force it but it will not come / You can taste it but it will not form / You can crush it but it's always here / You can crush it but it's always near." This "it" is genuine power, as Arendt understands it. The more that empowered violence attempts to force its citizens to submit, the more its own power, which rests in these very citizens, will slip away until it is gone and power is transferred to a new leader or governing body. For Arendt, revolution and resistance are always part and parcel of political subjects' response to tyranny and totalitarian authority.

Hail to the Thief's "I Will" portrays Radiohead's take on this understanding of resistance perhaps better than any other track in their corpus. Yorke proclaims that, after hiding in a bunker, he will rise up, refusing to let harm come to his family: "I won't let this happen to my children." It is a clear and transparent message of a citizen resisting violence, a form of Arendt's political action, in the face of overwhelming odds.

Yorke finishes "I Will" with the repeated refrain of "little babies' eyes." It's almost as if he is alluding to the hope found in the infant's visual exploration of the world as ultimately the same as his hope that the social future of the newborn will be one of a just plurality, shorn of any and all tyrannical or totalitarian violence and terror. Arendt would say this outro expresses the power of natality, the hope found in the power of acting anew as a free political subject. And there is no doubt that they would both say that this power of natality, of new political birth, is one in which the gun can never be pointed at the people, the source of true political power and action. But if, and when, it does happen, when "absolute power corrupts absolutely" rings troublingly true again, then it is the responsibility of all political subjects to say: "I will rise up."[3]

3 This essay is dedicated to Aaron Cowan, Robert Sievert, and Joshua Hathaway, and the power found in friendship.

15.

Evil and Politics in "Hail to the Thief"

Jason Lee

> Everything begins and ends in eternity.
>
> —Thomas Newton (David Bowie), *The Man Who Fell to Earth*

> Be thankful for everything, for soon there will be nothing . . .
>
> —Tagline, *28 Days Later* (Danny Boyle, 2002)

On March 23rd, 2003, the United States bombed Baghdad. Some whooped with glee, believing this was an eye-for-an-eye victory against terrorism. But millions of others around the globe marched in protest. Saddam Hussein's extermination of the Kurds should not be forgotten, but Osama bin Laden and Iraq's alleged weapons of mass destruction were nowhere to be seen. Revenge, along with the lust for blood and oil, was the victor.

Hail to the Thief was made between September 2002 and February 2003. So it was complete when the second Iraq war began. But there had been a tense build-up to the war and it was natural for fans and the media to see the album as a response to the invasion.[1] With words like "FEAR" and "OIL" looming large on the album cover, this was a natural interpretation, invited even more by the apocalyptic lyrics of "The Gloaming" (Softly Open our Mouths in the Cold): "Go and tell the king that / The Sky is falling in." The next line, however, tempers this interpretation: "When it's not / Maybe not." And Thom Yorke's own ambiva-

---

1 See Kate Livett, *Australian Humanities Review* 41 (February 2007), available online at http://www.australianhumanitiesreview.org/archive/Issue-February-2007/Livett.html, accessed August 15 2008.

lence about the intended meaning of the album's title complicates things even more. He has stated that he believes the 2000 election was effectively stolen,[2] making "Hail to the Thief" seem like an obvious play on the traditional American presidential anthem, "Hail to the Chief." But in a *Rolling Stone* interview a year after the album's release, he said:

> they're not so much songs about politics as me desperately struggling to keep politics out. If I could have written about anything else, I would have. I tried really fucking hard. But how can any sensible person ignore what's been going on altogether? I couldn't, I really couldn't. Fuck, man, I would love to write lyrics free of politics! Send me on a retreat somewhere, where I can get it out of my system![3]

In fact, the "thief" in question, Yorke says, is John Quincy Adams, the sixth American president, who won the election of 1824 despite having received fewer votes than Andrew Jackson.[4] Yorke's title, then, is bigger than just a comment on the election of 2000. It points to the political metaphysics returned to again and again in the album's songs—an enduring metaphysics of deception, fear, violence, and want suggested by all the words on the album's cover, and allowing the album to transcend the specific wars, deceptions, and lives belonging to the period in which it happened to be made.

Getting All Literal

The line "Hail to the thief" appears in track one, "2 + 2 = 5", implying things are never as they seem. To begin to see what Radiohead is doing here, therefore, it might be useful to compare

---

2 Chuck Klosterman, "Radiohead: No More Knives," *Spin* (July 2003), pp. 64-70.

3 Serge Simonart, "Radiohead Tour Preview: A Show for the Head', *Rolling Stone* (May 2004), pp. 52-53.

4 BBC Radio 4 is thoroughly and quintessentially of the English establishment, but ironically it was here that allegations that the British government had "sexed up," as they put it, the dossier concerning reasons for going to war with Iraq were first made. This led to the Director General of the BBC, Greg Dyke, being forced to quit.

them to celebrated French philosopher Alain Badiou, who says that there's an ancient tie between philosophy and poetry. What that tie might be is suggested by French poet Arthur Rimbaud (1854–1891) who saw poetry as a kind of "les révoltes logiques", or logical revolts. Philosophy, like the best poetry and lyrics, pits thought against the defective state of the world and life.[5] It revolts against the world—something that seems to capture in a nutshell Radiohead's project.

But it's not that simple. For Radiohead is also probing the question in this album of what the boundaries, the limits, are between us and the world. And between people—as in "Where I End and You Begin. (The Sky Is Falling In.)" In light of Radiohead's interest in androids, this question becomes central. Recall here the Radiohead track "Paranoid Android," the lead track from their addictive third album *OK Computer* (1997).[6] The very idea of a sentient android blurs two of the fundamental categories through which we understand the world: mechanical objects and conscious beings. Inert, material substance and active, thinking souls, as Descartes believed everything in the world to be made up of. Or, radios that passively pick up signals and human heads with brains that think, act, decide and experience the world. A radiohead, or a person with a radiohead, would be some kind of blend between human and machine—perhaps like Newton, David Bowie's character in *The Man Who Fell to Earth* (Nicolas Roeg, 1976). Newton is an alien on Earth looking for water who comes to believe that Earth's television signals are coming from his own head.

What does this have to do with politics? Everything. If we are all radio heads, sponging up everything thrown at us through our very atmosphere, we are susceptible to being controlled by our elected leaders, instead of them being controlled by us. "We don't want the loonies taking over," as "Backdrifts" puts it. But one thief may have already done just that, at least in part because many

---

5 Alain Badiou, *Infinite Thought: Truth and the Return to Philosophy* (Continuum, 2004), p. 39.

6 The track's title is taken from Marvin the Paranoid Android in Douglas Adams's *The Hitchhiker's Guide to the Galaxy*, originally a radio comedy broadcast on BBC Radio 4 in 1978, variously adapted for page and screen.

yearn to be led and controlled. There is in some, Nietzsche said, "an overwhelmingly forceful and pleasurable desire to be a function," pure and simple.[7] Just ask one of the *Stepford Wives* (Bryan Forbes, 1974; Frank Oz, 2004).

The importance of personal, political boundaries is underscored by sociologist and philosopher Ernest Gellner (1925–1995). As Gellner sees it, looking at another, if there is no fixed sense of self, means we cannot comprehend another.[8] We only understand another through ourselves, yet we only understand ourselves through another. This helps make sense of the anxious dread within "Where I End and You Begin" (The sky is falling in)—especially with the lyric, repeated over and over, "I will eat you alive". Yorke seems to point to an ultimate fear, to evil itself, emerging within this question of boundaries between our self and the world, between what is familiar and friendly, and what is other, very hungry, and inspires our greatest fears.

One philosopher to look at a similar sense of dread inside everyday existence is Martin Heidegger (1889–1976).[9] Heidegger's view is that the Other or source of evil is not any particular thing, only the lack or defect. We fear nothingness or the nothing (*das Nichts*), but perhaps we should not: "Horror is produced in subjective existence by the threat of real evil. Nothingness does not kill; being does." Heidegger should know, given his controversial membership in the Nazi party before the Second World War.

Who Is This Devil in Disguise?

Elvis, like many before him, was singing about a woman. But "Hail to the Thief" could be referring to the evil done as we negotiate the boundaries, at once metaphysical and political, between ourselves and others in the world. In some ways, the songs on *Hail to the Thief* evoke a stately presidential parade of horrors, as if the undead of the twentieth century rose up to sicken us with their presence and the memories we usually repress or avoid.

7 Friedrich Nietzsche, *The Gay Science* (Vintage, 1974), p. 176.

8 Ernest Gellner, *The Psychoanalytic Movement: The Cunning of Unreason* (Fontana, 1993), p. 91.

9 Martin Heidegger, *Being and Time* (Harper and Row, 1962), p. 233.

Track two, "Sit down. Stand up" (Snakes and Ladders) evokes Auschwitz, with the command of the title, and "Walk into / The jaws of hell." "The raindrops" could be gas. "2 + 2 = 5," again, suggests that the thief in question might be the Devil of Dante's Inferno who punishes those who betray others by having their souls sent to hell before they die. A demon inhabits their bodies for the rest of their life, while their souls are frozen in a lake right next to Satan, himself another punished soul. The tragedy here is that once you're in, you're in (and it's much hotter than lukewarm): "It's the devil's way now / you can scream and you can shout / it is too late now." In a way, your condemnation is just, because you've done it to yourself: "you have not been paying attention."

From Hell, we go to human sacrifice. Track five "Go to Sleep" (Little Big Man being Erased) has instrumentation and structure reminiscent of the folk music from the cult film *The Wicker Man* (Robin Hardy, 1973) in which a virgin Christian policeman is burnt alive to appease the pagan gods and help the crops grow again. Each of these horrors, however, presupposes a certain easy metaphysics of the self, an easy division between ourselves and others (or "the Other," evil itself).

The Most Gigantic Truthful Mouth of All Time

The disturbing collection of videos that accompanied *Hail to the Thief*, in the form of *The Most Gigantic Lying Mouth of all Time*, explore this conception of evil and the Devil. For those that see the Devil everywhere, the title could refer to Bush junior, and the videos are actually presented by a demonic figure with archteypal horns and an obfuscated devilish voice. It's a parody of a number of genres, particularly the kids show and celebrity music program, with comments such as "if you would like to contact us write to us stating your age" and "all footage you're about to see has been prewatched by adults." The opening is akin to an episode of *The Brady Bunch*, with cheesy music and mug shots of the band, but with words such as "skinned alive," "strung up by the wrists," and "pointless" being flashed on the screen, we'd be forgiven for thinking this was purely an exercise in driving us deeper into a hole. A man holds up a sign saying "now we see you," confirming our paranoia. Lyrics such as "ice age coming," "this is really happening," and "take the money and run," suggest Yorke's political and social paranoia.

To create *The Most Gigantic Lying Mouth of all Time*, Radiohead put out a general call for videos and selected their favorites, with the initial idea of having their own television channel. The videos are interspersed with "ironic" interviews with the band, but how ironic are they? After all the media hype over the politicization of the band's music, Yorke reveals in two interviews that the best thing about being a celebrity is receiving free gasoline, although he did snog Robbie Williams and Richard Nixon. At least it's only a snog not a shag. Can we conclude, like those who see the devil personified in politicians, that we only see what what we want to see, only hear what we want to hear? Ebba Frikzon's "Cat Girl" video for "2 + 2 = 5" involves a cartoon rat teaching a class full of animals. The rat writes on the blackboard, "Today we are talking about animal rights."

Our perceptions of evil, though, begin to change when we see our complicity in them. The significance of *The Most Gigantic Lying Mouth* is, in part, Radiohead's participatory approach to their art— a move that prefigures both their pay-what-you-want model for marketing *In Rainbows* and, more broadly, their more optimistic, less apocalytpic view of the world after *Hail to the Thief*. Yorke perhaps had to go through the "Hail to the Thief" stage to reach this point of activism. He got involved in Friends of the Earth in 2003, after the UN report on climate change was published, and decided to support their Big Ask campaign for a strong climate change law. And he went public with his optimism:

> Unlike pessimists such as James Lovelock, I don't believe we are all doomed. It was good to hear Professor Sir David King recently saying he was an optimist and human behaviour is changing. As I heard George Monbiot saying not long ago, isn't it funny how in the space of a year we went from listening to sceptics who denied this was happening to suddenly saying we're all doomed – how interesting that both scenarios demand that we do nothing. That can't be right. You should never give up hope.

The Self and Politics

The key to this transformation may lie in the picture of evil *Hail to the Thief* explores. Does its metaphysics of self-and-other really make sense? It may have at one time when, under the ideals of the Enlightenment, human culture aspired to develop a complete and total knowledge of the world. What remained outside, what could not be assimilated or known, remained a threat to this ideal. Michel Foucault identifies this remainder or unreason with madness itself, and traces its rise to the classical age of enlightenment. If the essential quality of humans is their rationality and reason, then exceptions to the order of reason or rational discourse cannot be truly human and become identified with evil. In other words, what is classified as inhuman comes to be feared as parasitic or, in the case of our current political situation, potential terrorists.

But the ideal fails to understand how reason is in fact enmeshed in the world, and not sovereign over it. This is why Badiou's and Rimbaud's conception of philosophy as a kind of poetry-of-revolt is important for understanding Radiohead. Because philosophy navigates and creates the border between self and other, it creates the space of politics within which we think and experience the world and do philosophy. Philosophy is part of the world, not above it, and therefore must reflect and learn from those transformations happening in contemporary situations. Philosophy is no longer sovereign. Rather, it is as if philosophy has finally heard that cry addressed to it for decades, a cry voiced by so many artists, scientists, activists and lovers whose activities it has deafly appropriated from on high: You have not been paying attention.

Thinking in Rainbows

And you have not been acting. For Yorke's optimism seems not only connected to a new way of thinking, but also a new way of behaving and acting in the world. Radiohead embraced the notion of acting without reciprocity when they left their label EMI, and offered *In Rainbows* for download at whatever price people wanted to pay for it. And perhaps interpretations of Radiohead's earlier music that compared it to Pink Floyd and stressed its negativity were wrong. Once again, "You Have Not Been Paying Attention". Although this does sound like a vicious school teacher barking at a child, as depicted in Pink Floyd's 1982 film, the point was, and still is, act before it's too late, as the tagline for *28 Days Later* that began this chapter suggests.

There is in much of this music an encounter with a feared Other, but discourse with the Other is a discourse of continual revelation. Like listening to the music and finding hidden revelatory depths, its tongue is that of the absolute Other, and its name is responsibility, the call to respond ethically. It all depends on you.

Radiohead, Heidegger, and Technology. *(Our Iron Lungs.)*

16.

The Mutilation of Voice in "Kid A" (Or, My John Mayer Problem)

Adam Koehler

When I was a kid, back in the era of cassettes, my friend Brandon made me a copy of *Pablo Honey*. He pressed his stereo up against mine, hit "play," and then hit "record" on mine. Since we used the external mic on my stereo, *Pablo Honey* came through layered with echoed static and the sounds of Brandon trying to be quiet: taps set to the beat of the songs, his dog running through the halls in the background, and later, Brandon's mother calling him over to eat. You can also hear him shout: *Quiet, Mom! I'm recording!*

I loved that tape. Before it went the way of all my cassettes, that copy of *Pablo Honey* accompanied me to school; it was with me while I was on the bus; it played between mix-tapes of songs I'd recorded off the radio (complete with DJs' voices bleeding into and out of songs); and it took its rightful place next to *Mellow Gold*, *Ten*, and *Nevermind* in my tape collection.

Yes, *rightful* place—I know people who cringe when I tell them that I love *Pablo Honey*. Of course, I agree that *The Bends* is brilliant and that *OK Computer* and *Kid A* are masterpieces. But I still love *Pablo Honey* not only because "Anyone Can Play Guitar" is beautiful and "Creep" (despite what anyone—even Radiohead themselves—says about it) is one excellent song. I love it also because of the sounds of the springs in Brandon's bed squeaking as he got up, because I loved hearing him tap along when he sat back down, because I loved his dog, Benny, and because I'll never know what got Benny so excited so as to run up and down the hallway, paws clacking the length of their apartment. I loved that Brandon's mother called him over to eat. It reminded me that someone *made* this for me.

But it wasn't until I heard *Kid A* that any of this made sense to me.

Surprises and Alarms

As most Radiohead fans remember, *Kid A* was kind of shocking when it was released. One friend of mine, when I asked him what he thought, said that he couldn't listen to their old stuff anymore. Their core *sound* had changed. Radiohead had *evolved*. They'd picked up electronic music, yet couldn't quite be called "electronic" themselves. They had abandoned the naturalistic realism of rock albums and embraced the very technology used to record them. They weren't pretending that a person playing an acoustic guitar and singing into a microphone was any less technologically determined than a band that drew from drum samples, distorted vocals, and software. When we hear Thom Yorke's voice at the beginning of "Everything in its Right Place," we hear it disfigured—cycled frontwards and backwards through some machine. It's spooky, weird, and clearly marked a new direction for the band.

One thing that I still love about *Kid A*—and which is, no doubt, one of the shocking things about it—is that you're always reminded that someone *made* this. The music doesn't disappear into the transparency of recording technologies—even "How to Disappear Completely" uses guitars as easily as it does studio effects. At nearly every turn, we're reminded of the synthetic quality of the songs and the technology used to compose the album— or, at least, the texture of that technology. Years after its release, when I was teaching writing, one of my students was surprised that I had never seen the band live. I was (relatively) young at the time, but my response was, *I don't think I have to.*

I said that because seeing the band live didn't seem to be the point. (Later, when *I Might Be Wrong: Live Recordings* came out, I learned that I might be wrong about that.) At the time, though, the whole point was artifice. Radiohead had long been lamenting the artificiality of things early in their career (with, for example, "Fake Plastic Trees" and "Fitter, Happier") and *Kid A*, as shocking as it was, seemed like a logical step: use the technology that alienates us, crawl into it, and turn it into something else *from the inside*. For the media-saturated youth-culture that rallied around *Kid A*, the album seemed to speak simultaneously from within the technology wrapped around us as well as about it. Where *OK Computer* was *about* the low-level panic and anxiety produced by living in "the information age," *Kid A* was an artifact *of* that information and that age, the first child born from the very technology rock music traveled. (Okay. Maybe not the *first*. But let's not get hung up on origin myths.)

To me, the album is inseparable from the artifice used to compose it. And it's inseparable from what I see as *Kid A's* technologically determined conundrum—the question: how does the withdrawal and making-evident of artifice shape anything *Kid A* might say? Does this inseparability of music and the technology used to create it mute, mutilate, or magnify Radiohead's voice? Is it part of some larger comment by the band on the ways technology is thinned out into a nearly invisible backdrop against which we live? Consider this chapter my attempt to figure this out and record what I hear in *Kid A*. And I'll try to be quiet while the tape plays.

Kid A, Heidegger, and the Question of Technology

Science fiction writer William Gibson says that cyberspace is where telephone conversations take place. I imagine this is the same place where we listen to *In Rainbows* (and a case could be made for that, I'm sure), but what interests me most about Gibson's definition is not necessarily the space we occupy when on the phone, but the role of the phone itself. It shimmies between connection (as it presents our voice to the person on the other end) and distortion (as it makes that voice different, distorted, and electronic). The telephone determines and enables. Conversations may take place in cyberspace, but they get there through an electrocution that seems to manipulate and facilitate our voices equally. Or, switching metaphors, imagine listening to your voice played back on tape. That's not what you sound like. Is it? *Yep, Kid A* says, *that's you.*

That's the best way I can explain the kind of anxiety I feel when I listen to *Kid A*. Actually, scratch that—it's not anxiety. It's familiarity, philosophically speaking, especially when I hear Yorke's distorted voice, digitally bubbling up, saying something like "Kid A, Kid A/Kid A, Kid A." This kind of disfigurement recurs again after the distorted voice of "Everything in Its Right Place" blurs and repeats. It asks, "What was that you tried to say?" while the disfigured samples cycle through their own continual distortions in the background. The album's title track, "Kid A," is so disfigured we can't even understand it. We hear the technology. Its part of the song. *Somebody made this*, it says. *Listen.*

Martin Heidegger had a lot to say about such disfigurement in his analysis of *Being* and the notion of *presence* in western philosophy. In *Being and Time*, he claimed that technology amounted to a collective human effort to control and manipulate nature, at the expense of understanding the ways in which technology turns around and controls and manipulates us. This is a lesson that we've learned well from Radiohead. It's right there in the band's name (bringing to mind images of machine-like brains working through millions of signals that register and millions that don't). It's there in *OK Computer* ("I might be paranoid, but not an android," the computerized voice reassures us). And it's there in *Kid A* ("Strobe lights and blown speakers / fireworks and hurricanes / I'm not here / This isn't happening"). The world of *Kid A*, after all, is one in which we're here, but we're not here. "In Limbo" says we're "living in a fantasy world," and then "Idioteque" tells us "this is really happening." We've shimmied in between space and cyberspace. And we get there through the technological atmosphere *Kid A* orchestrates around us.

In *Being and Time*, Heidegger argues that most of our everydayness is spent firmly in the realm of the ordinary—we need to study, go to work, buy groceries, pay bills. In the process, much of what enables such ordinariness retreats from our attention and becomes invisible to us. For Heidegger, western philosophy has spent far too much time investigating what is present to us—or presence (or existence), more generally—and too little time investigating the ways such presence tends to erase that which enables it by virtue of rendering it ordinary. Technology is one of mankind's biggest enablers of ordinary lives, and yet, when all is working appropriately, it retreats from our daily attention. The *dan-*

gers of technology (such as the risks of identity theft or car accidents on the way to the grocery store) actually help right this imbalance by pointing us to the world that lies ordinarily withdrawn from view or experience—an absence that is so very important for Heidegger's ongoing critique of the persistence of presence in philosophy.

Heidegger's demand that western philosophy re-think what it means by presence—and his point that attempts to investigate the nature of existence, therefore, will always privilege the presence implied by the word "is"—centers around the concept *Dasein*. Put simply, *Dasein*, as its German definition suggests, refers to "being"—specifically, *human* "being." In Heidegger's scheme, human "being" is not something static—it is not exclusively presence—but rather something bound up in its particular temporal and material circumstances. It's a movement through a world of material possibilities. So to privilege what "is," according to Heidegger, is to ignore that which has withdrawn from "being," but which, nevertheless enables that "being." To privilege presence is to erase its conditions as well as the many opportunities that may be possible when we re-imagine what has enabled those opportunities. Technology, he argues, is one of the primary withdrawn tools that enables that "is" to the degree that we don't think about it—or see its alternative potentials. Think email. Think cell phones. Think cars. Think iPods. Think laptops, even tables and chairs. Think *Pablo Honey*.

Technology is an invisible backdrop in *Pablo Honey*. It's merely the vehicle for hearing (in my opinion) damn fine alternative rock. We'd expect the band to sound much the same playing live. Who cares about the ways studios provide technological environments that quite seriously shape the music we hear? I want guitars. I want drums. I want infectious bass lines. I want microphones amplifying screams. Forget that these are technologies themselves. But in *Kid A*, it's different. Technological environs become very, *very* important. The studio *is* an instrument. Sound and technology merge. New possibilities arise. Who cares about standard guitar rock? I want samples. I want drum machines. I want disfigured vocals. Think email viruses. Think dropped calls. Think strobe lights and blown speakers. Think *Kid A*.

We're shaken out of our ordinary understanding of rock
music—and the ways it renders its technologies invisible. And
that's kinda scary. But it's also very familiar. I've been assaulted by
technology in ways designed to attack me (computer viruses, identity theft) and I've been assaulted by technology in ways designed
to "help" me (advertisements in every virtual and physical place
my eyes can go, dropped calls, laptops that crash while I'm working, and yes, even car crashes). When technology makes itself vis-
ible, I usually don't want to see it. I'm sure this would be different
if I were a programmer. Or an engineer. But I'm not. I'm a
teacher. I require that the equipment that surrounds me work
properly so that I can get through my day. When it doesn't, I'm
pissed. I don't have the time to worry about it making itself visi-
ble. I want it to shut up and do its job. I *want* it to withdraw.

Which helps explain the particular, familiar, anxiety or panic
that domes *Kid A*. My desire for withdrawal, *Kid A* says, is a fantasy. There's no such thing. Maybe the anxieties produced by my
technologically situated lifestyle are something that haven't found
adequate expression in the culture of "the information age"—the
culture into which I was born. The synthetic opening keyboard of
"Everything in its Right Place" immediately announces that this is
not the standard guitar-driven, withdrawal of technological and
musical opportunity. Perhaps this making-evident of artifice is the
depiction of a new kind of pop music. Perhaps this is a new voice
articulating something we haven't heard pop music say before.
Maybe *that's* why it sounds disfigured.

Making Sense by Not Making Sense

The song "Kid A" itself is striking not only because its voice is disfigured to the point of unintelligibility. Nor is it only because it's
the second in a trio of opening songs that dramatically announce
a new direction for a very popular band. To me, "Kid A" is striking because it is beautiful—and I'm not sure why. The electrocution of (I assume) Yorke's voice doesn't enable what technology
usually enables: communication, connection, (the illusion of) clarity. The song doesn't communicate in the way we ordinarily communicate, and the degree to which anything sung is at the mercy
of the technology presenting it to us should send shivers down

our (very human) spines. And it does. So how is that song so beautiful?

First, it's willful. No matter how oppressive the technological marring becomes, the voice still sings. It may be trapped, but it's not going to quit. It may not be understood, but it's still going to sing. And the evocative quality is as intoxicating as it is terrifying. Human expression may be entrapped, our avenues of expression becoming more and more ways toward dead ends rather than entry-points into effective, clear communication. But the digitally soaked voice of that song doesn't care. So what if its very humanity is scarred by the very technologies meant to announce it? That's no reason not to try.

And second, its failure makes it *feel* human. This is how Radiohead can embrace electronic music with *Kid A* without actually *becoming* electronic. In fact, they still remain inside the realm of pop music. It wasn't as if Radiohead heard some interesting avant-garde electronic music and thought that they should imitate it for artistic or (even less likely) commercial success. Rather, the synthetic feel of *Kid A* seems more the product of a band exploring their surrounding technologies—technologies that were ready-at-hand when *Kid A* was recorded—and using those technologies to express something very human: the anxiety of living in an information age that claims to want to help us, yet feels more like an imposition than anything else. The song "Kid A" and its electronic saturation feel very much like a saturation in which we operate daily, whether through television, radio, internet, or phone lines.

Just as Gibson noticed, much of our lives are lived through the circuitry that enables our lifestyles. And the music we listen to is an important part of that electronic saturation. Radiohead's evolution from *Pablo Honey* to *Kid A* itself reflects the degree to which we have become electronic in order to survive in "the information age." "Kid A" is as much *of* technology as it is *about* technology. It disfigures voice as much as it is concerned with singing about disfiguring voice. Such an accommodation suggests that in order for humans to say anything in "the information age" we must become partly technological ourselves (or acknowledge how dependent on technology we always have been). Humanity itself isn't enough. We need to use our technological environs. We need *help*.

I listened to the song "Kid A" for seven years before I became in any way interested in what the lyrics were saying. As far as I was concerned, for seven years, when that song emerged from the silence following "Everything in its Right Place" all I cared about was being washed in the strange familiarity of the way it feels, rather than the acknowledgement of anything particular that the lyrics might say. That was a beautiful experience because it felt, actually *felt*, like there was suddenly a band out there in mainstream global pop culture that knew how inarticulate I felt in the torrent of media I swam through daily, how trapped and protected I felt in my little world of global connection. How was it possible to say anything that might be heard, let alone *understood*, in a globalized culture that, no matter how much I depended on it, created a technological environment that trapped me as much as it protected me? The benefits of the world wide web, cell phones, laptops, television—all that stuff—were benefits that I depended on, but didn't understand. So I lived with a low-level anxiety about the technology that surrounded me. The bands I listened to didn't seem to understand this, or know how to articulate it. Radiohead did. And they did it by being inarticulate.

At Ease

I became interested in the lyrics of "Kid A" when I came across John Mayer's acoustic cover of it. I listened because I thought, *No, there's no way this guy covered Radiohead. This must be a different "Kid A."* But there was his acoustic guitar muting the rhythm of "Kid A." And there, in just the places where the voice of Radiohead's "Kid A" kicked in, he started singing. *Oh man,* I thought, *this guy just doesn't get it.* Now, I've got nothing against John Mayer and I'm not interested in being a snob about rock music. He seems like a perfectly nice guy and I genuinely think he loves what he does (which is more than I can say for many artists). And, in a way, he did me a favor. Because as soon as I realized that this was indeed Radiohead's "Kid A," I took the opportunity to listen intently and try to figure out what the lyrics were saying. As Mayer told MTV, he covered the song in order to bring out the lyrics and melody:

> There's a tune there, but it was almost purposefully obscured, like a robot was singing it. It was one of the few songs I could do something with—if you're gonna do a cover, leave the song

somewhere different than where you picked it up. (March 17th, 2004, MTV.com)

But it's also good not to leave a knife plunged into the song. I could hardly pay attention to the lyrics, overshadowed as they were by the clash between the two renditions. Think Dylan's (or even The Byrd's) "Mr. Tambourine Man" compared to William Shatner's stilted and clueless performance. Who's the real robot here?

The clash suggested to me a kind of spectrum with which to make Heideggerian sense of Radiohead's conundrum—an axis between understanding plain-spoken words articulated by Mayer (or Shatner) at one end, and being able to understand by *not* being able to hear the words that are *not* articulated, at the other. And it lets me articulate (!) why the original is so much more effective than Mayer's cover.

Kid A is an album that at once shows us how popular rock music can point us toward the synthetic, technological textures of our lives that we've come to depend on while at the same time enacting how we have come to accommodate the dangers and anxieties that such dependencies produce. It's popular music that reconfigures what we consider popular not in terms of fashion or trend, but in terms of what we use in order to connect fashions and trends. It asks popular music to start thinking about *how* we rally around our (globalized) culture. How does the circuitry that brings us together also breed alienation? How can popular music think through this? The result is often panicky music, shaking with anxiety, and nearly cyborg-like in its depiction of humanity. The title track of *Kid A*, if at all meant to be emblematic of the album, and by extension, the new direction the band took at the time, seems, to me, to suggest that, while there are no easy solutions, the attempt to think through these issues means risking not making sense—and that risk is becoming more and more a daily requirement.

John Mayer's cover seems to work as a comforting moment in an otherwise difficult existence. Sure, I hear the words articulated. But do I understand what is being said? This is where I find Radiohead's original more (and ironically so) comforting: the risk of trying to make sense means as much to me (perhaps more) than any sense made. I admire the will to face the technological saturation of our cultural moment and to try not only to make sense out of it, but to make it sing. *Kid A*, it seems to me, does just that. It shakes us out of our ordinary dependencies and shows us the risks we take on a daily level. It's not always easy to hear that, and often requires that we listen to the layers around us. It asks us to listen not just to the songs, but to the fact that there are people and technologies at work in the background who have produced those songs—and that there is a whole other life withdrawn from what we ordinarily hear. Our responsibility is not only to listen, but to understand. And that's not easy. But it can be beautiful.

17.

Why a Rock Band in a Desolate Time?

MATTHEW LAMPERT

In the age of the world's night, the abyss of the world must be experienced and must be endured. However, for this it is necessary that there are those who reach into the abyss.

—Martin Heidegger, "Why Poets?"

In the time of hedonist fascism nobody dares scream or judge what is so pathetically suspended in mid-air, which is life itself—nobody till now, that is. Meaning that if you aren't mad you're crazy—we are being eaten body and soul and no one is fighting. In fact practically no one sees it, but if you listen to the poets you will hear, and vomit up your rage.

—Lester Bangs, "Richard Hell: Death Means Never Having to Say You're Incomplete," in *Psychotic Reactions and Carburetor Dung*

If you ask, "What is Radiohead's music *about*?" one answer crops up more than any other: "alienation." All Music Guide says that Radiohead tells "tortured, twisted tales of angst and alienation," while Paul Cantin's review of *OK Computer* for the *Ottawa Sun* (to take one typical example) calls it a "superbly realized collection of songs focused vaguely on the alienating effects of modern living" (August 19th, 1997). But I have a problem with this answer—the same problem I'd have if you explained that my favorite food is made of "food."

For starters, alienation is hardly unique in Radiohead. It runs throughout Radiohead's discography as well as that of their influences: Pixies, My Bloody Valentine, DJ Shadow, Pink Floyd, and Bowie. Plus, we can find alienation within the music of a host of other rock bands: Bauhaus, Joy Division, The Stooges, The Clash, The Doors, Ramones . . . This list could go on forever and run through Reggae (as well as its ancestors, ska and rocksteady), rap music (from The Sugarhill Gang, through Public Enemy, to The Roots, Outkast, and Eminem), to industrial music (Nine Inch Nails is the obvious example, but certainly also think about Skinny Puppy, Ministry, or even—especially?—Throbbing Gristle). And then there's the Blues! My point is not that alienation is a played-out theme or that Radiohead is unoriginal for writing songs that express this theme in some way (any more than I should refuse to eat my dinner because "it's only made of food"). Rather, my point is that alienation is a central theme in all of culture, especially as it's expressed in music.

But if that's the case, then *why* is it the case? What is this "alienation" that mass culture seems to be reflecting back at us? For fear that we get carried away playing "armchair philosopher" and stagger off into the dizzying heights of abstract speculative questioning, let's begin by asking not "What is Radiohead's music about?" but rather, "*How* does Radiohead express the theme of alienation in their music?"

Aliens Hover

For reasons I'll come back to later, it seems to me that we can divide Radiohead's music into (at least) two major stages. The first begins with their debut album *Pablo Honey* (and its predecessor, the *Drill* EP) and culminates with *OK Computer*. The second stage begins with *Kid A* and *Amnesiac*, and has carried through the present. For now, notice two things that signal the "break" marked by *Kid A*: first, the return to album liner notes with no printed lyrics sheets (*Pablo Honey* did not have lyrics sheets, but both of the following two albums had them); second, the introduction of the theme of "disappearance" ("How to Disappear Completely"), which will become a major theme in not only the subsequent Radiohead albums, but Thom Yorke's solo work as well (*The Eraser*).

So how is the theme of alienation expressed in Radiohead's early work? It comes through most clearly as the feeling—a feeling that is given almost constant expression in Radiohead's music—that one doesn't *belong*, that one is *not at home* in one's surroundings (not at home *in the world*, even). This is central to the band's first hit single, "Creep"—"What the hell am I doing here? / I don't belong here." But notice how often it crops up in different forms throughout the whole album. "Creep" gives us a first-hand account of the feeling of alienation, while the very next track on *Pablo Honey*, "How Do You?" puts it in the third-person perspective (with far less sympathetic results). This track narrates the story of a man who "wants to be loved and he wants to belong / He wants you to listen, he wants us to weep." Like the protagonist of "Creep," this man is desperately unable to connect with others. He struggles against this inability to form meaningful relationships, attempts to maintain control, but ends up further alienating others in the process. The same feeling forms the backdrop for "Stop Whispering"—"the feeling . . . that there's something wrong"—as well as "Anyone Can Play Guitar." Alienation is the looming threat in "Ripcord," permeates the tragedy at the center of "Vegetable," and is the "strange and creeping doubt" that drives "I Can't." *Pablo Honey*, you might say, establishes the base problem that will drive the rest of Radiohead's work: the feeling of being cut off from others, unable to connect, fundamentally not at home.

It's tempting—as so many have done—to chalk all of this "alienation nonsense" up to "the loser/slacker zeitgeist of the early 1990s" (as Radiohead fansite "Green Plastic Radiohead" puts it). But we would be hasty to simply smell the same old "teen spirit" in Yorke and company's portrait (or, better, we'd be mistaken to think it's *only* adolescence that "Smells Like Teen Spirit"). Alienation, as presented by Radiohead, is not simply a problem of some marginalized sector of society (teenagers, art school kids, scrawny Brits); it's a bigger problem. As "Subterranean Homesick Alien" on *OK Computer* puts it, it's a problem "of *all* these weird creatures / who lock up their spirits / drill holes in themselves / and live for their secrets." It's *the human condition*. It's not "they" who can't connect; it's *us*. But why not?

Everything Is Broken

One thing's certain: this inability to connect is not for lack of trying. It's not "I Won't," but, "Even though I might, even though I try, I can't." Alongside the more obvious manifestation of alienation, there is another constant theme: passivity and the loss of control. Again, "Creep" introduces this loss ("I don't care if it hurts / I want to have control / I want a perfect body / I want a

perfect soul"), and it is a *constant* companion to the theme of alienation. In fact, this has been the fundamental problem with alienation all along: we only feel cut off, feel like we "don't belong
here," *because* we cannot connect with others. The hostility of the
world and our inability to act within it are in this way *dependent on*
one another. We cannot simply explain the hostility of the world
through our inability to engage with it, but neither can we simply
blame our inability to engage with the world on its hostility; we
need to understand our attunement to the world, and the character of the world itself, as somehow fundamentally connected. We
are headed, that is, toward a *phenomenological* analysis of alienation—one that doesn't split the world from our experience of it.

Using this as our way forward, let's look at the albums *Pablo
Honey*, *The Bends*, and *OK Computer* where this inability is expressed
in two ways (not one after another, but simultaneously): first, as a
passivity (the inability to act); and second, as an "emptying" of the
self (having nothing to give, contribute, or call upon). The first is
found in songs like "Prove Yourself" ("I want to breathe, I want
to grow / I'd say I want it, but I don't know how") and (obviously) "I Can't." But it echoes as well through "The Bends" ("Fall
asleep beside the window pane / My blood will thicken"), "High
and Dry" ("Drying up in conversation / you'll be the one who
cannot talk / All your insides fall to pieces / you just sit there
wishing you could still make love"), and even "Karma Police"
("hysterical and useless"). Here the passive person (whether narrated first-, second-, or third-person) is unable to pursue his or her
desires, and is instead either acted *upon* by the world (as in "Karma
Police"), or is simply thrown to the disposal or mercy *of* the hostile world (again, "Karma Police" fits, but also "High and Dry," "I
Can't," and others). This inability to act, then, is more precisely an
inability to be responsible for oneself or to decide one's own fate
(think of the helpless appeals to "destiny" to "save me from the
world" that start off "Anyone Can Play Guitar"). German philosopher Martin Heidegger calls this inability "inauthenticity," and it's
at the root of his phenomenological analysis of alienation.

In his masterwork *Being and Time* (Harper and Row, 1962),
Heidegger says that to be authentic is to "choose" yourself and
"win" yourself (p. 68), to take over and bear full responsibility for
the meaning of your own existence. Inauthenticity, on the other
hand, means accepting for your understanding of yourself the

meanings and possibilities placed upon you by an impersonal society—what Heidegger calls *"das Man"* (German for "the They" or "the One," though the echoes of the American expression "the Man" shouldn't be entirely dismissed). It's an idea with which—terminology aside—we're already intimately familiar as Radiohead fans. If "Fitter Happier" on *OK Computer* is supposed to be bleakly ironic, then this experience of inauthenticity is *exactly* what it's about: "Not drinking too much / regular exercise at the gym"; "getting on better with your associate employee contemporaries"; "keep in contact with old friends / (enjoy a drink now and then)"; "fond but not in love"; "an empowered and informed member of society." The list slowly grows more menacing as the song progresses, but what are its essential contents? Platitudes. The 'obvious' goals of everybody in the 'good society'; this is *society's picture of the good life*. But *who* is "society"? "Them." "One says it is like this." *Das Man*. In choosing to become what society wants us to become, we essentially choose to abandon ourselves only to wind up high and dry: "You'd kill yourself for recognition / kill yourself to never, ever stop / You broke another mirror / you're turning into something you are not." And from this abandonment of self comes the feeling of powerlessness and passivity; "Drying up in conversation / you'll be the one who cannot talk."

Open Up Your Skull

This leads us to the other manifestation of powerlessness, the "emptying" of self. As Yorke sings in "The Bends": "I need to wash myself again to hide all the dirt and pain / 'Cos I'd be scared that there's nothing underneath." "Let Down" speaks of "the *emptiest* of feelings." And in "Karma Police," the crescendo finds the narrator exclaiming, "For a minute there I lost myself." But if the self is "emptied," where does it "go"? Again, this is where the *phenomenological* account of alienation is so powerful: scientifically speaking, our thoughts are always in our heads, while the world remains apart and outside. But if you pay attention to your *experience* of the world, you will notice that on any average day you spend a lot of time *not* lost "in your head," as we like to say, but rather *absorbed in the world*. This empty feeling is closely connected with a dissolution of the self into whatever activities happen to be going on. Heidegger writes that "this 'absorption in . . .' has most-ly the character of Being-lost in the publicness of the 'they'" (p. 220). To be inauthentic is to have "fallen into the 'world'. 'Fallenness' into the 'world' means an absorption in Being-with-one-another, in so far as the latter is guided by idle talk, curiosity, and ambiguity."

But what happens when we "fall into the world"? Isn't it just to "lose yourself in the moment"? (Note the two meanings of the word "lose" in play here: in getting *lost* in the moment, we *lose*—we don't *win*—ourselves. Thus Heidegger's description of authen-ticity as not just "choosing" yourself, but also "winning" yourself.) "Karma Police" plays nicely on the Hindu and Buddhist reference suggested by the word karma when the narrator speaks of "los-ing" himself: to be absorbed in the world, to be lost in the moment, is, as my yoga teacher always says, to "exist in the moment." But what alternatives are there? We can "exist in the past," of course, as one might say of someone constantly trying to recapture their "glory days." But we can also exist *in the future*: we can, as Heidegger says, "project" ourselves. The play on the word "project" here is important, as well: to "project" is to cast-ahead (as a projector does with an image, or I might do with my voice when addressing a crowd); but we project *ourselves* by setting *proj-ects* for ourselves, tasks we mean to work on, goals we strive toward. In becoming lost in the moment, we do not project our-selves into the future; both future and past fade away, and we exist only in the "now." Now *never* becomes the future or the past; instead, having emptied myself into the present, time stands still: I am held "In Limbo." Held in limbo in the present, I fall into the world—"I spiral down." Is the narrator of "In Limbo" not right to warn me, "You're living in a fantasy world"?

Nice Dream

Let's own up to something: we live in our fantasies because they are more pleasant than the hostile world of reality. What catches my attention in "Karma Police" is the line that immediately fol-lows the first round of "For a minute there / I lost myself, I lost myself." It appears in the liner notes (significantly) as: "(Phew) for a minute there / I lost myself, I lost myself." It signals a sense of relief, as if the burden, the *responsibility* of "choosing" oneself, has been suspended. Heidegger describes a related tranquility: "Through the self-certainty and decidedness of the 'they'," we are encouraged to believe "that there is no need of authentic under-standing or the state-of-mind that goes with it. The supposition of the 'they' that one is leading and sustaining a full and genuine [read "Fitter Happier"] 'life' brings [us] a *tranquility*, for which everything is 'in the best of order'" ("Everything in its right place," as it were). Falling into the world, which Heidegger calls a "tempta-tion," "is at the same time *tranquilizing*" (p. 222).

But if inauthentic falling into the world is "tranquilizing," we should by no means assume that it is idle. Heidegger continues:

> However, this tranquility in inauthentic Being does not seduce one into stagnation and inactivity, but drives one into uninhib-ited 'hustle'. Being-fallen into the 'world' does not now some-how come to rest. The tempting tranquilization *aggravates* the falling. . . . When [the inauthentic subject], tranquilized . . . thus compares itself with everything, it drifts along towards an alien-ation in which its ownmost potentiality-for-Being is hidden from it. Falling Being-in-the-world is not only tempting and tranquilizing; it is at the same time *alienating*.

Getting "lost in the moment" is not simply to drift quietly in the stillness of yogic repose. The times in which we are the *most* "lost in the moment" tend to be the very *busiest* of times: commut-ing during rush hour; rushing to meet a deadline at work; running errands over our lunch break. At our busiest, we "fall into the world," giving ourselves over to this "uninhibited 'hustle'." "Ripcord" really puts it best:

> Aeroplane do I mean what I mean?
> Oh it's inevitable, inevitable, oh aeroplane.
> A thousand miles an hour
> On politics and power
> That she don't understand
> No ripcord, no ripcord,
> No ripcord, no ripcord.

The "relief" that comes with "losing ourselves" is at the same time the emptying out of ourselves, the giving-over of ourselves to the demands of an impersonal society. And in shirking our responsibility to "choose" and "win" ourselves, we become alienated from that very world in which we are lost. Heidegger calls this movement the "downward plunge" (p. 223) and makes the central metaphor of "Ripcord"—falling out of an airplane without a parachute—no mere coincidence. It recurs frequently in Radiohead's work; "The Tourist" gives expression to the same idea when the narrator says, "They ask me where the hell I'm going/At a thousand feet per second/hey man, slow down, slow down." That feeling of falling, of flying by, *is* the feeling of alienation; stuck in the limbo of the present, the world is nonetheless moving too quickly, and we cannot keep up.

They Fed Us on Little White Lies

Having analyzed the phenomenon of alienation, however, we've run headlong into a rather nasty bind. Alienation arises from our absorption into the world; this absorption, meanwhile, is a symptom of inauthenticity, of giving ourselves over to the role society provides us. This inauthenticity has two (mutually reinforcing) consequences: first, as "tranquilizing," inauthenticity carries with it the delusion that authenticity is unnecessary. In other words, inauthenticity carries with it the illusion that it is not the source of alienation. Second, to be inauthentic and absorbed in the world is to empty oneself; our alienated state thus also carries with it the feeling that we have no power to be otherwise, that "it's inevitable, inevitable, it's a soul destroyed." Part of being alienated, we might say, is an inability to determine exactly what's wrong; the other part is the impression that we couldn't change things, even if we did know. "Dear sir, I have a complaint/can't remember what it is/doesn't matter anyway" ("Stop Whispering").

Placing Radiohead's early work back into the context of the early 1990s "loser/slacker zeitgeist," we can perhaps see where so much of the *angst* comes from. The pent-up frustration of grunge seems the most natural of reactions to an experience of alienation, the certainty that something is wrong coupled with the equal certainty that it cannot be changed. And at its worst, grunge had a tendency to slide toward nihilism (either the active nihilism of suicide, which ended authentic grunge in April of 1994, or the passive nihilism of "if you can't beat 'em, join 'em," which saw grunge slide into mainstream pop after about 1991, under the unintentionally ironic banner of "alternative music"). But Radiohead has never been a nihilistic band. In addition to the problem of alienation, Radiohead offers us a solution. Or, I should say, *two* solutions, an early solution on *Pablo Honey*, and then a rethinking of this solution that moves from *OK Computer* into *Kid A*.

Back to Save the Universe

Radiohead's first solution to the problem of alienation is a romantic solution, and one that reveals their debt to the punk scene of the late 1970s. It's stated most clearly in the refrain to "Anyone Can Play Guitar," perhaps the only truly optimistic song on the entire album:

> And if the world does turn and if London burns,
> I'll be standing on the beach with my guitar.
> I want to be in a band when I get to heaven,
> Anyone can play guitar and they won't be a nothing anymore.

The first line picks up on the apocalyptic imagery that runs through the album: destruction, inevitable doom, "You and me and everything caught in the fire / I can see me drowning, caught in the fire," as the opening track, "You," puts it. Fire, decay, and Armageddon flag world-alienation here—*complete* world alienation. The first line of the chorus sees this as a possibility: *if* the world does turn, and *if* London burns, that is to say, if we should prove able to hit rock-bottom, and experience complete and total alienation.

But why hit bottom? This sounds like nihilism, except that the second line offers us a promise: should alienation reach its completion, things will not in fact end. Instead, the narrator vows, "I'll be standing on the beach with my guitar." On the other side of complete devastation is a heaven where the narrator declares his/her intention to "be in a band." What's going on here? In Heidegger's lecture series, *The Fundamental Concepts of Metaphysics:*

World, Finitude, Solitude (Bloomington: Indiana University Press, 1995), he asks:

> Why do we find no meaning for ourselves, i.e., no essential pos-
> sibility of being? Is it because an *indifference* yawns at us out of
> all things, an indifference whose grounds we do not know? Yet
> who can speak in such a way when world trade, technology, and
> the economy seize hold of man and keep him moving? And
> nevertheless *we* seek a *role for ourselves*. "What is happening
> here?" we ask anew. Must we first make ourselves interesting to
> ourselves again? Why *must* we do this? Perhaps because we our-
> selves have become *bored* with ourselves? . . . Yet how are we to
> find ourselves . . . in such a way that we are thereby *given back* to
> ourselves, that is, given back to *ourselves*, so that we are *given over*
> to ourselves, given over to the task of becoming who we are?
> . . . Will we find ourselves via this indication of that *profound
> boredom*, which perhaps none of us knows at first? Is this ques-
> tionable profound boredom actually supposed to be the *sought-
> after fundamental attunement* that must be *awakened*? (p. 77)

Part of being inauthentic, again, is not really *understanding* that you're inauthentic. But by "hitting bottom," so to speak, we dive into the abyss; by turning to face the problem head-on, we finally come to see our own inauthenticity. Heidegger here calls this expe-rience "profound boredom" (in *Being and Time*, he will talk about the same turning-point in terms of "anxiety"), by which he means something like Radiohead's "emptiest of feelings"—not merely "empty," but something worse and more profound. The turning point happens at the empti*est* of feelings.

And then what? Heidegger says that, face-to-face with our own inauthenticity, we might finally *take back* ourselves. "We may not, therefore, flee from ourselves in some convoluted idle talk about culture, nor pursue ourselves in a psychology motivated by curiosity. Rather we must find ourselves by binding ourselves to our being-there and by letting such *being*-there become what is *sin-gularly* binding for us" (*Fundamental Concepts*, p. 77). By finally fac-ing up to our own alienation, then, we might finally stop looking to the world 'outside' of ourselves for meaning and instead take up the responsibility of *creating* that meaning *for* ourselves. We "bind" ourselves "to" ourselves, and *create* ourselves, almost like a work of art: we create a "role" for ourselves, something like the part played by the guitarist in a rock and roll band.

Think of the famous diagram from the punk 'zine *Sniffin' Glue* (or was it *Sideburns?*) with three guitar chords and the captions: "This is a chord; This is another; This is a third; Now form a band." Inauthentic life assures us that music can only come from musicians. Everybody plays their special role. "Everything in its right place." In the face of this, punks, Radiohead, and all the dis-alienated insist: *anyone* can play guitar, *anyone* can take control of their own lives, *anyone* can be the star. Stop worshipping false (American) Idols, and start your own band. "Stop whispering; start shouting."

Starting and then Stopping

And it might really be that simple to overcome alienation, were it not for "the alienating *effects* of *modern living*" as Paul Cantin's review of *OK Computer* put it. In both the early Heidegger and the early Radiohead, we find a proposed solution to alienation that hides a simplifying assumption: authenticity and inauthenticity are equally possible for us—it's simply a matter of choosing or not choosing ourselves, winning or losing ourselves. But in the pursuit of authenticity, seeking "bottom" and its turning-point, both Heidegger and Radiohead look more closely at the *roots* of inau-thenticity and make some rather startling conclusions.

Read against the picture of alienation in *Pablo Honey*, "Planet Telex"—the opening track of *The Bends*—becomes a sliver of nag-ging doubt: "You can force it but it will not come." It is as if, two years on from *Pablo Honey*, we're still waiting for the return to authenticity to happen, and we've started to wonder: what's gone wrong? "Everyone is, everything is broken / Why can't you for-get?"

The song's title is a clue: "Planet Telex" was in fact originally called "Planet Xerox." This image of an entire world filled with artificially reproduced items and copies seems to be more than just a metaphor for inauthenticity and its consumer-society trappings. Where *Pablo Honey* was filled with natural images (the sun, the moon, the stars, and—oh yes—fire, lots of fire), *The Bends* creates a aural world where nature is slowly pushed out by the creeping tide of technology, a tide that will become a flood by the crisis point of *OK Computer*. While *Pablo Honey* has a few technological metaphors for alienation (the buildings of "Stop Whispering," the airplane in "Ripcord," and the gun and cathode ray of "Prove Yourself"), most of the metaphors take the form of illnesses and human failings.

The paradigm of this metaphoric trend is "Lurgee," a wonderfully layered British slang word. Lurgee can be a vague, unspecified (and even sometimes imaginary) disease—one might complain of having "the dreaded lurgee" when either sick with a generic flu bug or when calling in sick from work. But British children will also use the word lurgee the way Americans use the term "cooties"; in other words, it will mark a person as "unclean" and, hence, *alienated* from the group. In Northern Britain "fever-lurgee" is slang for lazy or idle—in other words, *passive, inactive*. These biological metaphors are used to build a picture of the fundamentally individualistic, *human* condition of alienation in *Pablo Honey*. But the power chords opening up "The Bends" jettison these human, biological and psychological metaphors and replace them with technology. On its own, the song contains more technological imagery than all twelve tracks of *Pablo Honey* put together.[1] Two tracks later, "Fake Plastic Trees" offers a new standard for thinking about the problem of alienation: It's not simply that we can't act in a world we find hostile, but rather that all action is meaningless (and "wears me out") in a world that is *itself* inauthentic.

Why does the problem need to be rethought in terms of technology? Because of our plan to deliberately retake "possession" of ourselves. As Heidegger points out in his 1946 essay, "Why Poets?" animals can act "in" the world, but humans act "on" it. An animal (or even a plant) interacts within a world, but does not really transform its environment. Yet when someone takes a "properly human" action, he or she transforms raw, given nature *into* a meaningful world. To create ourselves as meaningful, authentic

---

1 Okay, thirteen if you're American and thus have both versions of "Creep" on your disc. But notice that whether you're "fucking special" or just "very special," the alienation expressed here is still strictly psychological, and thus confined to the individual and his or her experience.

individuals, we must take "possession" of our entire world; in other words, we must act "technologically." Heidegger writes:

> Accordingly, human willing can also be in the mode of self-assertion only by forcing everything into its realm in advance, even before it surveys anything. For this will, everything, already in advance and therefore in the consequence, is relentlessly turned into the material of self-asserting production. Earth and its atmosphere are turned into raw material. Man becomes a human material that is applied to goals that have been set out before him. The absolute self-assertion of the deliberate production of the world is unconditionally established as the condition of human command; this is a process that comes out of the hidden essence of technology. ("Why Poets," pp. 216–17)

In order for the voluntary, romantic action proposed in *Pablo Honey* to be possible as a solution to alienation, we must identify ourselves with our *will*, acting upon both nature *and ourselves* as "raw material."

This Machine Will Not Communicate

Both Radiohead and Heidegger relate this way of looking at things to technology; but this does not mean that we should demonize technology itself. On *The Bends*, the metaphors for alienation are unequivocally technological, yet we are clearly reminded that technology is what supports, sometimes even *makes human life possible*: the iron lung ("my life support," the narrator calls it), the "Prozac painkillers." *OK Computer* will do an even better job of thinking about both sides of the issue, opening with the "Airbag" that "saved my life."

So what then is the problem with technology? It has to do with the "hidden essence of technology" Heidegger speaks of. In "The Question Concerning Technology," Heidegger takes us looking for this "hidden essence of technology" and says that we are accustomed to thinking about technology as a human contrivance, an instrument that serves as a means to an end (p. 312). In this sense, technology is something we *use* for some *further purpose*; "Everything depends on our manipulating technology in the proper manner as a means. We will, as we say, 'get' technology 'intelligently in hand'. We will master it. The will to mastery becomes all the more urgent the more technology threatens to slip from human control" (p. 313).

The problem is this slippery slope: though we begin by using technology, we must quickly shift our focus toward controlling it. Or, to put it another way: humans, weak and fragile by nature, develop and adapt tools to help them get by. But these tools, in turn, make us dependent upon them, weaken us, require us to adapt to using them. (Think about the new afflictions that face our generation: "Nintendo thumb," email-induced carpal-tunnel syndrome, and the twin curses of the MTV generation, ADD and ADHD). Few of us are not dependent on some kind of "iron lung" or another. "I'm not paranoid; I'm an android."

As long as we think about technology as a means to an end, we never see the *real* problem. Thinking like this always leads us to believe that we are not trying hard enough, that we need to develop a better strategy to control technology, and so on. (Think about nuclear nonproliferation treaties; bio-ethics panels; modern-day morality plays like *Terminator* and *The Matrix*.) We need to look deeper, Heidegger says, at the real essence of modern technology: the very *framework* or world-view that makes developing technology *possible* in the first place. He calls this deeper essence of technology "*Ge-stell*," a German word that roughly translates as "framework" or "skeleton" (to understand technology, "you've got to feel it in your bones," we might say). Modern technology is set apart by the framework through which we see all of nature as a "standing reserve"; instead of simply "working on the earth," the way more primitive societies did, for us technology comes first: the earth simply exists as a storehouse of resources. "The earth now reveals itself as a coal mining district, the soil as a mineral deposit. . . . Agriculture is not the mechanized food industry. Air is now set upon to yield nitrogen, the earth to yield ore, ore to yield uranium . . . uranium is set upon to yield atomic energy, which can be unleashed either for destructive or for peaceful purposes" (p. 320). But it doesn't even stop there: for Heidegger (as, I think, for Radiohead—"we are the dollars and cents/and the pounds and the pence," as one track on *Amnesiac* has it), such modern notions as "human resources" are more than ominous metaphors, they are a sign about the fundamental way we experience the world.

This Is the Panic Office

The danger is that this way of seeing things blots out any other ways of experiencing the world; the river is never just a river again. It's either a reserve of hydroelectric power, or a reserve for tourist attraction—or, like the Hoover Dam, it's both. Seeing the world through the framework of means/ends calculation and as a repository of resources to be exploited *only* allows for "technological" solutions (again, the very idea that technology might be a means that we could put to a better end is a *technological solution to the problem of technology*).

At the same time, this framework of technology has *produced* the modern form of alienation. Inauthenticity thus takes on an even *more* illusory character: for even if we can *see* the problem of inauthenticity—which was the *entirety* of our problem as recently as "The Bends," a past which already seems blissfully naïve ("I wish it was the 60s / I wish we could be happy . . .")—the framework of technology now ensures that we can only come up with technological (and, hence, *further* alienating) solutions to the problem (as if "her green plastic watering can" could make her "fake plastic tree" any less fake). We have gone from "anyone can play guitar" to "this is our new song / just like the last one / a total waste of time." By *OK Computer*, Radiohead will be warning us that "ambition makes you look pretty ugly."

Again, we can't simply discard technology completely to try and solve the problem, as it is also what's keeping us alive (all of those iron lungs and airbags . . .). "The genie" has been "let out of the bottle," as "The Gloaming" puts it. "2 + 2 = 5" is more direct: "It's the devil's way now/there is no way out." We can't live with it, and we can't live without it; so how is this problem to be solved? I might remind you that I really do believe what I said before: Radiohead has never been a nihilistic band. And in the face of the renewed problem of alienation, I'd like to point out that the very last line on *The Bends* is, "Immerse your soul in love." But how?

I Feel My Luck Could Change

Modern life takes place in a world ruled by technology (in both the every-day and essential senses); these are dark times, indeed. But when Heidegger asks the question, "Why Poets?" he is taking up a question asked by the German poet Hölderlin: "And why poets in a desolate time?" Even in a world where technology holds sway, there is yet another way of looking at things: "poetically." It's the poets who are still capable of showing us the truth.

Technology acts to further obscure the roots of alienation, but those roots remain, in one sense at least, intact: alienation is still a symptom of inauthenticity, the handing ourselves over to an impersonal system, and a simultaneous inability to see that this is what we are doing. The first step toward disalienation, then, still must be a recognition of our true alienation. We still have to see— and then really understand—the problem before we can even think of solving it. If we are to ever attempt a non-technological solution to the problem of technology, we must stop trying to master it long enough to look around and really understand our-selves and our human condition within the modern world. This is the role Heidegger sees for "poets" (and the role Lester Bangs and I see for authentic rock'n'roll bands—the true poets of the mod-ern age).

The true poet's job is not to *solve* the problem of alienation, but to experience it *in its fullness* and help *us* experience that alien-ation in its fullness. "Those who risk more experience defenseless-ness in unwholeness," Heidegger says; "Those who risk more, as singers of what is whole, are 'poets in a desolate time'" ("Why Poets?" p. 240). If our alienation is characterized by the ignorance of our own true alienation, poets set themselves the task of open-ing our eyes, that we might all experience our alienation together. To do this they must truly experience the "defenselessness" of our existence in the void; they must truly experience the "unwhole-ness" of the human condition; and they must "sing" this whole of the human condition back to us, that we might experience it as well.

If You Think that You're Strong Enough . . .

In a typically sarcastic passage, Bangs writes:

> Shit. Who needs songs like that, that give off such bad vibes? We got a groovy, beautifully insular hip community, maybe a nation, budding here, and our art is a celebration of ourselves as liberated individuals and masses of such—the People, dig? And antisocial art simply don't fit in, brothers and sisters. Who wants to be depressed, anyway? (*Psychotic Reactions*, p. 32)

Bangs is defending the "antisocial art" of The Stooges. But the spirit of his defense applies just as well to Radiohead. The demand that all art be uplifting and celebrate the human spirit is only the demand that art lie to us, help us pretend that we are not alienated. Instead, what we need are the poets who can help us experience our alienation *as* alienation, so that we might begin to really own up to and understand the problem.

To avoid falling back into technological attempts to solve the problem, however, the poet needs to limit him or herself to a genuine experience and understanding of alienation. True art must be limited to staring into the abyss (at least, "standing on the edge") in order to better understand it. Radiohead has moved in this direction with each successive album following *Pablo Honey*; *OK Computer* already shows a more complete understanding of the technological character of modernity than its predecessor *The Bends*, which is why it's so often (and rightly) referred to as a masterpiece of alienation. But *OK Computer* still carries the prescriptive, action-oriented content of Radiohead's early punk-roots. The central message of the album crops up again and again: "Stop the noise," "slow down," the album still holds out the hope that if the poet can "show them the stars and the meaning of life," that "they'd shut me away / but I'd be alright." Aliens step in to take the place of destiny (or Jim Morrison), but there's still hope that some outside power might swoop in and save us before it's too late.

Heidegger's retort is simple: "The turning of an age does not occur at just any time by the eruption of a new God or by the new eruption of an old God from an ambush. Where is he supposed to turn to, upon his return, if men have not already prepared for him his residence?" ("Why Poets?" p. 201). They're not going to "sweep down in a country lane," in other words, and "show me the world as I'd love to see it." Not, that is, until we can turn and welcome them: "The gods who 'were once here' 'return' only 'at the proper time'—namely, when there is a turn among men in the right place in the right way" ("Why Poets?" p. 201).

Kid A, then, marks a break with the previous albums, as Radiohead steps up to fill their role as our modern poets. And while the album is still decidedly Radiohead, all the same I can't escape the feeling that everything is new. The missing lyrics sheet, Thom explained to *NY Rock* in December of 2000, is because there's "no point in taking the lyrics alone, apart from the music. That's one of the reasons why we won't have a lyric sheet with the album. You just can't separate it." The album presents not a *picture* of alienation, but *the experience of it*. The band's much-discussed move into "electronica" territory brings the listener inside the alienation of modernity, shot through with technology. And a new theme emerges: disappearance. Staring the danger right in the face, the poet now "risks more," facing the possibility of disappearing completely. (But isn't this also the point? After all, as Yorke says on his solo album, "The more you try to erase me / The more that I appear.") All of this is risked, though, to allow us to really understand what it means to be inauthentic and alienated; from the technological ordering of "Everything in its Right Place," to the dumb isolation of "Idioteque," we can stare into the abyss and find it staring back. Critics who complained that the album lacked "soul," "warmth," or "humanity" cut right to the heart of the matter while missing the point completely.

So if we ask, "What is Radiohead's music about?" the answer "alienation" is correct, as far as it goes. Still, it seems inadequate on a more fundamental level. Radiohead's music is not "about" alienation; it *is* alienation. But rather than it being nihilistic, their music offers us the only real hope we have: as Heidegger tells us, paraphrasing Hölderlin, "The closer we come to the danger, the more brightly do the ways into the saving power begin to shine and the more questioning we become. For questioning is the piety of thought."

18.

The Signature of Time in "Pyramid Song"

Michael Thompson

After hearing "Pyramid Song" from *Amnesiac*, most people say, "Something's not quite right with that song." Still, the song is entrancing. It could be Thom Yorke's lilting howl, an oddly soothing wail, that draws us in. Or it could be the haunting lyrics that float over the piano—"a room full of stars and astral cars"—that sets imaginations wandering. These lyrics describe jumping into rivers, swimming with black-eyed angels, and going to heaven in a little row-boat to find all of your lovers—a story that has inspired much speculation about the real meanings and references in play. (Among others, the most popular contrivances include linking the lyrics to Dante's inferno and the Greek river Styx, Tom Waits' "Clap Hands" and themes of suicide.) Yet neither the vocals nor Yorke's delivery seems to account for the arresting qualities of "Pyramid Song." It is, rather, the mood of the song that seems to grab and keep your attention. And that mood has everything to do with the song's rhythm.

The rhythm of the song seems skewed. As it plays, you might ask, "why does it sound like the notes are played a split-second too late?" It's because the song has a complex time signature that leads to rhythms that are out of joint with those of our ordinary experience. This is what is so compelling about "Pyramid Song." Its timing, rhythm, and beat are literally out of sync with the way we ordinarily experience the world.

Rhythm and Time Signatures

A debate rages, mostly in the blogosphere, about whether "Pyramid Song" has an odd time signature or whether the time signature changes through the course of the song. Amateur and professional musicians, pundits, and fans have weighed in. One view is that the timing is plain old 4/4, but with syncopated stress points. 4/4 time is the most common signature you find in music, with four quarter notes in a measure (the rhythmic grouping of the song). This is the strong, regular beat of the Christmas favorite "Jingle Bells." Normally, each of the sounds that make up the rhythm of singing ji / ngle / bells/ (rest) / receives equal emphasis. But you could syncopate "Jingle Bells" by putting stress on one of the beats and singing, for example, ji / NGLE / bells / (rest) /. This creates an unexpected rhythm. Bloggers who favor this theory about "Pyramid Song" argue that Radiohead does not fully deviate from popular music timing formulas, but, simply creates a disturbing impression by stressing beats we are not accustomed to hearing stressed.

But many disagree. People with classical musical backgrounds typically approach "Pyramid Song" like conspiracy theorists. The complicated formulas they concoct seem almost as other-wordly as the song itself. One theory holds that the song's timing is 8/8 (eight eighth notes per measure) but with a grouping of notes into pairs and trios. The first three notes are heard as if they belong to a group of three that are followed by a second group and then, finally, two notes that end the sequence and tie all the notes together. Another elaborate theory argues that the song can be broken down into clusters of sixteen eighth-notes, 16/8, with the notes arranged in 3 / 3 / 4 / 3 / 3 groupings. Both theories have some merit, depending on how you group and arrange the sounds yourself. Do you hear things in small clusters or can you hear larger groups of sounds and their inter-relations?

Perhaps the oddest theory you can find is one that argues that the timing itself alters periodically throughout the song. This theory claims the signature varies from a 5/4 time signature to a 4/4 followed by another 4/4 grouping and ends with 3/4. In the first grouping you find five quarter-notes arranged together, then two groups of four quarter-notes establishing a rhythm and then a shift to three quarter-notes.

Unfortunately, Radiohead has been either unwilling or unable to settle the debate. In an interview, Yorke stated that the song has no definite time signature, that it is simply *felt* as the song is played. This makes sense of the effects the song has and suggests that different listeners may in fact hear the song differently—that the debate about time signature rests on the subjectivity of perception Yorke points to. If you tend to see life as a sequence of small clusters of events with strange emphases, a simpler time signature is what you will recognize in the song. If you see life as a larger sequence with regular patterns and rhythms, you will hear a more complicated time signature. If you see life as a constantly shifting series of events, some smaller, some larger, and recognize the cyclicality of these events, you will hear shifting time signatures.

How Radiohead uses time and rhythm in "Pyramid Song" raises questions about how time affects our experiences and perceptions and points us toward the relationships between the rhythms of our lives and the events and interconnections within them. Radiohead may be unwilling to settle the question, but it seems unlikely that they are unaware of the history and precedence it has. Purposefully manipulating the timing and rhythm of a musical score to make listeners confront and become aware of time is a technique found in the music of Frédéric Chopin.

Time Signature and Mood in Chopin

Born in 1810 and living until 1849, Chopin lived and worked in the middle of nineteenth-century romanticism. Other great composers of this movement include Ludwig Beethoven, Richard Wagner and Franz Schubert. Like theirs, Chopin's music celebrates the creative capacity of the human spirit while recognizing how short life can be. Nineteenth-century Europe was wracked by wars, political instability, widespread disease and economic upheaval. Romantic authors and composers therefore celebrated the achievements we are capable of during such short and fragile lives. For Chopin it is the subtlety and poetry of his piano music that captures this spirit and sets him apart from his contemporaries.

Chopin achieved distinction for his virtuosity, but it was mostly his nocturnes that secured his fame. Nocturnes were a new musical genre that are inspired by the night—the time when things slow down and we can reflect upon the activities of the day and the shortness of life. Chopin's sound is melancholy and nostalgic, at least partly because Chopin himself was prone to such moods. Exiled from his homeland, Poland, by fortune and war, he moved to Paris to continue his musical education and establish his career as a composer and performer. Lest he forget his homeland, Chopin collected a small silver cup of his native soil and carried it with him for the rest of his life. During his journey to Paris, that soil became bloody as Poland erupted in civil war and, in what was to become known as the November Uprising of 1830–1831, Polish nationalists revolted against the Russian-backed government. They were defeated, however, and Chopin never went back to his homeland.

Chopin's use of various time signatures and signature changes reflects his melancholy and nostalgia for his beloved homeland, their other-worldly tone evoking a far-off, forbidden place. The term nostalgia is comprised of two Greek works, *nostos*, for returning home, and *algos*, for pain. Literally, it refers to the feeling of pain we get when we think of home or the longing for a return to our home. Often, we find ourselves nostalgic for a time past or event long ago; we wish to return to more youthful days of spring or when times were better. If we give in to the pain of our longing for places or times not present, our mood can darken into melancholy. We become sad and lethargic, not wanting to see or do anything. We sit on our hands and remember times past and rue that we cannot return to better times. In works like Nocturne in G, op. 37, No. 2 we find Chopin at his most ethereal, painting idyllic auditory landscapes a child might imagine. In Nocturne in C minor, op. 48, No. 1, there is a note of despair. Chopin's contemporary Jan Kleczynski described it as "the tale of a still greater grief told in an agitated recitando" and calls it "The Contrition of a Sinner."

This comment takes us a step closer to the philosophical significance of these Nocturnes. For what is needed for confession or contrition is precisely some account of one's life as it has unfolded in time—a remembrance and phenomenological self-awareness. In order to understand his exile, Chopin had to remember and long for the home to which he could never return. His nocturnes seem to do just this.

Temporality

Crucial to this kind of self-awareness is an awareness of time itself. Chopin uses changes in time signature to this effect in his Nocturnes and so does Radiohead in "Pyramid Song." Both are drenched in feelings of nostalgia and a burgeoning awareness of our existence in time. By disturbing the regular rhythms we are accustomed to feeling in our everyday lives, these peculiar, other-worldly works demand that we sit up and take account of the experiences of our lives as embedded in time. This has been a major focus of philosophical phenomenology. Philosophers such as Husserl, Heidegger, Gadamer, Sartre, Merleau-Ponty and others have struggled to specify exactly how and in what ways time affects our lives and our understanding and experience of ourselves.

Against the conventional view that we simply live *through* time as disconnected observers (like an audience at a concert that will go on regardless of whether this or that audience member leaves or never shows up), most of these philosophers insist very differently that temporality is the very fabric or foundation of our experience that has made us who we are. Heidegger's student Hans-Georg Gadamer, for example, introduced the concept of "historically affected consciousness" to capture the way that our awareness is determined by our specific pasts. "I want to say," Gadamer wrote in his classic *Truth and Method*, "that our consciousness is really historically determined, that is . . . determined by real events rather than left on its own to float free over the past." But this doesn't mean our consciousness is fully controlled by events or epochs (such as those dividing Chopin's exile from his earlier life in Poland), because we can develop an understanding of this "historically effected consciousness" itself and become conscious of the way time works on our understanding: "On the other hand, I want to say that it is important to produce within ourselves a consciousness of this operativeness" (*Truth and Method*, 1972, p. 238)

Heidegger placed less emphasis on history and more on the phenomenological significance of the human body. All our experience, while particular and unique among individuals, possesses certain structural necessities arising from the fact that we are embodied. Having a body or, better, being a body is one fundamental fact that we cannot escape in this human existence. Having a body itself has several ramifications. We experience things through our body—even ideas are experienced in reference to the understanding we all have of our unique selves as possessing this particular body. For example, we imagine ourselves trying to accomplish something for the first time, say playing a musical instrument. We imagine our clumsy, untrained hands fumbling for the keys or strings. It is not some ideal body we imagine, but our own unique body with all its incapacities and abilities.

By combining the structural necessities of our body with the passage of time, Heidegger as well as Maurice Merleau-Ponty emphasize the rhythmic qualities of daily life. Every morning we rise from slumber and begin going through the paces of our day. These days have a regular rhythm marked by things like rising and brewing coffee, walking dogs, taking showers, preparing for work, packing a suitcase, finishing homework, greeting our families, and downloading *In Rainbows*. The redundancy and regularity of these activities establishes a rhythm and unity that we guide our lives by. Merleau-Pointy points out, in his major work *The Phenomenology of Perception*, that the body is "a nexus of living meaning" and that our habits "enable us to understand the general synthesis of our own body" (*Phenomenology of Perception*, 1962, p. 175). The redundancy of our habits and the rhythm of our embodied lives are found in the interconnections of our bodily activities and these provide us with a sense of unity to our lives.

One danger that both these philosophers and musicians like Chopin and Radiohead speak to is the way that we can become insensitive to these rhythms and find each day similar to the next. Obviously, there are deviations and extraordinary events. But these are exceptions to the pulse of life in which we find ourselves. According to Heidegger, our ordinary lives are characterized as a slipping into everydayness. In everydayness days bleed into days, months into months, and years into years. No longer are our lives unified, but in the most superficial way of the seemingly endless succession of moments. The danger involved in everydayness is the tendency for us to overlook how our lives are shaped by both our past and our futures. Failing to recognize our historically affected consciousness, we slip into an automatic lifestyle, one in which we fail to recognize not only who we are, but also how we have come to be who we are.

Knives Out

But Radiohead and Chopin break with this mundane routine. By chopping and slicing time in their music, they break us away from ordinary existence and its ordinary rhythms. They violate our temporal expectations and routine and force an awareness of time. They compel us to ask ourselves how we arrived at this particular place in our lives. For Chopin, his musical career in Paris is always framed by the remembrance of his native Warsaw and the family he left behind. With "Pyramid Song," Radiohead forces us in two directions at once. Whether it's a mere emphasis or a changing time signature, the song's rhythmic qualities push us out of our normal awareness of time (one where we are barely even aware of its passing). At the same time (!), however, it invites us to a take a synoptic view of our entire life (or, at least, Thom Yorke's life) from beginning to end:

> I jumped in the river and what did I see?
> . . .
> All the figures I used to see
> All my lovers were there with me
> All my past and futures

The result is like one of Chopin's nostalgic reflections as well as a Heideggerian moment of clarity, a flash of insight by which one sees one's past, present, and future as an organic whole. It is an invitation to reconcile our current embodied lives with our past and the future they together will create, like a river whose parts are interconnected and moving together.

Taken seriously as a philosophical moment, the song can spark a lasting insight. To realize that our present is informed and shaped by our past is to realize a historically affected consciousness, to no longer trudge through our days without realizing these operative interconnections. As we see how the past informs our present, we also realize that our past and present are constantly shaping our future and that our plans for the future shape our present. Who we are, what we do, how we experience life is not merely a consequence of what has come before, but also of what is to come in light of our plans—themselves conditioned, and made possible (or impossible) by our pasts.

The rhythmic oddness of "Pyramid Song" is then an opportunity to become aware of temporality itself. By breaking from the regular rhythms we expect to hear in popular music, Radiohead nudges us to adopt phenomenological perspectives on time—something one must do with caution. Remembrance and recognition of our lives in the past can be painful, as it seems to be for Chopin. For others it can lead to a difficult realization about death and finitude. But Radiohead seems to offer a twist on this, as well. Perhaps echoing Talking Head's "Heaven" ("a place where nothing, nothing ever happens") on *Fear of Music,* Yorke offers a consolation for those who realize that a heaven apart from life itself may be nothing more than a fantasy island you can reach "in a little row boat."

If so, this invites a more obvious comparison of "Pyramid Song" to Talking Head's "Once in a Lifetime," David Byrne and Brian Eno's study of sudden insights about the temporality of life: "And you may ask yourself, how do I work this? / . . . how did I get here? / . . . my God, what have I done?" Both Byrne and Yorke depict time as flowing water that sustains life silently and without drawing attention to itself (Byrne's time flows "underground"). Unlike Radiohead's, however, Talking Heads' song remains locked in a steady 4/4 rhythm and therefore does not use the temporality of their song to point directly at time and temporality itself.

If you can jump in the river of time and see your life in its historical embeddedness, there is nothing more outside of it:

> And we all went to heaven in a little row boat
> There was nothing to fear and nothing to doubt

With past, present and future united, there is no pain from the past and no fear of an uncertain future. We do not need to hide from or lament our past lives. Becoming aware of who we are now in relief of the past and anticipations for the future may be dangerous, but it can also be liberating.

19.

Fitter Happier Rolling a Large Rock Up a Hill

LINDSEY FIORELLI

When I first heard *OK Computer*, I was (of course) working at my computer. It was 2005 and I'd heard it over and over: "Radiohead is the best band in the world." So I decided to give this band a chance, starting at the beginning of their discography. *Pablo Honey* didn't sound too different from other alternative rock of the early 1990s. But *The Bends* impressed me more, partly because of "High and Dry" and "Fake Plastic Trees," and partly because I could hear a different band emerging. Some of their harder songs were giving way to more subtle, acoustic melodies, and I could hear Yorke's voice more clearly.

I expected their third album to move in the same direction, perhaps a little farther. But, something—a couple things—happened. With most great albums, I stick to my favorites, that handful of songs that makes them great. But with *OK Computer* I couldn't find any favorites. I loved them all. Day after day I played it, let go of my other favorite bands, and let Radiohead take center stage. When my friends asked what was going on, the only reply I had was: "You just have to listen to them. I can't explain it." And I couldn't even explain it to myself.

Up Above, Alienation Hovers

Now that *OK Computer* has dominated a good part of my listening life, I have a better idea of why and how it captivated me. It seemed, first of all, that each track had something different—and important—it wanted me to hear. At the same time, these messages seemed to belong together, to make sense together. What I found as I investigated further was a striking link to Albert Camus's *The Myth of Sisyphus*. For Camus, the world is meaningless and isolating, a view that also seems to be replicated in *OK Computer*. But what is the connection in play here? What exactly do Radiohead and Camus find so alienating, and how does each respond to it?

Back to *Pablo Honey* and *The Bends*: Here, Radiohead takes on isolation head on: "I'm a creep; I'm a weirdo; what the hell am I doing here?" "Black Star" talks of the alienation that comes with separating from a lover. "My Iron Lung" and "Fake Plastic Trees" look at the artificiality of life and relationships. In *OK Computer*, however, Yorke wasn't writing about separation from other people—he's separating from the world itself. Take "Subterranean Homesick Alien," in which he sings about a stifling town where "you can't smell a thing"—a town that threatens to fall apart, as people who "lock up their spirits" watch the ground for emerging cracks. Instead, Yorke looks up, to the sky, longing for a spaceship to take him onboard so that he can search for the "meaning of life," a meaning that he cannot find in the world he inhabits.

What has sucked meaning from the world of *OK Computer* is technology. The world has become as monotonous as it is structured, as empty as it is electronic. Dominated by the Internet and electronic communication, industry and modern transportation, the world has no place for human spirit. And this is what Yorke screams out in various tracks—how technology alienates us from ourselves.

"Fitter Happier," perhaps more than any other track, makes this conclusion inescapable. It isn't Yorke's voice we hear. It's robotic and lists all the ways in which this unhuman being will better his life and find ways to fit in with humans. He'll get along with his employees; he'll get more sleep; he'll get rid of his paranoia (maybe). He'll belong. But, to belong, he must become a pig "in a cage on antibiotics." To be human, the track seems to say, you must be inhuman, technological, artificial, or android. Otherwise, all this universe offers is isolation and emptiness.

Yet becoming a part of the technological world, becoming a paranoid android, doesn't seem attractive. No one wants to be trapped like a pig on antibiotics. So, Radiohead seem to say, we should try to escape from the technology of this world. In "Let Down," for example, there's a world of "transport, motorways, and tramlines." This world is chaotic and noisy, unsettled, always in motion. But it offers only the "emptiest of feelings." Yorke sings of being "crushed like a bug," insignificant and broken. So, what does he wish to do? To escape. To grow wings. To fly away.

For Radiohead, technology isn't something admirable and impressive. It's estranging, debilitating and quite confusing—as "Paranoid Android" shows. The song, it seems, isn't meant to make sense. As a combination of three very different kinds of songs—the acoustic intro, the Cantata-like middle, and the hard-rock parts surrounding it—it seems to represent a psyche that is confused. The narrator has "chicken voices" in his head and wants to be King. Technology has made his world dirty and dangerous—filled with panic and vomit, "yuppies networking," and that wishful-thinking robot repeating "I may be paranoid but not an android." The singer is human, but the non-human voice says he isn't. He's so wrapped up in technology that he doesn't even know it. If you stay here, it seems to say, you'll become a part of the dust and screaming. You'll rely on airbags to save your life. And you'll become just as confused about your humanity.

Kid Absurdity

In several of his writings, but especially *The Myth of Sisyphus* and *The Stranger*, Albert Camus writes about what he calls "absurdity." Absurdity is the clash between our longing for the world to have meaning and an irrational world that offers none. Absurdity can grab us at any moment—when we're walking down the street, when we're talking to a friend, simply while we're going through our daily routines. There are different types or levels of absurdity in life as Camus sees it. There is the absurdity of our realization of death (How are our actions significant if we're all going to die?); there's the absurdity of realizing the absence of any objective goodness in the world; and there's the absurdity that comes when we realize the lack of clarity and unity in the world. But they all point to the fact that the world offers no meaning, and our search for it is futile. Now, what happens once we're confronted with the absurd? Strangeness overcomes us. We feel divorced from everyone and everything. We're trapped in a dark world we can no longer call home.

In *The Myth of Sisyphus*,[1] Camus tells the story of a mythical figure he calls the absurd hero. Because he betrayed the gods, Sisyphus is sent to the underworld and given the endless task of rolling a large rock up a hill only to have it roll back down each time. Having to perform this futile struggle, Sisyphus's life is a meaningless one. His effort is "measured by skyless space and time without depth," and his purpose, although always achieved, falls back down upon him (p. 121). As the rock rolls back down the hill, Sisyphus must brace himself to perform the same task that has now become his fate. His effort comes to nothing. His routine accomplishes nothing. His life is one of mechanical gesture and meaningless struggle. And this is the absurd life.

For Camus, Sisyphus's futile struggle is our own. Like him, we partake in mechanical lives, as we go through our routines "Monday Tuesday Wednesday Thursday Friday and Saturday according to the same rhythm" (pp. 12, 13). But a moment comes when the "'why' arises" (p. 13). And in this moment, we're confronted with the absurd. For, rather than finding our actions to be meaningful, we see how futile our efforts are. Everything is robotic, much like Sisyphus's task. We're caught in a mechanical world of routine, strangers to ourselves because we realize how devoid of meaning our lives are. All along, we'd thought that everything made sense. But we realize that none of it does. Our tasks are interminable and insignificant. And the world retains none of the meaning we'd searched for. With this realization, we feel estranged.

This notion of "man faced with the absurd" is even more apparent in Camus's *The Stranger*.[2] The novel's protagonist, Meursault, is indifferent to the events that befall him. Robotic and emotionless, Meursault's thoughts and actions are entirely irrational, a fact that makes him a "stranger" to society. It's the con-

1 Albert Camus, *The Myth of Sisyphus* (Vintage, 1991)

2 Albert Camus, *The Stranger* (Vintage, 1989)

frontation between his irrationality and his society's search for meaning that elucidates absurdity as Camus sees it. When Meursault kills a man without any reasoning behind it, his society is faced with an instance of the world's meaninglessness. No human action, as Meursault's deed shows, is rational. Unable to deal with this irrationality, Meursault's society calls the murder premeditated and claims that he doesn't have a soul—all attempts to make sense of what they cannot make sense of, all efforts to give the universe a meaning in the face of its irrationality.

As Meursault's deed shows, human action (for Camus) doesn't make sense. The world just is irrational. Our attempts to give the world meaning are futile, an idea that is further developed when Meursault himself becomes aware of absurdity. While in jail awaiting the guillotine, he realizes that death is the only certainty. Now conscious of this fact, Meursault becomes aware that "I had lived my life one way and I could just as well have lived it another . . . Nothing, nothing mattered" (p. 121). Because life only leads to a certain and unavoidable death, it makes no difference how it's lived. His actions, like all human action, have always been insignificant and the world indifferent.

Pull Me Out, or Leave Me In, the Aircrash

Camus's outlook has no special place (or blame) for technology. But, except for that, Camus's sense of the absurd and the strange is familiar terrain in Radiohead's music. They are both artists exploring exile and estrangement, the feeling that we don't belong in this irrational universe. But there's another crucial difference. For Camus, the only correct response to absurdity is to live with it. We must continue searching for meaning even though we know that this search is futile. But isn't this response cowardly? Aren't we just giving up if we don't try and get rid of this meaninglessness? No, for Camus, it's just the opposite. Living with an acceptance of our absurdity and the eternal meaninglessness of Sisyphus's endless task is, in fact, a brazen and brave revolt *against* absurdity. We're keeping the absurd alive and not attempting to escape from what we can't escape. Not to accept absurdity, according to Camus, would be to deny one of absurdity's terms (1. our search for meaning and 2. the irrationality of the world). We'd either have to give up our search for meaning, or find that the world does possess a meaning. Instead, we must live with the absurdity we've discovered.

But, *why* revolt? *Why* live with this meaninglessness? Because, for Camus, revolt brings happiness, or as he puts it—"happiness and the absurd are two sons of the same earth" (*Sisyphus*, p. 122). The responses Sisyphus and Meursault have to their absurdity point to this fact. When Sisyphus watches the rock roll back, he becomes aware of the absurdity that comes with his endless task. He recognizes that his act has no relevance, that this world is irrational. And what does he do? He walks with "heavy yet measured step toward the torment of which he will never know the end" (p. 121). He pushes the rock each time with all of his strength, trying to give his task a meaning even though he knows it has none. This embrace of absurdity makes Sisyphus content to roll the rock up the hill. Since he doesn't hope for a better life, he can accept his destiny without reservations, without horror. And he now becomes "master of his days" because he is choosing to undergo his struggle for what it is (p. 123). He accepts its meaninglessness and, in doing so, can be happy with his alienated existence. For, he knows that his life is what he makes of it.

Similarly, Meursault accepts absurdity and, through this acceptance, finds happiness within his alienation. Once he realizes the inevitability of death, Meursault sees how pointless hope is. Even if he escapes his execution, he'll eventually die anyways. Knowing this, Meursault can accept his fate and revolt. And "for the first time…I opened myself to the gentle indifference of the world . . . I felt that I had been happy and that I was happy again" (p. 123). Accepting the fact that he'll die whether he escapes his execution or not, Meursault can be content. He fully acknowledges his destiny, and can live out his remaining days for what they are.

Like Camus's two absurd characters, we must accept absurdity. For, "the absurd man, when he contemplates his torment, silences all the idols" (*Sisyphus*, p. 123). Our constant consciousness of our struggle is the very thing that makes it less horrifying. We don't compare our destiny to one more preferable. Instead, we continue our quest for meaning and live with the futility of this search. We persist in our mechanical lives, persist in our struggle to find the meaning to it all. And we can then embrace the world's irrationality, and live our lives without reservations. Refusing to hope for something better, refusing to escape, we know that (although it is irrational) life is what we make of it. Like Sisyphus and Meursault, we come to love our alienated existence.

This is where Camus departs from *OK Computer*. For—lyrically speaking—Radiohead often focus on the escape Camus denounces. Yorke wants to take flight; he wants to be taken away on a spaceship; he wants to grow wings. The meaninglessness this technological world has to offer is too much. He isn't ready to revolt by engaging this absurdity; he'd rather try to escape, or long for escaping, even though he knows it's impossible. There are no spaceships, really, and by the time "No Surprises" comes around he seems quite resigned to a quiet life that merely minimizes, but does not escape, any realizations or existential crises life may hold from here on out.

Phew, for a Minute There, I Lost Myself in Technology

OK Computer may begin in a similar, alienating place as Camus, but it ends elsewhere—or so I thought before I added another crucial element to the discussion. What about the music, the actual "sound" of Radiohead? Once we include such a discussion, things get more complicated and ambiguous. Yorke's words suggest a wish to leave behind the alienating and dangerous technological chaos. But, the sounds Radiohead adopt only pull him right back into it.

Especially compared to the less treated guitars and drums of the first two albums, these tracks are loud, electronic, technological, and strangely addictive. "Airbag" takes us into the technological world immediately. The sound is hard, frightening, and lacerated by drummer Phil Selway's brittle, electronically distorted drums. Even the songs that do have natural, acoustic foundations (the piano in "Karma Police" or the soothing guitars of "The Tourist") are saturated with technological treatments, interjections and interruptions. The original human voices recorded on Jonny Greenwood's mellotron, for instance, on "The Tourist" sound menacing and garbled, not unlike the voice in "Fitter Happier." The result is sometimes beautiful, too. "Climbing Up the Walls" is hypnotic and gorgeous (despite the screaming) and makes me want to listen to it again and again.

Technology is at home here, which is why Radiohead seem to move in two directions, existentially speaking. They hate the technological world. They feel separated from it, and yearn for escape. But, they've also become a part of it (or it's become a part of them). Their music is technological. And they weren't pulled into this involuntarily (by aliens, say, who demanded they start using computers and synthesizers). Yorke & Co. plainly *chose* these sounds. And they chose, for *OK Computer*, to embrace technology in a big way. So how can they want escape from technology while simultaneously becoming a part of it?

This puzzle is not only a problem for understanding *OK Computer*. This turn to technology also seems to put Radiohead more at odds with Camus. Why? Because Radiohead opted for a kind of an escape from alienation—they've eliminated it. They've found a way to belong by becoming a part of technology itself. Camus didn't want his absurd man to become a part of the world. He wanted him to notice, every moment of every day, that this wasn't a place for him, that there was no meaning here. Radiohead have turned away from isolation and toward connection, a decision which is just the sort Camus despised.

A Large Rock Saved My Life

It's pretty simple to resolve one issue we can see between Camus and Radiohead—they are each responding to the absurdity of the world in their own, different ways. But isn't Radiohead's response, on its own terms, still puzzling and contradictory? How can Radiohead want to escape from technology when they've chosen to be a part of it all the while? It's not as though they changed their mind, after all. The lyrical search for escape from technology and the musical embrace of it happen simultaneously—and they are presented to us together. So, we need to ask ourselves if this contradiction matters. At the end of the day, does it make sense for Radiohead to simultaneously want escape and immersion in the technological world?

Of course it does, and for at least two different reasons. One, if you really come to terms with the kind of world that both Camus and Radiohead see—not an *irrational* world as much as an a-rational world (the "gentle indifference of the world," as Camus's Mersault put it) then there really isn't a sensible response to alienation in the first place. We may seek a reason, a strategy, and underlying logic, but they remain ours. The world does not participate in our logic, our categories, ideas and arguments. It's neither against us nor for us.

On the other hand, Radiohead might be responding to the alienating world in much the way Camus did (though Camus probably wouldn't admit that this was what he was doing). Sure, it might seem contradictory for Radiohead to yearn for escape from the alienating world while choosing to be musically immersed in it, but there's nothing paradoxical about working within the technology (or instances of it) that alienates us from the world in an effort to overcome that very alienation. Camus wrote novels about an alienating world and overcame alienation by connecting with his readers. So, too, Radiohead use their music, their instruments and computers and synthesizers, to connect with their fellow band members and, by extension, us.

If Sisyphus's rock is our modern technology, Radiohead have shown us one way to respond—to carve it up, to make new and marvelous sounds with it. After them, there's no way that rolling it up the hill over and over will be as boring, or as alienating, as it was for Sisyphus.

Radiohead and the Postmodern. *(Not Here. Isn't Happening.)*

20.

"Kid A" as a Musing on the Postmodern Condition

BRADLEY KAYE

It's difficult to classify *Kid A*. Musically, it has everything from the hard rock anthems and free jazz of "National Anthem" to the poppy dance-techno on "Idioteque." There's even the sappy film-score melodrama of "Motion Picture Soundtrack." The album is a motley painting of many types of music, mixed and bended in playful and satirical ways, that cannot be boxed into any neat compartment.

However, despite all of the musical challenges it presented to its audience, the album won a Grammy in 2001 for Best Alternative Album of the Year. Traditionally, the "alternative" label has been used to categorize music that exists outside of the more established genres such as rock, pop, country, or jazz. Ever since the rise of grunge, this category has helped the music industry make sense of albums that defy standard musical clichés. So there's a certain irony in trying to label such a kaleidoscopic artistic creation like *Kid A* as "alternative" when its very existence, it seems, is an attempt to transcend all contemporaneous labels and move beyond the status quo. In essence, *Kid A* is Radiohead's answer to the astronomical worldwide success of *OK Computer*. It's an attempt to play, explore, experiment, and stretch the boundaries of mainstream music.

Kid A breaks rules in an artistically creative act of transgression that remains, at its core, ambiguous. Unlike other famous concept albums (such as Pink Floyd's *The Wall,* or *Animals*), there is no seemingly clear or definitive message that unwinds through the playing of *Kid A*. Instead, Radiohead deconstructs the very idea of a conceptually themed album in a way that connects directly to what French philosopher Jean-François Lyotard (1924–1998) calls our postmodern condition.

Lyotard says, "Postmodern (or pagan) would be the condition of the literatures and arts that have no assigned addressee and no regulating ideal, yet in which value is regularly measured on the stock of experimentation."[1] *Kid A* is precisely this—an album whose value lies in its experimentation. The band had no intention to play things commercially safe when they released it in 2000. Although a couple of tracks were released for radio play (mainly "Optimistic"), none stands out as a radio-ready pop single and none gained any lasting success on the pop charts. Reception for the album was initially mixed, as well. One reviewer said it was, "just awful,"[2] another said, "plain frustrating." Even Nigel Godrich, the album's producer, had his doubts. Thom Yorke recounted Nigel's first impression by saying, "He didn't understand why, if we had such a strength in one thing, we would want to do something else. But at the same time he trusted me to have an idea of what I wanted, even though he didn't understand what it was for ages." The fact that the album's producer had no idea why Radiohead wanted to create that particular album shows how challenging the band was becoming.

What Was That You Tried to Say?

According to Lyotard, the key postmodern concept of "the differend" refers to "the unstable state and instance of language wherein something that must be able to be put into phrases cannot yet be . . . What is at stake in a certain literature, in a philosophy, or perhaps even in a certain politics, is to bear witness to differends

---

1 Jean-François Lyotard, *The Postmodern Condition: A Report on Knowledge* (University of Minnesota Press, 1984), p. 16.

2 "I Think I'm Meant to be Dead," *Guardian* (22nd September, 2000).

by finding idioms for them"[3] *Kid A* begins by bearing witness to something like this by undercutting the idea of a stable language. In sharp contrast to the cataclysmic opening track on *OK Computer*, the otherwordly "Airbag," *Kid A* begins with the quiet, calm mood of "Everything in Its Right Place." For a few moments as the song takes shape, everything can be taken into account. All is perfectly situated within a pristine, predictable, knowable sonic order of things. Nothing outside of the ordinary has occurred yet. Then the tone of the song changes and it becomes slightly ominous. Yorke sings "Yesterday I woke up sucking a lemon," and then questions, "There are two colors in my head, what was that you tried to say?"

Something unpredictable, some event, has happened. The predictable order has broken down, leaving the singer with a sour taste in his mouth. The "two colors in my head" are a way of attempting to make sense of the unexpected event by resorting to binary oppositions. But there's no sense to be made, it seems, because Yorke cannot understand what it was "you tried to say." As the music swells, what was once a pleasant song about a perfect order of things becomes a kind of organized chaos while Yorke's vocals grow more and more desperate. The message that is being conveyed is not so easily put into words that once made sense, when everything was stable and predictable. Here we have our first encounter with the postmodern condition. When we slip into an unpredictable, inexplicable or uncanny situation, we find ourselves squarely within the postmodern condition. When this condition occurs, Lyotard continues from the earlier quotation, it's "measured by the stock of its experimentation, in which it is measured by the distortion that is inflicted upon the materials, the forms and the structures of sensibility and thought. Postmodern is not to be taken in a periodizing sense."

So the postmodern is not simply some period or epoch *after* modernism, but rather a violation or rejection of ordinary parameters of what is thinkable, perceptible, and sensible. Where we once thought that things were in their right place, we now realize that in a moment it could all change. When an artist puts us in this

3 Jean-François Lyotard, *The Differend* (University of Minnesota Press, 1984), p. 13.

condition, we as an audience are in a sense reborn and recreated outside of our expectations and in ways that are irreducible to the standard conventions of language. In a sense we all say, "What was that you tried to say?"

"Kid A" continues the theme begun in "Everything in Its Right Place." It begins with music sounding like a lullaby interspersed with barely audible lyrics which, just like the first track, push the same questions of "What is being said? What does this mean?" Evading categorization is one of the many trademarks of Lyotard's postmodernism. In his first book, *Discours, Figure*, he wrote:

> This book protests that the given is not a text, that there is within it a density, or rather a constitutive difference, which is not to be read, but to be seen, and that this difference, and the immobile mobility which reveals it, is what is continually forgotten in the process of signification. (*Discours, Figure*, Paris, 1971, p. 9)

There are certain ideas or feelings that evade signification by words. Words cannot touch these feelings or express them, Lyotard says, because of this gap of "constitutive difference" between what is there to be seen but cannot be "read" into words. The opening of "Kid A," in this light, is a kind of fable about how we respond to the linguistic situation: Yorke's murmuring is so provocative, and repetitive, that people begin to mimic its articulations. "We've got heads on sticks," the lyric goes, "and you've got ventriloquists"—copycats, plagiarists, or epigones, perhaps—who mimic the initial articulation. The song finally settles into a pied piper motif, where the people play follow the leader, and Yorke sings in a computerized voice, "The rats and children follow me out of town, The rats and children follow me out of their homes, Come on Kids." In a sense, these lyrics from "Kid A" can also be seen as an attempt to lure the listener out of the safety and security of modern, mainstream music, a moment that rightly stands as an expression of Lyotard's conception of the differend as an idiom for what cannot be put into precise terms just yet, but which still must be articulated.

Epigones in Their Right Place

There's a well-known interview on MTV during which Radiohead was asked: "How do you feel about the fact that bands like Travis, Coldplay, and Muse are making a career sounding exactly like your records did in 1997?" Yorke replied, "Good luck with *Kid A*" (Wikipedia entry on Radiohead). Lyotard (and his many followers, perhaps) see a postmodern counterpart to this phenomenon, as well, in the way that "a vanguard machine" first produces values and ideas that shape the identity of those who follow them. Once a work of art is understood in common parlance, it is often co-opted by the mainstream and reduced to a commodity for mass consumption, an idea that German philosopher Walter Benjamin highlighted quite specifically in the early twentieth century in his essay, "The Work of Art in the Age of Mechanical Reproduction." In the postmodern condition which Lyotard describes, the production of knowledge creates a system that "seems to be a vanguard machine dragging humanity after it, dehumanizing it in order to rehumanize it at a different level of normative capacity" (*Postmodern Condition* , p. 63).

Many artists, like Radiohead, seem to think of themselves as a vanguard in this sense. Their goal is to effectively criticize and transform values, rather than simply make money as entertainers. In this sense, we can see *Kid A* as a message to other bands who may get more airtime on the radio and television, but whose music comes off as nothing more than artistic ventriloquism. They are like the rats following Radiohead out of town (to be drowned). But with *Kid A*, Yorke's point is clear. Good luck following along.

Dissecting National Anthems

After "Kid A" comes the steamrolling force of "National Anthem," where Yorke sings "Everyone is so near, everyone has got the fear, it's holding on." Another defining characteristic of Lyotard's postmodern condition is an "incredulity toward grand-narratives." This means that when one slips into the postmodern condition, even if it happens for a moment, the stories that used to make sense, such as stories about nationalism and patriotism that move people on a large-scale social level, suddenly fail to inspire. For a moment we hesitate to believe that (for example) progress is occurring, or that the United States is forever building a more perfect union as a nation. Yet we still have to live within a social system that is dictated by meta-narratives, or large-scale storytelling.

The national anthem is an example of the use of meta-narratives within society. Even though we may carry doubts about nationalism, we realize that "it's holding on" because these national anthems serve a necessary social function by providing a sense of national unity. Lyotard responds to this circumstance in *The Postmodern Condition*, in which he touts the importance of "little narratives" along with the proliferation of multiple narratives within a single culture. These smaller stories can undercut grand-narratives and produce what he calls "language games" that multiply and criss-cross throughout society. This dissemination of little narratives creates a society which enables individuals to create their own narratives rather than subordinating their thinking to the logic of a large-scale nationalistic grand-narrative.

Lyotard is a pluralist. Creating a pluralistic society where everyone has a voice can seem a bit chaotic (not unlike the battling horns at the end of "National Anthem"). But Lyotard's pluralism is not chaotic or frivolous. He advocates that we play the game of the just (as in "justice") and play by the rules and preserve the autonomy of these rules in different language games in local, decentralized narratives. Instead of deriving justice from the meta-narratives of national anthems, society justice should think of justice as local, multiple, and provisional, and subject to contestation and transformation. For Lyotard, justice is never eternal, like that portrayed in a national anthem for instance, but is rather the result of the contingency of social circumstances through which it is produced.

This One's Optimistic

Another unexpected turn is found on "How to Disappear Completely." With the lyrics "I'm not here, this isn't happening" and "in a little while, I'll be gone, the moment's already gone, yeah, yeah, yeah," Yorke becomes a person who doubts his existence. This too, Lyotard suggests, reflects a residue of modernity.

"Modernity, in whatever age it appears," he writes, "cannot exist without a shattering of belief and without the discovery of the 'lack of reality', of reality together with the invention of other realities" (p. 77). In the postmodern we must learn to live within this pluralism of realities and, consequently, suffer pervasive doubts about our own being.

As if to drive that point home, "How to Disappear Completely" is followed by the instrumental "Treefingers." Yorke has disappeared leaving us with another postmodern moment of silence:

> In the differend, something 'asks' to be put into phrases, and suffers from the wrong of not being able to be put into phrases right away. This is when the human beings who thought they could use language as an instrument of communication learn through the feeling of pain which accompanies silence. (*The Differend*, p. 13)

Some things resist being said and are best communicated by saying nothing at all. "Treefingers" is absent all narrative—it's just a space, with a mood, for introspection.

Yorke returns in "Optimistic," an odd choice for the first radio single from *Kid A*. The chorus is a line inspired by Yorke's partner, who reportedly said to him when he felt worn down from the grind of touring, "you can try the best you can, the best you can is good enough." If this is indeed a postmodern slogan, then it eschews becoming a grand and definitive recipe for success or happiness. There's not much of that around, after all, as Yorke sings on "Optimistic" about "flies buzzing 'round my head, vultures circling the dead, picking up every last crumb, the big fish eat the little ones, the big fish eat the little ones, not my problem, give me some." Later in the song Yorke croons, "this one drops a payload, fodder for the animals, living on animal farm." This reference no doubt alludes to George Orwell's political allegory, *Animal Farm*, which compares the labor of animals on a farm, managed by a well-intentioned farmer, to modern capitalism. Lamenting this situation, where the strong exploit (and possibly eat) the weak, Yorke empathetically sings, "I'd really like to help you man." But it seems he can't do much "floating around on a prison ship" except try the best he can.

Not everything's in its right place at this point. In the social structure depicted by Yorke, something is terribly wrong. Characteristically, Radiohead want to disturb us, not comfort us, by joining Lyotard in a challenge to think about suffering in a post-modern sense. This means, for example, believing that most of the suffering in the world can be alleviated by changing our narrative structures on a micro-political level; by saying from one person to another, "I'd really like to help you man." This is an ironic optimism, not a simple-minded moral prescription from feel-good new age gurus who think optimism will magically transform an animal-farm society. But, in the midst of a social system that alienates people from one another, one can find temporary solace on a local or micro-political level. Through the unexpected optimism of a friend or loved one, the animal farm can become bearable. Even if the meta-narratives that have so far held society together are antiquated but still dominant (like the "Dinosaurs roaming the earth" at the end of the song), we can still keep our wits by caring for those around us in a local, interpersonal way. Postmodern optimism must be ironic as well as cautious. As Lyotard asks in *The Differend*, "What assurance is there that humans will become more cultivated than they are?" (p. 181). None, but you can be optimistic.

You're Living in a Fantasy World

The postmodernism lurking in *Kid A* is not articulated only by Lyotard. The last four songs of the album, "In Limbo," "Idioteque," "Morning Bell," and "Motion Picture Soundtrack," connect to the writings of another French postmodern thinker, Jean Baudrillard (1929–2007). With "In Limbo," for example, we take a step from Lyotard toward Baudrillard by being immersed in distorted vocals, layers of sounds and effects that again point to Lyotard's conception of a postmodern message without an addressee, "I got a message I can't read." The song's chorus declares, "You're living in a fantasy world," and repeats this a number of times. According to Jean Baudrillard, capitalist society is saturated by fantasies and, specifically, representations. These representations of things have so much power that it's impossible to distinguish between reality and these many representations of it.

Baudrillard uses the terms "simulacrum" and "hyperreality" to articulate this understanding. We are now, he says, in a new historical era based on simulation in which computerization, information processing, media, and the organization of society according to simulation codes and models replace production as the organizing principle of society. He tells us: "Information dissolves meaning and the social into a sort of nebulous state leading not at all to a surfeit of innovation but to the very contrary, to total entropy."[4] To, that is, a kind of limbo.

According to Baudrillard, technological communication systems and networks are not marks of human advancement or progress, but rather of a stasis in human development. We're stuck in an information and entertainment glut where messages are sent but not necessarily understood and fantasy and reality are routinely confused. Baudrillard's book *TV World* discusses how the image of the television doctor is sometimes taken for a real doctor, specifically telling the story of how Robert Young, a television actor popular as "Marcus Welby" in the 1960s and 1970s, received thousands of letters asking for medical advice. The fact that he later appeared in commercials to advise viewers about the wonders of decaffeinated coffee only reinforced the confusion. Similarly, Baudrillard notes, the actor Raymond Burr (known as defense lawyer Perry Mason) received thousands of letters asking for legal advice in the 1950s. This "hyperreality," in Radiohead terms, would amount to asking Johnny Greenwood or Thom Yorke for advice about fixing a laptop because, after all, they recorded an album entitled *OK Computer*.

Hyperreality blurs together real life and representational, simulated life. That's why we need to be reminded that in many ways life is "not like the movies," as Yorke croons on "Motion Picture Soundtrack." Less than optimistic, Baudrillard sees us believing in the hyperreal because we are so far removed from the original reality that it becomes difficult to give conclusive evidence that there is a reality outside of hyperreality (think *The Matrix* here). The scale models of the United States on display in Disneyland—another famous Baudrillardian example of this—are hyperreal

4 Jean Baudrillard, *The Ecstasy of Communication* (Semiotext(e), 1983), p. 100.

because they maintain and promote a certain conception of reality that is more readily accepted and circulated through representations by the Disney Corporation than what we might believe to be "real" homes that actually exist in the United States. The representation is more real, in this way, than reality.[5] Radiohead concludes *Kid A* by pointing to these curious features of our world, beckoning us to reject the hyperreal (if that is even possible anymore), by reminding us "it's not like the movies" (even if the governor of California was an action film star, and people still write to Perry Mason for legal advice).

Today I Woke Up Sucking a Grammy

So what kind of album is *Kid A* (really)? One problem with "Best Alternative Album of 2001" is that it presupposes the reality, perhaps hyperreality, of the very kinds of categories that *Kid A* lyrically and musically rebels against. "Alternative" may not be precise, but along with every other category it presumes there exist certain stable qualities and categories of albums, of musical experiences, to be labeled and named—all of which becomes doubtful when viewed through the postmodern lenses the album itself puts on us. Perhaps the choice of "Optimistic" as an airplay-single makes a lot of sense. Even if we know the limitations of our language, and the way some ideas and things resist being said, understood, or seen through the fog of postmodernity, we have to use language and, when we do, acknowledge these limits and try the best we can.

5 Jean Baudrillard, *Simulations* (Semiotext(e), 1983), p. 25.

21.

Hyperreally Saying Something

Tim Footman

> It is the fantasy of seizing reality live that continues—
> ever since Narcissus bent over his spring.
>
> —Jean Baudrillard

The search for 'reality' and 'authenticity' has long been a preoccupation of philosophers. Consider Plato's analogy of the cave, in which the shadows of puppets on a wall form the only reality known by chained prisoners, or René Descartes's well known introspective mantra: "I think therefore I am." We can also see this search for authenticity in George Berkeley's questioning of whether or not an unobserved event truly happens or in Martin Heidegger's musing on the ultimate meaning of the verb 'to be' in human existence.

This philosophical tradition has been recently furthered by French cultural thinker Jean Baudrillard (1929–2007). Baudrillard argued that modern culture and media have effectively destroyed any notion of authenticity, replacing it instead with a succession of images that purport to represent reality while, in fact, masking it from view. One of the key concepts most associated with Baudrillard is the simulacrum, which he defined as the image's inevitable victory over reality. He saw this simulacrum as progressing in four stages:

it is the reflection of a profound reality;

it masks and denatures a profound reality;

it masks the absence of a profound reality;

it has no relation to reality whatsoever: it is its own pure simulacrum.[1]

This triumph of the simulacrum—the state in which a simulation doesn't just represent a reality, it actually takes its place—leads to what Baudrillard calls *hyperreality*, the state in which people are unable to distinguish the real from the fake. Think of the way the architectures of Disneyland and Las Vegas ape entire cultures, dazzling consumers with ersatz exotica, and lulling them into a dazed receptiveness to the all-important corporate message/massage. Or consumer branding, the logic of which dictates that we choose to purchase a feeling of crypto-bohemian comfort rather than a coffee; a swoosh rather than a sports shoe; a vague notion of authenticity ("The Real Thing", which actually isn't real) rather than a sweet, fizzy, brown drink (which is the reality).

An entity such as Radiohead almost by default sets itself up in opposition to such manifestations of capitalist mind control via the simulacrum. They are a rock band, with all the connotations of rebellion and non-conformity that this implies. That said, much of their music transcends the clichés that attend such a simplistic definition: in search of inspiration, they are more likely to delve into the traditions of electronic dance music, or the classical avant garde, than they are to mine the back catalogs of, say, Led Zeppelin. But their place in modern culture remains that of a rock band: they are reviewed by rock critics, their music plays on rock stations, and if record shops still exist by the time you read this, their CDs are shelved alongside the Red Hot Chilli Peppers and the Rolling Stones, not Rimsky-Korsakov or Ravi Shankar. At concerts, Radiohead fans tend to wear Converse sneakers and don't drink overpriced Chardonnay or talk about skiing holidays in the concert interval.

Moreover, the band labors under that equally unsatisfactory tag of 'alternative rock', a core characteristic of which has always been an insistence on 'authenticity' and an admission of human frailty and imperfection. No inconvenient truth may be swept

1 Baudrillard, *Simulacra and Simulation* (University of Michigan Press, 1994), p. 6.

under the mat, no bum note may be excised, and no zit may be air-brushed. In the words that Richey James Edwards, of the Welsh band Manic Street Preachers, hacked into his scrawny arm in 1991, the most important thing is to be "4REAL." (The guitarist, who had a history of depression and self-harm, cut himself during an argument with *NME* journalist Steve Lamacq, who had questioned the Manics' integrity. In 1995, Edwards disappeared—completely?—and was legally declared dead in November 2008.)

Radiohead go further to oppose corporate simulacra. In their song lyrics, their public statements and their activities as a band, they criticize the pervasive influence of global capitalism and its effect on culture and society. But can a successful rock band, operating within the landscape of the modern media, avoid the processes that Baudrillard envisaged? How does Radiohead avoid becoming a tawdry simulacrum of itself?

I Wish I Was Special

In the early years of the band's existence, philosophical conundrums about perception and reality were hardly an issue. At the time of the first album, *Pablo Honey*, and the successful single, "Creep," Radiohead were lumped together with Nirvana and Pearl Jam in the then-current grunge movement (for no better reason than that they looked unhappy, and sounded as if they might have listened to Sonic Youth when they were young). By 1995, with the release of *The Bends*, Radiohead were often classified as Britpop (see Oasis, Blur), because they were British and had guitars.

While the band members didn't fit neatly into the stereotypical rock mold (too middle-class and not disposed to throwing televisions out of hotel windows) they were awkward and intense enough to slot into any number of indie sub-genres. Moreover, they were patently 4REAL, to the extent that they were the antithesis of a manufactured pop act. With their down-to-earth demeanour, it was clear no record company executive could have dreamed them up. Even their looks attested to their authenticity: a stunted, squinting singer; a gangling giant of a guitarist; a pudgy, bald drummer; and two brothers who had great cheekbones, but still managed to look a bit weird. These boys were hardly a boy band.

Not that this market-driven pigeonholing required much of a philosophical response on the band's part. With a few exceptions (for example, the anti-corporate 'Banana Co.', issued as a B-side in 1993 and 1996), Thom Yorke's early lyrics tended to solipsism and self-pity. Any sense of political awareness, or engagement with the wider world, was reserved by band members for press interviews, although they did give the impression that they found the latter aspect of showbiz about as enjoyable as root-canal work without anaesthetic. It seemed they disliked the corporate crassness that required them to play "Creep" in front of a bevy of jiggling biki-ni babes, as they did on MTV's *Beach Party* show, but they went ahead with it.

No Chance of Escape

The band's social comment became more acute (albeit still only implicitly political) with the release of *The Bends*. "Fake Plastic Trees," for example, offers a chilling snapshot of the hyperreal environment to which Baudrillard alerts us, and the remorseless logic that takes us from thoughtless consumerism to an entirely artificial existence. As in a theme park, nature (represented by plants and earth) is rendered in plastic; then come the polystyrene people. Even lust, that primal motivator rock'n'roll mythology, becomes synthetic. "She tastes like the real thing"; she's a geneti-cally-engineered, focus-group-driven simulacrum of what a woman ought to be, packed with "nature-identical" flavorings; the unreal reality of a Coke ad. But that's good enough for an admir-er who can only offer his "fake plastic love" in return.

The socio-political content came into much sharper focus in 1997, with *OK Computer*. Now, as well as the articulation of self-loathing to which fans and critics had become accustomed, the band seemed to be striving for a bigger picture, concocting a cri-tique of modern society stumbling towards the new millennium, dazzled by the banal neon of global capitalism.

The most explicit example of this on the album was the sev-enth track, "Fitter Happier." Delivered in an emotionless, comput-erized voice over a minimal backing track, it expresses the vacuity of contemporary consumer culture as a string of disjointed phras-es. The emotional impact comes from hearing a non-human voice expressing sentiments of such all-too-human banality ("on

Sundays ring road supermarket") and poignancy ("like a cat tied to a stick"). It conjures up memories of the quietly deranged computer HAL, from *2001: A Space Odyssey* and the confusions between real and unreal, analogue and digital, raised by the virtual worlds that arose with globalized computer technology. These online worlds, such as Second Life or World of Warcraft, gave new impetus to Baudrillard's warnings about society's inability to perceive its own drunken lurch into a state of hyperreality.

In Baudrillard's terms, "Fitter Happier" presents us with a simulacrum, comprising not visual images, but words. The haunting slogans, many of them apparently drawn from company training manuals, reveal the rhetoric with which capitalism disguises its own hollowness ("an empowered and informed member of society"). Silent Gray's cover of "Fitter Happier," on the tribute album *Anyone Can Play Radiohead* (Vitamin, 2001), uses the same voice program to 'speak' the slogans. Although the passage isn't physically copied from Radiohead's original (in the sense of sampling a section from a record), it is a copy in the Baudrillard sense, sonically identical, a simulacrum in sound.

Radiohead may have been taking a few tips from the Situationists, à European avant-garde artistic collective with roots in Marxist criticism of capitalism. This groups often utilized paradoxical slogans such as "Be reasonable; demand the impossible!" that offered a running commentary on the student-led upheavals of 1968, and have informed the more creative and imaginative strands of political activism ever since.

"Fitter Happier" is, in many ways, the band's first successful attempt to break away from the orthodoxies of alternative rock, which had become as restrictive as the clichés it had sought to escape. This move towards electronic experimentalism forced the band and listeners alike into a reappraisal of what popular music has become. As Joseph Tate put it: "The band's music, I argue, is not a distortion of 'real rock', but an uncovering of its absence, its phantasmic structure."[2] If Yorke and his colleagues were seeking to expose the void at the heart of capitalism, how could they

---

2 Joseph Tate, "Radiohead's Antivideos: Works of Art in the Age of Electronic Reproduction," in Joseph Tate, ed., *The Music and Art of Radiohead* (Aldershot: Ashgate, 2005), p. 107.

exploit as their preferred medium a genre that was equally empty, equally dishonest?

This Just Feels Like Spinning Plates

The band's retreat from the traditions of guitar-based rock music became even more evident on the subsequent two albums, *Kid A* (2000) and *Amnesiac* (2001). In place of old favourites such as the Pixies and the Smiths, the band drew from a variety of new musical traditions. On these records, the influence of dance-floor electronica (in particular acts associated with the Sheffield-based Warp label), New Orleans jazz, early-1970s Krautrock and the challenging works of twentieth-century composers like Olivier Messiaen, Krzysztof Penderecki, and Paul Lansky can all be heard.

However, simply replacing guitars with samplers, aesthetically satisfying as it may have been, wasn't dealing with the problem. It wasn't just rock music that had become a simulacrum of half-remembered flakes of folklore, most of them nothing to do with music *per se* (Elvis from the waist up on the Sullivan show; Bowie announcing his bisexuality; the newsflash of the Lennon shooting; that embarrassing Milli Vanilli track to which you lost your virginity). For Radiohead, it was the entire mode of production and transmission that had become a glossy fraud.

Yorke had long been brooding about this contradiction. His lyrics about the evils of global capitalism, encouraged by his readings of Noam Chomsky, Will Hutton, Naomi Klein and others, were transmitted around the world thanks to global capitalism. In attempting to expose the simulacrum, he was adding more layers to it. As early as 1998, he admitted the extent to which he was implicated in the scam:

> Then there's the false authority in mass-producing a work which gives it a false sense of significance. The thing of taking responsibility for your work is to a high extent bullshit because a big part of it is simply that yours is being mass-produced and someone else's isn't. Yours is getting marketed in ways that other people's isn't, and that's part of how people approach it, independent from the work itself. (Mary Gaitskill, "Radiohead: Alarms and Surprises," *Alternative Press*, April 1998)

Later, as technological developments conspired to make the traditional record company structure redundant, Yorke further
expressed his frustration:

> I like the people at our record company, but the time is at hand
> when you have to ask why anyone needs one. And, yes, it prob-
> ably would give us some perverse pleasure to say 'F—— you' to
> this decaying business model. (Josh Tyrangiel, "Radiohead Says:
> Pay What You Want," *Time*, October 1st, 2007)

From 2000, Radiohead began extending the scope of their subver-
sion from the nature of the music itself to the way it was presented to the audience. There were no singles from the *Kid A* album.
Press interviews were all but non-existent, and communication
with listeners came in the form of cryptic postings on the website
and viral blips. Most significantly, the whole album appeared
online three weeks before the official release date, and rumours
persist that, far from being an act of copyright piracy, the leak was
a premeditated decision by the band.

It seems as though Radiohead's purpose was, in part, political.
By disrupting the normal modes of communication between cultural producer and cultural consumer, they were encouraging the
latter to question the economic and power structures that under-
pin the entertainment industry. Fans were being provoked to ask
fundamental questions, not least among them, "What is this thing
called Radiohead?"

Then a Sheer Drop

The culmination of this methodology came in October 2007
when the band announced the release of their first album in four
years, *In Rainbows*. At the time, Radiohead were not contracted to
any record company, and elected to make the album available as a
download. This was already becoming a popular method of distribution, especially among acts with committed fan bases. However,
Radiohead struck fear into the heart of the record industry by
insisting that 'buyers' of *In Rainbows* should pay only what they
wanted to pay, if anything at all.

This was interpreted by many as representing the band's last,
desperate attempt to escape the compromises that they were

forced to make as agents of commercial production. By eliminating the obligation upon listeners to pay money for product, Radiohead had apparently absolved themselves of any incriminating links with capitalism.

But the pay-what-you-like model had a more profound impact on the perception of Radiohead. It stripped away much of the extraneous interference that distanced the listener from the music. No accompanying marketing campaign, no in-store displays, not even any cover art to pore over. The short time between the announcement of the project (a seemingly casual comment from Jonny Greenwood on the band's Dead Air Space site) and the release of the download itself meant that no advanced copies were sent to critics, who lost their privileged role as mediators between artist and fan. By the time the hacks had began their frantically typed appraisals, fan-led reaction and analysis was already populating blogs and message boards across the planet. Here is the music, Radiohead seemed to be saying, in ones and zeroes: take it or leave it. As far as modern technology allowed, the simulacrum had been pushed aside, and authenticity was permitted to poke its pale, pimply nose into the sunlight for the first time in ages.

At any rate, that may have been what was supposed to happen. Instead, the unorthodox method of delivery, and the 'honesty-box' mode of payment, became a new story, a new simulacrum, one that obscured the music as completely as a conventional marketing campaign would have done. Once it had been exposed to the fierce glare of the media, *In Rainbows* became not so much a collection of ten songs, beginning with "15 Step" and ending with "Videotape," but more a narrative about itself, about the anti-commercial perversity of its creators and its own mongrel status. You couldn't buy it in record shops; it didn't have a sleeve; it wasn't eligible for the charts; was it a 'real' album or wasn't it? For example, the critic Paul Morley, of the *Observer Music Monthly*, 'live-blogged' his thoughts as he listened to the album for the first time on the morning of its release, and allocated his own recommended retail price to each track (http://blogs.guardian.co.uk/observermusic/2007/10/rainbow_warriors.html).

The joke was that there was a real album on the way, available in various desirable combinations of CD, vinyl, and hardback book, for sale at a normal, non-negotiable retail price, under the auspices of a normal record company. The band, of course, could not live by digital goodwill alone, and it soon became apparent that the free download was little more than advance publicity for the hard-copy album. Essentially, the digital 'pay what you want' record was only a simulacrum of something that had yet to come into existence. A *rainbow* is essentially an optical illusion and, as such, doesn't exist for anyone or anything to be *in* it, a fact that may or may not be coincidental.

Rather than feeling duped, the consumers loyally sent the ('real') album to the top of the charts in Britain, the United States, and beyond. One is irresistibly reminded of Graham Chapman in *Monty Python's Life of Brian*, urging his unwanted followers away from conformity, only for them to declare: "Yes! We're all individuals!"

In the end, it was the intrusion of reality at its most mundane (the need on the band's part to feed the children, pay the electricity bill, maybe buy that nice new guitar; the wage-slave mentality that Yorke had skewered in "Fitter Happier") that necessitated the maintenance of the original simulacrum, the hyperreal version of what 'Radiohead' really is. And the punters, bless them, bought it.

This Isn't Happening

Baudrillard exaggerates, and his hyperbole is part of his charm. For the most part, there is some sort of reality behind the simulacrum. Las Vegas and Disneyland and your nearest McDonald's exist as concrete and steel and glass. Baudrillard's notorious contention that "The Gulf War Did Not Take Place"[3] is true only in the sense that the interrelation of media and politics and economics meant that Joe Blow sitting at home watching CNN had a false impression of what was going on. Bullets still got fired and people still got killed.

And, despite the distractions of music and video and interviews and website posts and even a book about their relationship with philosophy, Radiohead do exist, in the sense that five Englishmen come together with guitars and computers to make noise, and when they're happy with the noise, it is deemed to be Radiohead music.

---

3 Jean Baudrillard, *The Gulf War Did Not Take Place* (Indiana University Press, 1995).

To an extent, it's that deeming, that discrimination, that brings down the shutters, and makes what we hear in their music a simulation of the 'real' Radiohead. Even when we hear music that's supposedly in its raw, unadorned state, we only hear it by permission. For example, the song "How I Made My Millions" (an extra track on the "No Surprises" single, released in January 1998) consists of little more than Thom Yorke mumbling and noodling in his living room on a piano, while his partner does the housework in the background. It sounds 'real', but it's only a packaged sliver of reality, like a few seconds of *Big Brother*. And it's only in the universe of our perception because Yorke and our colleagues allowed it to be there.

A live gig is as close as most of us will get to an 'authentic' experience of Radiohead (especially because the band tend to eschew fancy, theatrical effects, and there's always the delicious prospect of events sliding beyond their control) but even in this context, authenticity is compromised. The atmosphere, the excitement, the consumption of drink or drugs, even the weather can affect the spectator's objectivity. And then there's hindsight, especially when delivered in the form of music journalism. The journalist Paul Trynka made this comment on the band's performance at the Glastonbury Festival in June, 1997:

> When I've talked to people since who witnessed that performance, it's been galling to hear the odd person describe it as merely 'a good gig'. It wasn't. It was something far more profound.[4]

Just as it has been decided by pundits that *In Rainbows* is really more about the pay-what-you-like hoopla that surrounded its own release rather than the music, so this Radiohead performance in the south-west of England in the summer of 1997 has been pigeonholed as "profound." Baudrillard might reasonably have argued that, like the Gulf War, the Glastonbury Festival (and Woodstock, Monterey, Coachella, and others) Did Not Take Place, because the combination of nostalgia, hype, dope, senility and heatstroke make an objective reality impossible to ascertain.

Thom Yorke had come to a similar conclusion only a few days before the Glastonbury performance. On stage at a concert in Dublin, he had an experience that might best be described as a

4 Quoted in Jim Irvin, "We Have Lift Off," *Mojo* (September 1997).

mixture of acute dissociation, stage fright, and an out-of-body experience. Under the collective gaze of the 38,000-strong crowd, he was overwhelmed by the desire not to be there; in fact, the urge not to be at all.

Yorke's creative response to the episode was eventually released as "How to Disappear Completely," on *Kid A*. It's an intriguing document of a man in crisis, and it goes some way to reconcile the two conflicting aspects of Radiohead as a collective persona. Yes, they are hugely successful rock stars, part of millennial rock royalty alongside REM and U2, and they know all about "Strobe lights and blown speakers / Fireworks and hurricanes," night after night. This is the hyperreality of the public Radiohead. The fans see an entity they know as Thom Yorke, standing five-foot-five on the stage, but the real Thom might be floating down the Liffey, if he exists at all.

How to Reappear Completely

Don't forget that the band's roots lie in alternative rock, the twenty-first-century manifestation of existential, outsider culture. The desire for invisibility, for absence, that first brought Radiohead to global attention, and which still permeates their music ("I don't belong here" in "Creep"; "I'm not here" in "How to Disappear Completely") speaks to a tradition that goes back as far as Shakespeare's *Hamlet*, encompasses Dostoevsky, Kafka, and Camus and still has resonance in the life and work of Ian Curtis of Joy Division and Nirvana's Kurt Cobain.

They and Yorke and Morrissey and Michael Stipe and Pete Wentz and the other titans of anguished alt-rock might appear to be diametrically opposed to the extravagant simulacra of showbiz. But their angst is not really a challenge to the fakery of modern media. It's only because mainstream culture is so inescapably unreal that a little bit of misery feels refreshing once in a while. As Baudrillard put it: "Melancholia is the brutal disaffection that characterizes our saturated systems."[5] Radiohead's glumness is just a way of dealing with the hyperreal world, of coming to terms with it, and, in fact, of manifesting themselves within it.

5 Baudrillard, *Simulacra and Simulation*, p. 162.

Which makes it seem as if Radiohead have failed in their post-*OK Computer* quest to oppose, to subvert, to demystify the systems and structures that rule us with their superficial luster. Their best attempt comes in the pleasing articulation of gloom and inadequacy that fills their discography and in their attempts at a different model of consumer capitalism. Which is not to dismiss them, because as Yorke opines in "Optimistic" from *Kid A*: "You can try the best you can / The best you can is good enough."

22.

Sexier More Seductive

PERRY OWEN WRIGHT

After albums addressing themes as diverse as techno-phobia, techno-politics, and techno-honey, Radiohead has released an album principally about sex: *In Rainbows*. While it initially struck me as odd that a band I tend to consider interested in more cerebral pursuits would take things below the waist, it doesn't require philosophers with difficult names representing incomprehensible schools of thought to tell us that sex is everywhere.

It's in the siren songs of the ads that call us to delicious consumption and in the ruby red lips of our cartoon rabbits in drag. It's the burning light under the bushel of David Bowie's codpiece-eyeliner mélange. In fact, I think we can go so far as to say that the ubiquity of sex has spread more widely than the contact high in front of the main stage at Bonnaroo.

But we currently find ourselves in a historical epoch at odds with itself. While the historical and philosophical movement known as the Enlightenment hardly offered a uniform philosophical worldview, or even a distinct and easily definable period, the movement did in fact march its parade to the tune of a broadly identifiable foundation of presuppositions. With the simultaneous rise of the notions of individual rights and the nation-state, a bevy of revolutions sprang up against political and religious institutions. Slave traders in The People Business™ were out; rationalism, the scientific method, and Natural Law were in. In the broadest sense, rationality and observation were taken to be the predominant avenues to objective truths and reality.

And so we inherited a world propped up by these Enlightenment ideas. Myths and gods were killed off in the name of science and the real. Bodies were dissected and diagramed, effectively disenchanted from their prior hidden mysteries by the observations of biology. Our anatomy became our destiny, our biology our fate, as the objective truths of our bodies were discerned.

Et Cetera Et Cetera

Even our definition of sex has been reduced to a biological system of physical intercourse and genitals, with its repeated proof of existence evidenced in the orgasm. In this reduction, however, sex has been handed down its own death sentence, since in the strict biology of the orgasm, the only proof that it ever existed is in its ending.

If we want to reclaim sex as something enchanted and mysterious, what we need is a challenge to the current course of things. Something to divert us from where we are and lead us aside into a world that still contains the mystery before sex was repackaged, commoditized, and outsourced as desire and biology. According to French philosopher Jean Baudrillard, what we need is not desire, but seduction (*se-ducere*: to take aside, to divert from one's path).

> Seduction's enchantment puts an end to all libidinal economies, and every sexual or psychological contract, replacing them with a dizzying spiral of responses and counter-responses. It is never an investment but a risk; never a contract but a pact; never individual but duel*; never psychological but ritual; never natural but artificial. It is no one's strategy, but a destiny.[1]

---

* Translator's note: In French, the word *duel* means both duel and dual; Baudrillard plays with the double meaning, simultaneously agonal/agonist relations and reciprocal challenges, so it gets translated "duel" even in the adjectival form.

1 Jean Baudrillard, *Seduction* (St. Martin's Press, 1990 [1979]), pp. 82-83.

Seduction challenges the sex-killing anatomical reduction by being a game without end, without regard to intercourse or the orgasm. What *In Rainbows* does so well is excavate the problematic nature of the current course of sexuality and offer a penetrating aesthetic consideration in the wake of this receding Enlightenment.

Fifteen Steps then a Sheer Drop

Enlightenment sexuality is understood in terms of the individual and Natural Law, but seduction reminds us that sex is never about the individual and always about the interplay of relation. This dizzying feedback loop of seduction creates the possibility for sex to break from individualized sexuality, dissolving the need for the individual-as-subject because "there is no active or passive mode in seduction, no subject or object, no interior or exterior: seduction plays on both sides, and there is no frontier separating them" (p. 81). What should have been circular all along, simultaneously playing on both sides, has become a flat earth, where, as "15 Step" reminds us, you can never end up back where you started.

The duel horizon of seduction, then, can be understood as a feedback loop with no concern for traditional subject-object mediation or meaningful acts in search of the real. Instead, seduction becomes "an ironic, alternative form, one that breaks the referentiality of sex and provides a space, not of desire, but of play and defiance" (p. 21). This play and defiance is the hope seduction offers the age, a game and a revolution.

I Am Trapped in This Body and Can't Get Out

For Baudrillard, there's no greater display of the Enlightenment's sexual reduction than in pornography, where headless bodies or genitals confirm the *truth* of sex to an era convinced that sex is nothing more than a scientific exchange of genitals, repeatedly proven by the orgasm. Why not fill the screen with the only things that matter in sex? In essence, pornography is a scientific and close-up version of intercourse, as one might find in a laboratory under a microscope.

The common belief about pornography is that it is an avenue for fantasizing about sex, but Baudrillard is convinced that "the only phantasy in pornography, if there is one, is not a phantasy of sex, but of the real, and its absorption into something other than the real, the hyperreal" (p. 29). He contends that in pornography, we're searching for real sex, based on our belief that sex can be reduced to a Natural Law of physical intercourse. In the end, however, this approach to sex only delivers a simulacrum, a simulation of the real.

Pornography is the High-Definition Television of sex. The irony implicit in the idea of HDTV is that its aim is to reproduce a more and more realistic image of a visual deception. By this irony, the images come ever closer to revealing that, wouldn't you know it, the bodysnatchers on the screen aren't really dismembering and inhabiting the body of that pretty mother-of-four. With HDTV, you can see clearly that those are men in rubber suits and makeup, and she's not really a blonde, she's wearing a wig. The irony is that as the quality of the visual reproduction increases, its ability to deceive you is destroyed. But the deception that has been lost was once, and is ostensibly still, the goal of both the filmmaker and the viewer. Like HDTV, pornography is a simulation of a sex that no one has ever had, and it is in ever more real depictions. This is what Baudrillard calls *hyperreal*.

As hyperreal, pornography can be understood as "the endless over-signification of a real that no longer exists, and of a body that never existed" (p. 33). As we're perpetually bombarded with pornography's version of sex, we forget that it isn't at all related to an experience of sex that anyone has ever had. Baudrillard asserts that this forgetting over time establishes an entire culture of hyperreality, as we develop simulations that are further and further from experience but with no ability to remember that they are not actually referring back to reality at all. Eventually, we achieve a repeated simulation of a thing that never existed in the first place, the hyperreal.

We can call this vision of sex a *simulacrum*, "a truth effect that hides the truth's non-existence" (p. 35), as this anatomy-determined simulation of sex is all that we can remember at this point. Pornography claims by its existence there must be sex like this somewhere, since it is the caricature and simulation of that sex, but this reveals that it is only a simulacrum of the truthless sex we inherited from the Enlightenment's reduction. And this reduction is not just found in pornography, but pornography is its most revealing simulation.

This is the entire troubled story of sex in this age, once mysterious and now rapidly approaching the hyperreal. This is the lament of "Bodysnatchers," as it paints for us an image of the ironic bodiless pornographic simulation extending beyond the borders of the screen and a vision of the new hyperreal body that simulation produces, a lie:

> You killed the sound
> Removed backbone
> A pale imitation with the edges sawn off
>
> They got a skin and they put me in
> On the lines wrapped round my face
> Are for anyone else to see
> I'm a lie

But if Baudrillard is right and the deterministic body is outstripped by seduction, where then is seduction's foothold? Seduction belongs to the world of aesthetics, and as such, belongs to the world of deception and appearances. The physical bodies must be transfigured into signs. What we have is a symbolic, not anatomical, fate.

You Paint Yourself White

Whereas pornography breaks the Natural Laws of the real it claims to simulate by creating the hyperreal and simulating an unreal, seduction eschews the real for the sake of the arbitrary artifice, the sign. Deception is one of its most powerful tools.

Among the arbitrary artifices of sex, none is more compelling than the body. Nudity, presence, even touch are not actions or objects but signifiers, because in the world of seduction, the body is not a means of accumulation or production but a sign among signs. And "the power of signs lies in their appearance and disappearance; that is how they efface the world" (p. 94). Even unreservedly arbitrary things like wearing cosmetics become intimately vital in the game of seduction for Baudrillard, for they create even more layers of artifice and secrecy. In seduction, the body itself becomes a fluid artifice, transfigured into a mere sign, stripped "Nude."

> Now that you've found it it's gone
> Now that you feel it you don't

As an offspring of the sphere of the aesthetic, seduction belongs to the world of immediacy and surface. This means that the signs of seduction are not concerned necessarily with meaning but rather with the game of being signs. The meaning of the signs is reserved, withheld for the sake of the immediate and endless play of the feedback loop of the game. As with cosmetics, seduction keeps play alive by abdicating its meaning to concealment and secrecy, creating a series of appearances and disappearances that efface the traditional subject-object relationship. Baudrillard calls this moment *aleatory suspension*, for seduction exists in the frozen, thrilling, pregnant moment between the throw of the dice and their landing, where everything is anticipation, hope, and faith, even though the game is bound only to arbitrary chance.

I Follow to the Edge of the Earth and Fall Off

The relation of seduction has required that we forsake our interpretation of the signs for the sake of the game. Enchanted sex is no longer about the orgasm, or even intercourse, but the play of the seductive relationship. The abyss before us now is not one of depth or meaning but of appearance and aleatory suspension, for seduction enchants us in the world of immediacy, not the world of meaning. Baudrillard calls this critical shift toward the aesthetic the *superficial abyss*. This transformation of meaning into appearance is our hope for a re-enchanted sex.

But what is a superficial abyss, beyond a contradiction? Consider it analogous to a mirror pointed at the sky. The mirror's reflection of the sky reflects the appearance of infinity, doubling the endless span and countless stars in the heavens, and yet it has no depth its own. It transforms the truth of the sky into pure appearance. Seduction has the power to work the same magic on sex as the mirror with the sky. This is seduction's transformative power over truth. We choose the sign over the object and the arbitrary over the meaningful for the sake of enchantment and endless play.

Your Eyes, They Turn Me

Baudrillard's example of this transformation is Narcissus. Narcissus is typically painted as a character too deeply in love with himself and his own image, but Baudrillard thinks that this explanation is too psychological. He contends that Narcissus was seduced by a version of himself that was appearance-only, not his attractive reflection. Narcissus was called into the water by the prospect of becoming a mere sign.

But this echoes the warning suggested by the parable of "Weird Fishes / Arpeggi," as the narrator is seduced in the depths by the dangling bright light of an anglerfish, mistaken for eyes. On the bottom of the ocean, seduction is leading the narrator off the edge of the earth. They sink deeper and deeper, until the narrator can no longer take the risk implicit in the seduction and escapes, leaving the game. As we find with Narcissus, the risk of seduction is simultaneously the risk of death.

Of course, this might not be particularly shocking news considering that seduction has already required us to rebel against the Enlightenment and transform meaning and truth into arbitrary signs. But the possibility of death always raises the stakes of a game, and it's no different here. If seduction is going to re-enchant sex, it must transform every sign, even death itself, into superficialities in an even greater deception.

I Am in the Middle of Your Picture

So what we need is a greater deception. Borrowing a term from the world of visual art, Baudrillard employs the *trompe l'oeil* ("trick the eye") as deception's sublime face. Whereas pornography was the truer-than-true, the *trompe l'oeil* is falser-than-false; whereas pornography was hyperreal, the *trompe l'oeil* is hypersimulation. Stemming from a long tradition throughout the history of visual art, and reified in the Baroque period, *trompe l'oeil* uses tricks of perspective in two dimensions to create optical illusions of a third.

Yet, crucially, *trompe l'oeil* does not intend to confuse itself with the real, but rather presents itself as a challenge to the real by an enchanted deception, just as seduction challenges Enlightenment sexuality. Unlike other visual techniques in art such as chiaroscuro, which uses the interplay of light and shadow to create a third dimension, *trompe l'oeil* forces the simulated third dimension specifically onto the viewer, transforming the viewer into the source of the perspective, the source of light. It's a seductive form of visual simulation because the artist compels the relation upon the viewer by creating another deceptive space in which the elements live together with the viewer. The third, artificial, dimension in which they relate is enchanted.

If the superficial abyss is a mirror that can reflect the infinite, transforming it into appearance and surface only, then the *trompe l'oeil* is a magic mirror, a superficial abyss that can re-enchant appearance. In this re-enchanted appearance, the *trompe l'oeil* draws the viewer into its deception and annihilates the subject-object relation in the aesthetic sphere of seduction.

In this enchantment, even death itself is a sign to be caught in the feedback loop, to be seduced and to seduce. "All I Need" is narrated by Death, personified as a stalking lover seeking a partner for its own seduction, as it has been re-enchanted in the middle of a picture, a superficial abyss that deceives by hypersimulation.

> I am the next act
> Waiting in the wings

Death unveils itself in "All I Need" through a series of metaphors: a doomed animal, an ignored day, an insect wandering in the night. But it's unveiling itself by further veiling itself in these metaphors, hovering in the wings of the stage and yet lurking ever-present in the tall grass, right there in the middle of any photograph of someone you love. From this voyeuristic position, death longs to seduce, as it has always already been seduced by life even unto its own end, as a moth drawn to its death by the illumination of a bright light.

There's No Real Reason

By entering the feedback loop of seduction, death offers itself as a sacrifice to artifice. The *trompe l'oeil*, or hypersimulation, re-enchants that artifice into the indefinite play of signs. The Enlightenment stripped us of our myths, our gods, and our eternal souls. The enchanted artifice is the only immortality we have left, as signs endlessly seduce each other. In this sacrifice, death itself shines by its absence and is transformed into a "brilliant and superficial appearance, that it is itself a seductive surface" (p. 97).

And yet there are many who find themselves in seduction who feel the risk is too great, as with the narrator of "Weird Fishes / Arpeggi." Often, they flee the seduction to return to the familiar and comfortable life of Enlightenment sexuality with its safe orgasms and objects. Still others attempt to maintain the relation of seduction, but at a distance great enough to allow them to keep one foot in the old Enlightenment sexuality, perhaps with another partner. In other words, some people are cheaters.

The Infrastructure Will Collapse

Cheating says, "Look around you! Your love and your marriage are arbitrary and meaningless contingencies! The Natural Law is survival and reproduction!" What cheating doesn't know is that in the risk of seduction, the arbitrary and aleatory have been embraced in the artificial perfection of the sign. Seduction already knows that it is a game of signs and not meaning.

Because seduction is a game, it follows the Rules of games and not the Natural Laws of the Enlightenment. The difference between Rules and Laws, Baudrillard says, is that "The Rule plays on an immanent sequence of arbitrary signs, while the Law is based on a transcendent sequence of necessary signs" (p. 130). Consider baseball. There is no universal Natural Law that says that when you hit a ball you must run to first base instead of third base. This is a completely arbitrary and meaningless response to hitting a ball with a stick, but for the sake of the game, it is observed. Unlike Laws, Rules are not believed but observed. The Rule is a *parodic simulacrum* of the Law; it ridicules the Law. That means it simulates a Natural Law that never existed as a way of challenging the Natural Law that says there are Natural Laws.

Rules are observed as a means of keeping the game alive. We embrace the meaningless Rule for the sake of play because we want it to continue. Games do not have finality. Sure, when nine innings are played in baseball, the team with the most runs *wins*—but they don't *win* Baseball, only a round of baseball, a simulation. This is because baseball doesn't ever end but constantly invites individuals to observe its arbitrary Rules again and again.

If games did have finality, the only true players would be the cheaters. Laws establish universal lines of the real, and in so doing, establish linear horizons that delimit but also reveal the beyond. That is to say, Laws draw a line that must be crossed because seeing the line always already suggests its other side. But Rules are arbitrary interdictions. They establish no horizon and, as such, one cannot transgress them, only fail to observe them. And if you aren't observing the Rules, then you aren't playing the game anymore.

The aesthetic problem with cheating in relationships is not that it breaks a universal Natural Law of fidelity. Cheating still operates in fidelity, but in fidelity to the disenchanted simulation of sex, the real, anatomical determinism and Law. Cheating substitutes the Law for the observation of the arbitrary Rules of seduction, hurling the cheater out of the feedback loop, the game of relation and signs. With regard to seduction's re-enchanted sex, cheaters simply aren't playing anymore.

Kiss Your Husband Goodnight

"House of Cards" traces this same idea by painting a marriage as a fragile and contingent stack of playing cards set upon each other to resemble a house. The narrator addresses another man's wife, making sexual advances toward her through precisely the same line of argument that we see from the Law: your marriage is an accidental contingency, a house of cards, and there is no reason you can't step outside the arbitrary Rules of fidelity to your husband.

> Forget about your house of cards
> And I'll do mine

But we know that if she assents, she has left the endless game of her marriage. This is not the same thing as an ethical or moral indictment of infidelity. Those indictments are still established in terms of Law, and as such, are perpetually transgressed. The aesthetic indictment simply removes her from the story without judgment. She was, perhaps, a sign seducing and being seduced and is no longer. But in leaving the game, she is also leaving sex for the sake of Enlightenment sexuality. She transforms seduction into its negative form, *production*, of which cheating is a simulation. And this is why her repeated response in "House of Cards," her only response to the aesthetic indictment, is a refutation: "Denial."

This Place Is on a Mission

So it is production, not seduction that tends to give seduction its bad name. Production dictates that "everything is to be transcribed in relations of force, systems of concepts or measurable energy; everything is to be said, accumulated, indexed and recorded" (pp. 34–35). The story of "Jigsaw Falling into Place" is a tale of this production, as the narrator lays out a strategy of production in the place where seduction should be. The song is a chess match, tracing the moves from the dance club to the bedroom, from sobriety to addiction. The sexual imagery is opaque and flippant, with a fumbling prosody leading us through the back alleys of sex-as-production. Everything in the song is scented with a tangible sexuality, even the description of the lines the narrator uses in his seduction.

> Words are blunt instruments
> Words are sawn off shotguns

The song presses harder and harder up against its sexual goal, the tension building, and finally releasing in the refrain.

> A jigsaw falling into place
> So there is nothing to explain

The production ends with the prospect of intercourse. The double-suggestion of the imagery perfectly reflecting the production, as the final piece of his negative seduction falls into place, strongly couched in the male-female image of a jigsaw puzzle piece, extending and receiving, his strategy and his phallus the same. This is the end, the limit, of seduction's negative form. It offers no immortality, no endless game beyond its singular, anatomical determinism, obtaining its brief and passing power through the meaning and strategy of the real. Yet again, the orgasm is the end of sex.

But to seduce is to die as reality and reconstitute the self and all signs as illusions in the great deception of the *trompe l'oeil*. We see that production obtains its power by producing real signs with fixed oppositions. But seduction, by producing only illusions, transfigures all powers. This transformation reveals production and reality to be illusions, returning them to the deceptions from whence they were produced, just as it challenged the Natural Law by mocking it with Rules.

You Are My Center when I Spin Away

What is the final word on seduction? Or how can we even settle on a final word for a challenge that refuses to end, an infinite game like seduction? While the world is filling up with Deleuzers, getting ever more Lyotarded, seduction sits back patiently, confidently. There is a great sense of predestination in seduction, as all tributaries inevitably wind their way to the feedback loop with nothing beyond it, precisely because there is nothing beyond it. But this is a bizarre sort of non-conclusion, cyclical and reversible as the signs of seduction.

"Videotape" stands us up at the pearly gates, again seating us at the foot of death as a way of establishing the severity of the moment. This is intensified further by bringing together many of the images from *In Rainbows* in this final scene in heaven: Faust's Mephistopheles and his abyssal hell, cameras, death, the imbalance and rippling of a spinning center, a reunion of the threads we have seen interact throughout the album as a whole, creating the eternity of the instant.

Musically, the churning cycles of the piano unfold and give way to consistent and calculated beats, which in turn give way to a final deception, as the rolling snare suggests a phase that will cycle through its entirety but never deliver on its promise, increasing the anxiety and subtextual disquiet in the pristinely quiet song.

The narrator considers his life in the eternity of the instant. What was once reflection is now a prismatic refraction of a digital projector's light as the movie of his life flickers on the screen.

> This is one for the good days
> I have it all here in red, blue, green

The movie of his life is at the same time a movie for those he loves, a way of saying goodbye in a home movie at some unknown date to come. It is a sort of non-conclusion for an eternal moment that hangs endlessly. Death may have the final word, but even that word is also a reversible sign to be seduced. To say that death is finality is to retread the abandoned anatomical determinism of our past. We have seen the signs transfigured before us in the ironic feedback loop of duel, agonistic relation, and by the transfiguring deception of the *trompe l'oeil*. There's no need for the game of seduction to end, even in the physical absence of a character. The remaining proliferating signs are an ironic, aesthetic simulation of sexual reproduction. "Videotape" suggests that we always leave behind a sign, even in our departure, and that sign is immortal.

How Come I End Up Where I Started?

The immediate and obvious rebuttal to all of this nonsense will of course be that it is completely self-defeating to attempt to use meaningful words and concepts to suggest the withholding of meaning for the sake of a game of endlessly reversible signs. Simply describing the concept sort of unravels the whole project, silly. Signs must have fixed meanings, otherwise how could concepts be explained in the first place? To this Baudrillard sighs, "Perhaps signs are not destined to enter into fixed oppositions for meaningful ends, that being only their present *destination*. Their actual *destiny* is perhaps quite different: to seduce each other and, thereby, seduce us" (p. 103).

This is seduction's irrefutable sleight of hand, to reclaim the infinite from the morgue where the Enlightenment has it dissected. In so doing, our sex and our existence can be re-enchanted in the never-ending play of seduction. Jean Baudrillard died in 2007, and yet here his signs have endlessly danced for our pleasure. Because he couldn't take them with him, they separate like ripples on a blank shore, in rainbows.

Selected chronological radiohead discography

Radiohead

Drill EP, 1992

"Prove Yourself" 2:32
"Stupid Car" 2:21
"You" 3:22
"Thinking About You" 2:17

Pablo Honey, 1993

"You" 3:29
"Creep" 3:56
"How Do You?" 2:12
"Stop Whispering" 5:26
"Thinking About You" 2:41
"Anyone Can Play Guitar" 3:38
"Ripcord" 3:10
"Vegetable" 3:13
"Prove Yourself" 2:25
"I Can't" 4:13
"Lurgee" 3:08
"Blow Out" 4:40

The Bends, 1995

"Planet Telex" 4:19
"The Bends" 4:04
"High and Dry" 4:20
"Fake Plastic Trees" 4:51
"Bones" 3:08
"(Nice Dream)" 3:54

For a full discogaphy, including singles and B-sides, see Wikipedia or greenplastic.com.

"Just" 3:54
"My Iron Lung" 4:37
"Bullet Proof . . . I Wish I Was" 3:29
"Black Star" 4:07
"Sulk" 3:43
"Street Spirit (Fade Out)" 4:12

OK Computer, 1997

"Airbag" 4:44
"Paranoid Android" 6:23
"Subterranean Homesick Alien" 4:27
"Exit Music (For a Film)" 4:24
"Let Down" 4:59
"Karma Police" 4:22
"Fitter Happier" 1:57
"Electioneering" 3:51
"Climbing Up the Walls" 4:45
"No Surprises" 3:49
"Lucky" 4:20
"The Tourist" 5:25

Airbag/How Am I Driving? EP, 1998

"Airbag" 4:46
"Pearly" 3:33
"Meeting in the Aisle" 3:09
"A Reminder" 3:51
"Polyethylene [Parts 1 & 2]" 4:22
"Melatonin" 2:09
"Palo Alto" 3:43

Kid A, 2000

"Everything in Its Right Place" 4:11
"Kid A" 4:44
"The National Anthem" 5:50
"How to Disappear Completely" 5:55
"Treefingers" 3:42
"Optimistic" 5:16
"In Limbo" 3:31

"Idioteque" 5:09
"Morning Bell" 4:29
"Motion Picture Soundtrack" 6:59

Amnesiac, 2001

"Packt Like Sardines in a Crushd Tin Box" 4:00
"Pyramid Song" 4:49
"Pulk/Pull Revolving Doors" 4:07
"You and Whose Army?" 3:11
"I Might Be Wrong" 4:54
"Knives Out" 4:15
"Morning Bell/Amnesiac" 3:14
"Dollars and Cents" 4:52
"Hunting Bears" 2:01
"Like Spinning Plates" 3:57
"Life in a Glasshouse" 4:34

I Might Be Wrong: Live Recordings EP, 2001

"The National Anthem" 4:57
"I Might Be Wrong" 4:52
"Morning Bell" 4:14
"Like Spinning Plates" 3:47
"Idioteque" 4:24
"Everything in Its Right Place" 7:42
"Dollars and Cents" 5:13
"True Love Waits" 5:02

Hail to the Thief, 2003

"2 + 2 = 5 (The Lukewarm.)" 3:19
"Sit down. Stand up. (Snakes & Ladders.)" 4:19
"Sail to the Moon. (Brush the Cobwebs out of the Sky.)" 4:18
"Backdrifts. (Honeymoon is Over.)" 5:22
"Go to Sleep. (Little Man being Erased.)" 3:21
"Where I End and You Begin. (The Sky is Falling in.)" 4:29
"We suck Young Blood. (Your Time is up.)" 4:56
"The Gloaming. (Softly Open our Mouths in the Cold.)" 3:32
"There There. (The Boney King of Nowhere.)" 5:23
"I will. (No man's Land.)" 1:59
"A Punchup at a Wedding. (No no no no no no no no.)" 4:57

"Myxomatosis. (Judge, Jury & Executioner.)" 3:52
"Scatterbrain. (As Dead as Leaves.)" 3:21
"A Wolf at the Door. (It Girl. Rag Doll.)" 3:23

COMLAG (2plus2is5) EP, 2004

"2 + 2 = 5" (Live at Earls Court, London, November 26th, 2003) 3:36
"Remyxomatosis" (Cristian Vogel Remix) 5:11
"I Will" (Los Angeles Version) 2:15
"Paperbag Writer" 4:01
"I Am a Wicked Child" 3:08
"I Am Citizen Insane" 3:34
"Skttrbrain" (Four Tet Remix) 4:28
"Gagging Order" 3:37
"Fog (Again)" (Live) 2:21
"Where Bluebirds Fly" 4:25

In Rainbows, 2007

"15 Step" 3:57
"Bodysnatchers" 4:02
"Nude" 4:15
"Weird Fishes/Arpeggi" 5:18
"All I Need" 3:48
"Faust Arp" 2:09
"Reckoner" 4:50
"House of Cards" 5:28
"Jigsaw Falling into Place" 4:08
"Videotape" 4:39

In Rainbows 2 (box set bonus disc), 2007

"MK 1" 1:04
"Down Is the New Up" 4:59
"Go Slowly" 3:48
"MK 2" 0:53
"Last Flowers" 4:27
"Up on the Ladder" 4:17
"Bangers + Mash" 3:20
"4 Minute Warning" 4:06

Thom Yorke

The Eraser, 2006

"The Eraser" 4:55
"Analyse" 4:02
"The Clock" 4:13
"Black Swan" 4:49
"Skip Divided" 3:35
"Atoms for Peace" 5:13
"And It Rained All Night" 4:15
"Harrowdown Hill" 4:38
"Cymbal Rush" 5:15

Where we got our big ideas

SEAN BURT lives in Tucson, where he teaches Hebrew Bible and ancient Jewish history and literature at the University of Arizona. By the time you read this he will have completed (knock on wood) a dissertation on narrative genre and ideology in the biblical book of Nehemiah. He paid full CD price for the *In Rainbows* mp3 files.

DAVID DARK is a Nashville-based educator who believes Radiohead and isn't afraid to say so. He thinks "You're All I Need" should be played (or sung) at the beginning of every working day at the United Nations. He is the author of *The Sacredness of Questioning Everything* and *Everyday Apocalypse: The Sacred Revealed in Radiohead, the Simpsons, and Other Pop Culture Icons.* He is currently pursuing a PhD in Religious Studies at Vanderbilt University.

MARK GREIF is a founding editor of *n+1* and Assistant Professor of Literary Studies at the New School in New York. He works on twentieth (and twenty-first) century intellectual history and the arts. One of his most prized possessions is a Christmas card from Radiohead cover-artist Stanley Donwood.

LINDSEY FIORELLI is an undergraduate at Oberlin College majoring in English and Philosophy. She began listening to Radiohead a few years ago, and became obsessed with *OK Computer.* This obsession resulted in her having a dream that was set to the video of "Paranoid Android" in which she was one of the cartoons in the video, one of the "androids." Needless to say, she woke up a bit confused and decided to not listen to "Paranoid Android" for quite some time afterwards. This is Lindsey's first publication.

TIM FOOTMAN is the author of *Welcome to the Machine: OK Computer and the Death of the Classic Album* (Chrome Dreams, 2007), and has also written for *The Guardian, Mojo, Plan B, Time Out,* and the *International Journal of Baudrillard Studies.* An alumnus of the University of Exeter (where he lived next door to the drummer from the Headless Chickens, and failed the only philosophy exam he ever took), he currently hovers somewhere on the metaphysical flight path between London and Bangkok, and at culturalsnow.blogspot.com. His favorite Radiohead lyric is the horn section from "The National Anthem."

BRANDON FORBES is a freelance writer, and occasional drummer, living in Chicago. He has written widely in music criticism and recently composed two volumes on Green Living for World Book. His first true experience of Radiohead's artistic power was in college, when late one night he was so completely freaked out while listening to "Climbing Up the Walls" alone in his dorm room that he was forced to turn off the CD and turn on some lights. He has an MTS from Duke University and would like to remind everyone that this is really happening.

BRADLEY KAYE is currently a Ph.D.candidate in SUNY Binghamton's Philosophy, Interpretation, and Culture Program. On October 3rd, 2000, the day *Kid A* was released, he was a pesky undergraduate at SUNY Fredonia. He had heard rumors that the album's title derived from a playing card set devoted to the work of the French Psychoanalyst Jacques Lacan called, "Kid A in Alphabet Land." Thom Yorke denied this connection. Unsatisfied with Yorke's rebuttal, Bradley did further research. Upon finding out that the card set was created by an American intellectual who hosted a webpage located at www.Freedonia.com (accessible now via The Wayback Machine), Bradley felt like a paranoid android. This discovery seemed scripted and Bradley had to remind himself, "it's not like the movies."

ADAM KOEHLER does it to himself. And that's why it really hurts. He's an Assistant Professor of English and Director of Composition at Manhattan College. He's also an editor for *The Avery Anthology,* which publishes innovative and experimental fiction by previously unpublished, emerging, and established writers (www.averyanthology.org). He lives in New York City.

MATTHEW LAMPERT is a Ph.D. Candidate at the New School for Social Research, where he also spent four years as an editor for the *Graduate Faculty Philosophy Journal.* Amidst the fog of his senior year in high school, spent mostly in front of MTV, one of the few things he remembers watching—really watching—is the video for "Paranoid Android." It both prepared him for the *Critique of Pure Reason* and sparked the insight that Radiohead (not Blur, and definitely not Oasis) is the only Britpop that matters.

JASON LEE was born as dust settled from the first lunar landing. He has worked in the Middle East, Eastern Europe, at six universities in the UK, and manages the film, media and creative writing programs at the University of Derby. Books include *Pervasive Perversions,* and the double volume *The Metaphysics of Mass Art.* On a plane to Melbourne, listening to *Hail to the Thief* for the first time, he got to the line "something for the rag and bone man, over my dead body." The CD player was on track repeat and dosing in and out of sleep he must have listened to it for over two hours. Realising this wasn't the actual length of the song he walked to the back of the plane. It plummeted. Hundreds of people asleep, Spanish lights like eyes burning brighter from below, but, what if, they went out, slowly, one by one . . . ?

MICAH LOTT is a doctoral candidate in philosophy at the University of Chicago. His interests in philosophy include ethics, philosophy of religion and ancient philosophy. He fondly remembers listening to "Creep" many years ago, while sitting in the passenger seat of a old brown station wagon, being driven to school by his brother Nathan.

DEVON LOUGHEED is a political theorist pursuing his Ph.D. at the University of British Columbia. He's a musician whose albums are available, following Radiohead, as pay-what-you-want downloads from www.DevonLougheed.com. He is a stand-up comedian who will make you laugh until your head comes off.

He can still remember the first time he heard "Paranoid Android" and the way it changed how he listened to music forever.

JÉRÔME MELANÇON lives in Camrose, Alberta, with his wife (who is much cooler than him) and his cat (also cooler). He studied in philosophy, sociology, and political science at the universities of Ottawa and Paris-Diderot and because as of this year he traded his student status for a suffix, he makes his living teaching political theory at the University of Alberta, Augustana Campus. He has notably published articles on people named Maurice, Pierre, and Walter (whom others call Merleau-Ponty, Bourdieu or Benjamin) and tries to write often in online publications. Having mastered the art of not being around when Radiohead come to town, he has only seen them live once, but did drive a ways and stood in line for almost ten hours to be in the exclusive area and all the way up in the front so he could feel special.

DAN MILSKY received his Ph.D. in philosophy from the University of Illinois at Chicago, and is assistant professor and head of the philosophy program at Northeastern Illinois University. His research is focused on the intersection between theoretical ecology and environmental ethics with a special emphasis on the concept of ecosystem health. In his spare time Dan likes to dress up in a King Canute costume and hand out recyclable drinking bottles at Lollapalooza.

GEORGE REISCH is the author of *How the Cold War Transformed Philosophy of Science* (Cambridge University Press, 2005) and series editor for Open Court's *Popular Culture and Philosophy* series. He runs Luxotone records, plays guitar in Bobby Vacant & The Weary, and became a Radiohead fan the first time he heard "Paranoid Android" and was smacked in the head by Jonny Greenwood's and Ed O'Brien's guitars at 2:42. Until that moment, he had not been paying attention.

EDWARD SLOWIK is a Professor in Philosophy at Winona State University, Winona, Minnesota, and a Resident Fellow at the Minnesota Center for Philosophy of Science, University of Minnesota. His main research interests are in the history and philosophy of science, with special emphasis on the philosophy of space, time, and motion. He's the author of *Cartesian Spacetime* (Kluwer, 2002), and many journal articles. One of Ed's favorite anecdotes about Radiohead concerns the band's weird (coincidental?) connection with the music of the twentieth-century Russian composer, Dmitri Shostakovich: a recording of the slow movement of the 7th String Quartet was played before the band took the stage during the *Kid A* tour; and Christopher O'Riley, who has recorded piano versions of Radiohead songs, has gone on tour playing these songs alongside Shostakovich's Preludes and Fugues for piano.

JERE O'NEILL SURBER is Professor of Philosophy and Cultural Theory at the University of Denver as well as a working musician. He was an (abject) graduate student at the Pennsylvania State University and the University of Bonn (Germany) and has taught at the University of Mainz (Germany) and the Katholieke Universiteit-Leuven (Belgium). He has long been intrigued by Julia Kristeva's idea of 'the abject' and its artistic expressions but never really knew what it sounded like until he started listening to Radiohead. He's written several books and articles (including some in the *Popular Culture and Philosophy* series) on German Idealism, Postmodern Philosophy and Culture, and Aesthetics.

JOHN SYLVIA IV is completing his M.A. in philosophy at The University of Southern Mississippi. During his undergraduate work at Mississippi State University, he had to road trip four hours to New Orleans in order to see Radiohead live. It's likely that this caused him to miss a few philosophy classes when he overslept the next morning. Now that he finds himself in the role of an instructor, he has so far been unable to convince his department that a field trip to a Radiohead concert is a worthy endeavor for his philosophy students (but perhaps this book will change that).

JOSEPH TATE published *The Music And Art Of Radiohead* (Ashgate) in 2005 and has lectured internationally on the band. "Lundy, Fastnet, Irish Sea," the lyrics beginning *Kid A*'s "In Limbo," confused Joseph so much he tracked down their source to a BBC Weather Shipping Forecast. He has cherished and nurtured his happy misunderstandings of Radiohead's obscurity since that time. He is a writer living in Seattle.

MICHAEL L. THOMPSON is currently finishing his dissertation for a Ph.D. at the University of South Florida. His research interests focus around Immanuel Kant and the Imagination. He has also published on the connection between sublimity and tragedy as well as African philosophy. His first appreciation of the power and refinement of Radiohead's music came during a long drive through the Rocky Mountains while listening to *Pablo Honey*.

DYLAN E. WITTKOWER teaches philosophy at Coastal Carolina University and studies how technology either encourages or prevents the formation of collaborative creative communities. In other words, he is like a "Web 2.0" tech geek, except with a whole lot more fretting, fussing, and Marxist rhetoric. He has recorded audiobooks of numerous philosophy texts, which may be downloaded at librivox.org. He edited *iPod and Philosophy* (2008). He also wants you to go to YouTube and watch the video for "All I Need."

PERRY OWEN WRIGHT lives in Raleigh, North Carolina, where he is a songwriter and musician, composing albums engaging the ideas of uncertainty and fidelity through a host of narrative frameworks as varied as the Jonestown event of 1978 to works of fiction and even tedious philosophy. Surprisingly, Radiohead has never asked his band, The Prayers and Tears of Arthur Digby Sellers, to open a world tour for them or even to get coffee. But this one time in Charlotte, Thom Yorke contextualized one of the songs from the *In Rainbows* material as, "This is when you just got laid," and sitting in the audience, Perry credited that as a follow-up interview with the artist for his chapter in this volume. He has a master's of divinity from Duke, where he traded the cow of his future financial security for three beans.

Index (for a book)

PINK FLOYD

AND
PHILOSOPHY

CAREFUL WITH THAT AXIOM, EUGENE!

EDITED BY GEORGE A. REISCH